Tolstoy, Woman, and Death

Tolstoy, Woman, and Death

A Study of *War and Peace* and *Anna Karenina*

David Holbrook

Madison • Teaneck
Fairleigh Dickinson University Press
London: Associated University Presses

Associated University Presses
440 Forsgate Drive
Cranbury, NJ 08512

Associated University Presses
16 Barter Street
London WC1A 2AH, England

Associated University Presses
P.O. Box 338, Port Credit
Mississauga, Ontario
Canada L5G 4L8

The paper used in this publication meets the requirements
of the American National Standard for Permanence of Paper
for Printed Library Materials Z39.48–1984.

Library of Congress Cataloging-in-Publication Data

Holbrook, David.
  Tolstoy, woman, and death : a study of War and Peace and Anna
Karenina / David Holbrook.
     p.   cm.
  Includes bibliographical references and index.
  ISBN 0-8386-3701-9 (alk. paper)
  1. Tolstoy, Leo, graf, 1828–1910. Voĭna i mir. 2. Tolstoy, Leo,
graf, 1828–1910. Anna Karenina. 3. Tolstoy, Leo, graf, 1828–1910—
Characters—Women. 4. Women in literature. 5. Death in
literature. I. Title.
PG3365.V65H58   1997
891.73′3—dc20   96-38804
                                                                                   CIP

PRINTED IN THE UNITED STATES OF AMERICA

For Margot, Suki, Kate,
Karen, Zoe, Ella,
Melissa, and Anna

Contents

1

Introduction

I have to admit that I do not know Russian, and that my discussions of *War and Peace* (1863–69) and of *Anna Karenina* (1873–78) are based entirely on English translations. I wonder what I have lost by this inadequacy. It seems extraordinary that these two novels should have such a tremendous effect on one's life, even though one knows them only in a translated form.

I apologize to modern language scholars for my intrusion into their sphere, but plead that Tolstoy's two greatest novels seem to be more powerful as art even in translation than much of British and American writing, although this is in our own language. There are no doubt aspects of this problem of which I am ignorant, so I hope all my readers will excuse my amateur enthusiasm.

*   *   *

To read these novels, for anyone responsive to the art of the novel, is perhaps the most powerful literary experience. They are enlivening and harrowing and force the reader to ponder values around love, relationships, and sexuality with great gravity. Of course, *War and Peace* raises other wider questions, of history, politics, and of the human proclivity for violence. But even here the attitudes of men to their roles in the world are centrally linked with the way they are inspired by women, or disillusioned by women. The problems of meaning and death underpin both novels.

Today their especial value lies in their quality of *gravitas*, about relationships between men and women. In our time, under the supposition that we have become more "free" over sexual matters, thoughts about love, sex, and relationships have come under severe pressure from falsification—not least from a new triviality. Today the prevalent belief seems to be that there is no wisdom about these matters—that there are no truths. Sex has been separated from the emotional life, as Rollo May has argued (in May,

Love and Will 1969) and is often treated at large with a lightheart-edness that borders on contempt. Yet at the same time the level of what may be called sexual casualties mounts while the degree of suffering caused by the breakdown of marriage and of relation-ships generally increases, under the effects of the persuasions of superficial attitudes.

Who would suppose, from today's atmosphere of 'enlighten-ment,' that sexual love can be one of the deepest sources of human value and meaning? And yet, as we know from the growing com-munity of psychotherapeutic work that it is in this area that people confess both their needs for self-fulfillment, and their need for authenticity, and strive, in the gravest dialogue, to achieve the very integrity of which the great novelists have written.

In today's atmosphere, especially the atmosphere of the "mod-ern novel," to say nothing of drama and film, a work such as *Anna Karenina* which shows human beings destroyed by sexual passion and by their failure to come to terms with reality, can barely be understood. In the current atmosphere of the arts, sexual reality has been so reduced to insignificance and to the trivial sensa-tionalism of a momentary distraction, that it can be said to be sunk in lies. In such a situation, we are cut off from tragedy, because the torments that arise from unresolved problems of sex-ual passion cannot be understood by us. And if we lose our capac-ity for tragedy, then we also lose our capacities for joy, reverence, creative responsibility, and respect for human nature. Tragedy is the cultural mark of high civilization, since it presses problems of the quality of existence to their limits, and asks, in the face of death, what it is that makes life worth living.

A society whose culture, dominated by commercial distortions, is given over largely to insults directed at women, sex, and rela-tionships becomes a decadent society. Insofar as it finds as its main goal what Viktor Frankl called "a thoroughly decadent sensu-alism," it comes to be overwhelmed by what the late E. W. F. Tomlin called "brothel culture," and nowhere is this more evident than in the present-day London culture of theater, film, and tele-vision, to say nothing of the novel and even poetry.

Tolstoy's greatest works are about as far as one could get from "brothel culture," while his gravity about his art is unquestionable, so attention to his work provides a valuable corrective to the de-pravity and corruption of our age and culture.

To try to understand his great novels, and to see where he is right (and where he goes wrong) may serve as a touchstone, and so help us perhaps to return to, or regain, something of the inheritance of serious European culture. This is urgent, for unless we recover our sense of values in the sphere of culture we are in danger of losing touch with our civilization—indeed, of losing our sense of what civilization is. If we do that, then we lose our sense of why civilization should go on existing, while forfeiting that sense of human value that makes it worth preserving.

However, this brings me to the question of what has happened to literary criticism since, roughly speaking, the decline of the influence of F. R. Leavis and the *Scrutiny* movement, which was once such a promising focus of serious discourse in the realm of literature and the arts.

In the course of preparing the present volume I have read a number of works on Tolstoy and this has brought me into the realm of the discipline of modern languages. There, I find, the influence of "literary theory" seems to have had a more profound impact than in English studies. In the latter I more or less accede to the point of view of Geoffrey Strickland in his distinguished book *Structuralism or Criticism?* (1981). The publishers' catalogs are now full of studies which invoke structuralism, deconstructionism, Marxism, and feminism, and, indeed, the whole academic world seems to be overwhelmed by these influences. Yet where are the seminal writings among the output of these fashionable positions? Where are the books which yield insights that illuminate one's reading—that send one back to the texts of works of art, with a new vision—as Leavis's used to, and as did the writing of such critics as I. A. Richards, William Empson, L. C. Knights, and D. W. Harding? What I have found, whenever I have made an effort to get to grips with any of the books in this area, is sterility. They seem to invoke elements of an unprofitable intellectualism, often with its roots in the French tendency to word-spin in an abstract and somewhat nihilistic way, with a tendency to take flight more and more from a gut-felt engagement with the text. The text, the works in question, are the last things to count, while authors seem unwilling to confront a work of art in such a way as to expose themselves to its creative dynamics, its essential revolutionary power. The commitment of the author has been undermined, and often one feels oneself floundering, unable to be oneself in response to the language of a work of art, in all its human challenge. It seems almost at times as though the primacy of "a work of art" has ceased to exist, and that all that is left is a tissue of "exagminations" [sic] about it.

Above all, one senses, it is the theory that must be preserved, along with its proponents: the reader will not need to be reminded of the leading protagonists—Derrida, Barthes, Sassure, Benveniste, etc. The jargon is formidable: in one critical volume on Tolstoy (Amy Mandelker, *Framing "Anna Karenina": Tolstoy, the Woman Question and the Victorian Novel* [1993]) I found the following:

> tropological, epigraphic, perí-modern, presymbolist, folkloric, post-realist, *passe-partout*, deconstruct, logocentrism, hypostatization, essentializing, biologizing, protofascistic, palimpsestic, heroinism, mythopoesis, entropy-producing, Peircean terminology, iconicity, emblematicize, a Kerotic Christ, ekphrasis, meta-aesthetic, energeaia, hypotyposis, feminocentric, phallogocentric, diglossic, chronotype, restructuration, semiotic, antimimetic, enantiomorphic, psychomachy, palendromic, askesis, anomastically, and metanymically.

This author actually says a few interesting things about Tolstoy and about his texts. But many of her quotations from Barthes, Derrida, and others seemed to add little or nothing to her own commentary, and yet serve as a screen to write nonsense. For instance she declares:

> Tolstoy deconstructs Western philosophy to reveal the gender bias implicit in its bifurcated categories, and draws on his native Eastern orthodox philosophical tradition to create a super-sublime category, that of Christian love that transcends gender and individual difference in promoting a community of aesthetic response. (Mandelker 1993, 7)

There were many passages like this against which I wrote "nonsense" in my notes. Yet in discussing (say) the Varenka scene of mushroom picking (Part 6) and the psychology of Anna Karenina being shown as divided against herself she was illuminating.

Those working in a field of criticism influenced by literary theory and feminism seem to be imprisoned by dogma. (On the other hand there are Christian critics who seek to interpret everything in art according to their faith's principles of which more later.) The critics in "literary theory" are deeply suspicious of earlier critics and commentators whom they believe to be imprisoned in their own political assumptions, which is also a characteristic Marxist ploy, as to dismiss opponents as "bourgeois." Yet at the same time, they seem unable to open themselves to a text, to let it work upon them, and to challenge their own adherences, while they are indifferent to questions of psychic reality and seem to ignore consciousness.

The author under discussion, Mandelker, for instance, is convinced that women, as shown in the nineteenth-century novel, are
entrapped in a male world, in which the alternatives to marriage
are severely limiting, from governessing to becoming a prostitute,
or death, so that (it is implied) no woman could ever fulfill herself
sexually, except in adultery. (That there could have been hundreds
of thousands of happily married couples, even bourgeois ones,
escapes notice altogether: of course, the novel is unlikely to interest itself in the normal, untroubled, and satisfying.) It is true
that she resists the allegation that Tolstoy is a misogynist who
characterizes marriage as a form of institutionalized prostitution,
but she takes it for granted that Tolstoy lives in a society in which
there is no escape from "the problematic nature of the sexual
contract," and that the "bourgeois institutionalization of marriage" meant "the failure of romantic love," and that this repre-
sented "the darker side of sexual politics." Thus "the sublime
becomes invested with heroic masculine attributes" while "the
beautiful is characterised as small, trivial, feminine." Women are
continually faced with the problem of being made, by the gaze of
men, into sex objects, with an acquisitive bias. From this women
can only escape, either by not having sex, thus removing themselves from the "entrapment" of the male gaze, or by not having
babies (as Simone de Beauvoir suggested) thus removing themselves politically from the whole degrading business of being confined in the home to do the chores and to bring up a family. (So
strong is the rejection of marriage, and even of sexuality, that one
often feels that the women who write feminist criticism do not
enjoy being women or even regard heterosexual sex as fit only
for rejection.)

Thus, she can pose the absurd question, "Is the opposite of
misogyny necessarily feminism?" And can accede to the suggestion that poor Dolly is the real heroine of *Anna Karenina* ("his
hypostatization of the 'ideal' woman into a de-sexed, plain Ma-
donna . . . Dolly.") Mary Evans, an English feminist writer, I note,
also says that "If there is a real heroine in *Anna Karenina* then the
honour might well go to Dolly, rather than Anna herself" (Evans,
Reflecting on Anna Karenina [1989]).

Mandelker approaches the complex problems of Tolstoy's views,
and of the astonishing perplexity of his penetrating portrayal of
women characters, through a confusing haze of what can only be
called propaganda. Whatever discussion is entered into, of Tolstoy's personality, of the nature of his art, and of his achievement,

what must be preserved is the political feminist position. So, she can actually say:

> Those with a post-modern feminist, post-Freudian perspective may question views that equate the expression of sexuality with positive self-assertion and creativity. (Mandelker, 30)

The implications of (say) thousands of reports on psychotherapeutic work with patients, that they seek fulfillment in good relationships and in sexual meetings, in the pursuit of a sense of meaning in life (in which sexual fulfillment is not necessarily a primary element, but often an important one) is ignored.

This author is afraid of being the subject of adverse political comment, if she commits herself in a moral way. She says that "the notion of practising a moral or ethical criticism is daunting since it exposes the critic to the dangers of political interpretation" (Ibid., 30). She thus reveals that her mind is not open, because it is haunted, not to say dominated, by a position upon which it is unprepared to be dislodged or even realigned, by the effect of a work of art—for fear of being found politically incorrect or of being forced to relinquish dogma. "The novel itself, especially the novel of adultery, is already ideological," and so the function of criticism, in its commitment to Socratic dialogue, around the meaning and value of texts, is inhibited.

So, Mandelker's criticism of *Anna Karenina* is confused: sometimes it is this perspective, sometimes that, and we see the novel in terms of perspectives (or, in her word "frames") that are so various as to allow us to make of it anything we want. At times she resists extreme feminist criticism (especially the view of Mary Evans that Anna is "a deviant and 'unnatural' woman") but here an essential feminism prevents her from confronting the tragedy itself. For example she says resisting the view of Evans that "the experience of maternity automatically generates higher moral values," "a woman's way of knowing," and a "different voice of a caring morality,"

> This theorizing runs the risk of essentializing and biologizing the experience of maternity to a degree that many critics have seen as being virtually protofascistic. . . . (Ibid., 51)

As one who regards himself as devoted to antifascism I was deeply shocked to find that the inferences, such as those of observers as various as D. W. Winnicott and Ann Ulanov, that women have a special mode of knowing, a deeper sense of being, and a finer morality in consequence of being potential mothers, is "protofascistic." Winnicott, a democrat if ever there was one, finds these feminine qualities and the family to be at its heart. So, one is left continually baffled by Mandelker's book, with its repetitive emphasis on the "enslavement" of women, the "dangerous bourgeois illusions of romantic love," and its prejudice against domesticity. She can even see Dolly (Oblonskaya), for example, as a portrait of the "victimization of woman . . . based on cowardice"— but what could poor Dolly have done?

I hope I have said enough about this critic to show how confused and confusing she is. The picture she gives of bourgeois life in the nineteenth century is one in which no woman was fulfilled, no marriage was successful, no family provided a secure and satisfying environment: and a present world in which women must virtually stand on their heads, resisting all impulses to fulfill themselves sexually, or to love, in case they fall into some "political entrapment" and become merely objects of the male gaze and of male sexual possession. One gets the impression that behind all this is a section of women who are dissatisfied with their sex, their sensuality, their maternal nature, and their procreativity, and are utterly confused by Tolstoy's tragedy of this exceptional character of a woman who seems to come to life, determined to fulfill herself and to find meaning in her life, even in spite of the prejudices and unconscious obsessions of her creator.

As F. R. Leavis said, life is a necessary word. The literary theorists write as though the work of art was created by an artist who was conscious of all nuances, and was always in control of his material. The novel is the product of "genres," of the influences of "narrative form" and techniques, consciously applied. The idea escapes them that a writer can only partly consciously cooperate and collaborate, in the creative process, with what emerges from his mind, and the psyche and unconscious play a strange and often betraying part in his creation. Often, as I hope I have demonstrated with D. H. Lawrence, and as I hope to demonstrate with Tolstoy, he can be taken over by unconscious dynamics, and falsifies his art and his own best intentions. He may even believe that, as an artist, he is pursuing truth, even deeper truths than what he believes to be truth at the level of rational discourse, when a studied view reveals that he is seriously wrong. The truth, implicit in *Anna Karenina*, is surely at odds with the implicit truth of *The Kreutzer Sonata* in which Tolstoy gives way to enthusiastic pathological drives, prompted by a hatred of women and sex.

It is the critic's duty to try to evaluate what the author offers as truth (for he offers it solemnly as truth even when he is seeking to generate beauty) in the light of what we believe to be truth from other disciplines. These include what I call philosophical anthropology, and this includes psychoanalysis, which will bring me, in a moment, to the problem of Freud.

But first let me show how this engagement with the human truth, and the need to judge whether what an author offers in its name is true or false, can be confused by literary theory. Mandelker writes:

> Women have lost their status as beautiful objects of the phenomenal world and become, instead, *objets d'art*. Beauty as a signifier (body of soul) becomes unstable and charged with anxiety in the male gaze as the would-be purchaser fears being duped by mere appearance. . . . (Mandelker, 86)

Thus, even our estimation of beauty and truth becomes subverted by political bias: more important than an open examination of the beauty of Anna Karenina and of her portrayal in the novel becomes the need to preserve the dogma of the enslavement of women.

I have said that some of Mandelker's psychological observations are rewarding, and this is particularly true when she invokes insights from Jung. But the feminist use of Freud has been, I believe, especially confusing. This is so because the feminists have concentrated on Freud's theories and works, which were certainly male orientated and the product of a male-dominated society, but which, in terms of therapeutic practice, are nearly a century out-of-date and have been developed by radical revisions.

I myself have traced the development of psychoanalytic theory (in *Human Hope and the Death Instinct* [1971]) and there have been many developments since. Some of the changes in point of view have virtually turned Freud on his head: for instance, instead of culture being, as it were, a sublimation of instinctual drives, the development of the capacity to symbolize has been brought to lie at the center of the development of a human sense of identity, in the psychological patterns of D. W. Winnicott. In this the natural response of the mother in her role of "creative reflection," in play with her infant, has come to the forefront. The need for meaning, rather than instinctual release, has come to the center of the stage, in the development of existential psychotherapy, as in the work of Viktor Frankl, Rollo May, and Irvin Yalom. So, it is impossible for

anyone who finds touchstones of human truth to lie in the reports
of such therapists on experience, to argue with those who take
psychoanalytic theory to be Freudian theory, or who believe it to
be still relevant. Freud made a major achievement in finding a
meaning in symptoms, dreams, and the symbols of ordinary life.
But his theories are felt to be abhorrent, false, and misleading,
by those who adhere to more recent theories: Harry Guntrip, for
instance, found Freudian theory repugnant and harmful: found
it to be a defense indeed against the deeper problems of the
schizoid problem of identity and of the meaning of life. The especial falsity of Freudian doctrine is associated with the belief that
our problems are fundamentally sexual and that the release of
sexual libido will cure them. There are many therapists who find
this view unprofitable. The more recent approach seems to be
that our essential problems are meaning and death: we know we
must die and we need to establish some meaning in our existence
before we are extinguished. Such a view, of course, throws a great
deal of light on *Anna Karenina,* and indeed on much of Tolstoy's
work, and it is unprofitable to anyone who has reached this view,
to engage with the interpretations of a critic stuck with the Freudian model. For instance, Mandelker's assertion that

> Feminist criticism has made us aware of the ways in which a literary
> figure of women reading literature is complicated by their immersion
> in an alien or other ("phallocentric") discourse. . . . (Mandelker, 129)

> The knife becomes a fetish, an enlarging substitute phallus that Anna
> must wield or woo to gain entrance into the world she encodes.
> (Ibid., 136)

This critic's view that Anna was led into adultery by reading a
romantic English novel ("the Victorian novel is actually phallocen-
tric in ethos") seems too simplistic, and based on a too facile application of Freudian concepts. On the other hand this critic's
discussion of the "shadow," a concept from Jung, makes a valuable
contribution to the debate.

She also offers an interesting insight into Anna's emotional du-
alism, as indicated by her dream of having two husbands, both
called Aleksei, though she does not explore this very far. And she
refers to the scene with Varenka and the mushroom gathering,
both by suggesting a connection with folklore, and the mushroom
as a symbol of both male and female sexuality: though I believe,
again, she is wrong in her politicized conclusions:

The character of Varenka and her escape from the life path of love
and marriage point the way to Tolstoy's ultimate view, that equality
between the sexes can only occur when there is an absence of the
sexual power relations and possession that are the inevitable accompa-
niments of nineteenth century bourgeois marriage. (Ibid., 178)

Surely Tolstoy does not celebrate Varenka's "escape" as a gain,
but shows it to be a sad disappointment. Later she relates Tolstoy's
view that sexual love is "something incomprehensible and repugnant, and offensive to human dignity," without attempting any
kind of diagnoses of this point of view. Surely, the normal view is
that, despite the anxiety and fear often associated with it, sexual
love is joyful and fulfilling, and a mysterious but rapturous way
of meeting another human being. And a path to finding one's
sense of significance in life. Rather Mandelker seems to endorse
something like the negative view, speaking of "freeing woman's
beauty from its economic and sexual entrapment."

In such attitudes I find the clue to my own rejection of the
kind of politics manifest in feminism, radical structuralism, and
Marxism. They ignore the unconscious factors in their own beliefs: they tend to believe that consciousness does not matter and
that individuals following these adherences fail to examine their
own unconscious motivation. They fail to accept psychic reality—
as by implying, as with "bourgeois marriage," that if only the
"social restraints" and economic determining factors were removed, human life and relationships would be improved. Would
female beauty be any better, "freed" from "economic and sexual
entrapment"? Those who think in this way seem to fail to notice
their own problems with ambivalence—the inevitable problem of
love and hate within one's own psyche, and the associated problem, since we all have mothers, of accepting on the one hand one's
sensuality, greed, and lust, and one's capacity to seek love and
higher ideals on the other. The feminists, strangely, seem to dis-
parage motherhood and the especially feminine virtues, such as
the uncanny capacity of women to know in certain ways, to "be
for," and to cherish being: characteristics eminently portrayed by
Tolstoy. So, one might say, they are impelled to deny the very
dynamics, of play and intersubjectivity, that make us human.
These, indeed, are dismissed as being concepts thrown over
women by men, as part of their "entrapment." They are thus
deeply faulted when it comes to explaining the nature of human
nature (and especially incompetent when it comes to examining
the work of an author so troubled by misogyny as Tolstoy).

In Marxism, it seems to me, the assumed views of the world and society are distorted by rationalizations which ignore the problems of human nature—intransigeance around which question has led in our century to misery and death for millions. On the one hand there is a utopianism that believes that once the economic drives of capitalism and the "icy waters of egoistical calculation" have been banished from the world, everyone will be able to fulfill themselves. On the other there is a ruthless impulse to bring about, and maintain, a system in which, while the economy is controlled in the interests of the socialist state, corruption, waste, pollution, and inefficiency flourish—yet this system must be maintained by imprisonment, starvation, enslavement, and murder. Yet the moral questions behind this dichotomy are simply not examined openly by the theoretical proponents while the psychic realities are implicitly denied. The essential problem of the need to find meaning in existence, in the face of death, is denied, by a manic activity which merely provides a mirror image of the manic activity of commerce. I have long since ceased to believe that Marxism and left-wing thought is capable of offering any help, to our pursuit of truth, and that this area of discourse has become anti-Socratic—that is, not open to genuine dialogue, in which truth can emerge. It is thus singularly unhelpful in literary criticism.

At the other extreme we find scholars who see everything in this author's work in terms of his religious belief. Prominent among these in a recent work is Richard F. Gustafson in *Leo Tolstoy, Resident and Stranger* (Princeton: Princeton University Press, 1986). Gustafson resists the prevalent view among Western critics, who regard Tolstoy's religious views as an aberration. In Russia, he declares, "art is a serious affair, for art is at the heart of its religion." The Russians are used to icons which are "pictures of the divine reality present to us," and there the images created by artists were taken seriously as words which reveal the Truth: "it is in this context that we must see the emblematic realism of Tolstoy." Tolstoy should not be judged by the criteria of realism: "his narratives tell of the divine call to love and man's response to that call." This surely ignores the fact that Tolstoy's conversion did not come about until about 1874, as delineated in his *Confession* of 1879, by which time *War and Peace* and *Anna Karenina* had been published: they were, surely, part of the process by which Tolstoy came to find and accept Christian belief.

Gustafson sees Dostoevskyan criticism as being "trivialised" by Freud. But some of his own observations on, and quotations from,

Tolstoy surely demand some kind of psychoanalytic investigation—for instance the fact on which he dwells that Tolstoy was an
orphan and that most of his major heroes are orphans, and that
in *A Confession* he sees himself as "a fledgling fallen from the
nest." "How can I love so that I will be loved and not be abandoned?"—that, says Gustafson, "was the question that pursued
Tolstoy all his life" (Ibid., 13) At the same time, this critic says,
"he found it so difficult to love and to let himself be loved that
he retreated into himself and in his self-centredness alienated
others" (Ibid., 20). The psychological predicament is surely more
primary than the beliefs which came with the conversion.

Gustafson does his own translations of passages from Tolstoy.
He is able to examine Tolstoy's prose in Russian and gives many
illuminating illustrations of the richness of ambiguities in his writing. One passage especially calls for psychoanalytic attention. It
is from Tolstoy's *Diaries*, written four years before his death:

> As in childhood I longed to cling to a being who loved me, who took
> pity on me, and to weep tenderly and be consoled. But who is that
> being to whom I would cling so? I go over all the people I love and
> none will do. To whom can I cling? I'd like to make myself small and
> cling to mother as I imagined her to myself. Yes, yes, Mommy, whom
> I had not even called by that name since I couldn't speak. Yes, she,
> my most exalted concept of pure love, not that cold, divine type, but
> a warm, earthy, motherly love. That's what my better but tired soul
> yearns for. Yes, Mommy, come cuddle me. All this is insane, but it is
> all true. (Jubilee edition, 1906, 55:374)*

It is true that Tolstoy's work as a whole was impelled by this
need to find love, which ideal of love was generated in those first
months of his life when he had to devise an ideal image of his
mother, after her death, as we shall see. But I believe that Gustafson, interpreting this love-quest in the Christian sense, tends to
bind Tolstoy's creative works too closely to this theme. This makes
him underestimate Tolstoy's achievement in portraying the most
positive elements in human relations in love. For instance, Gustafson says of Levin and Kitty in *Anna Karenina* that "joined, they
are still separate. . . ." while he equates them with Anna and Vronsky: each union is "marred by the isolation that distances the
characters from each other . . . harmony is elusive and often illu-

---

*Reference is made to the volume in the Jubilee edition, Polnoe Sobranie
Sochinenij (Moscow, 1928–58).

sive. . . ." (*Anna Karenina*, 46) Surely, as will be argued, the relationship between Levin and Kitty is intended to show the best a man and woman can do, and the best Tolstoy could do, in finding earthly human love, in its relationship with other people and with the whole of reality and the spiritual.

But Gustafson, it must be said, does not place much value on earthly love: he values more highly those moments in which the heroes are seized with a glimpse of transcendence, amid the suffering of war or in the face of death. In this, the woman has a role more like a catalyst than as a human being met in equal spirit. For instance he says that Prince Andrey "stumbles on the key to transcendence," by the "force of soul" he loves in Natasha, and learns it further when he sees Anatole Kuragin having his leg amputated. He feels

> a bliss he had not experienced for a long time . . . in his most distant childhood when he would be undressed and put to bed when his nanny would sing to him. . . . (*War and Peace*, 1026)

When he sees Natasha after he is wounded he sees love. "I experienced that love which is the very essence of the soul and for which there is *no need of an object*" (my italics). Gustafson pursues the image of the sky at moments of the culmination of the search for love, God, and meaning, with various heroes. He says that for Pierre Platon Karataev is "the emblem of love, of universal love that flows from the soul untouched by passion and suffering." For Gustafson, the quest in Tolstoy is, he says, through three stages, the "personal," the "pagan," and the "universal" or "divine" in which the boundary of the self is extended in the extreme: "the other becomes the 'All, everything that exists, God'" (Vsë, vsë surhchestvujushchee, Bog) (Gustafson, 87). "In this universal stage egocentric love is transformed."

From my point of view, this seems to accept Tolstoy's quest in terms of his need to rectify the serious dislocation of his relationship to the whole of reality, transmuted into a religious rationalization. The idealization of the divine image of his mother was so strong that it came to be thrown over the whole world. Being so idealistically spun, it could never find any satisfaction in any reality that was found, so Tolstoy was bound to remain forever frustrated, forever changing tack, in his attempt to find that supreme motherly embrace, that ultimate motherly meaning, of which he was deprived as an infant.

No earthly love, obviously, would do, and so Tolstoy's actual love relationships at the level of profane love, love of women, in marriage, were disastrous. And this element in Tolstoy's actual life Gustafson totally ignores. Not only, obviously, does he not think much of human sexual love or family love, but he ignores all the dreadful questions that arise, about Tolstoy pursuing all these grandiose spiritual goals, while, in the ordinary reality of the world and human affairs, behaving in such cruel and base ways to his own wife.

Gustafson takes the lofty Christian view: when Levin sees a glimpse of Kitty in the carriage, this critic utters an implicit disparagement of ordinary love.

> This hope is false, however, and Levin's mission to find his love is again destined to fail because he mistakes his personal love as his mission. (Ibid. 137)

Man must be on a higher plane and it is obvious that Gustafson prefers the way of the martyr:

> Pain is not an evil but an essential element in the dynamic of living. . . .
> If we did not suffer, we would not desire, and there would be no life, just meaningless existence. . . . (Ibid., 139)

Of course, mentally men suffer, and the existentialist view urges us to confront this suffering and to attempt to search for meaning in the face even of the ultimate suffering which is death. But to see suffering as an "essential element in the dynamic of loving" however courageous it sounds, is actually sentimental. And what can it possibly mean to say "If we did not suffer, we would not desire"? And what does Gustafson imply by saying that without suffering "there would be no life, just meaningless existence"? These comments seem to be put the wrong way round. Yes, there is suffering, but it is not the suffering that makes the positive significance of transcending it, but the existential courage of the sufferer. It is this courage that makes for meaning, not the suffering: this view is surely derived from the Christian obsession with the Cross. And the gloomy, morbid element in Christianity (viz., the obsession of medieval Christian art with punishment, pain, and death).

"For Tolstoy," he says, "suffering is not an evil": "Through suffering we are reborn to the spirit." This is a familiar Christian argument, but it leads to some convoluted argument in Gustafson over the motto to *Anna Karenina*: Vengeance Is Mine: I Will Repay.

Tolstoy, he argues, did not believe in a vengeful God. "The evil God, the one who avenges, punishes and causes suffering, is our creation, necessary to us for our own self-justification" (Ibid., 144) But he produces no convincing explanation of Tolstoy's use of this maxim. He quotes Tolstoy:

> "People so convince themselves that the bad they do is good that when they experience evil [*zlo*] they blame God rather than themselves and therefore in the depths of their souls they consider God evil, i.e. they deny Him and as a result receive no consolation from Him." That is Anna's story. (Ibid., 149)

The degree to which Gustafson misreads *Anna Karenina* can be worked out from this remark that accepts that this theme of blaming God is Anna's story. If it were so, and if Tolstoy had written a novel that was such an illustration of a Christian principle, that people "blame God" for experiencing evil, it would have been a boring religious tract. As it is, it is an exceptional European novel, not least because it cannot be pinned down to any such paradigm, but that it follows a complex woman's suffering with compassion. It is the work of an artist, not a Christian apologist, and it is this that I shall argue.

From his Christian point of view, Gustafson treats all of Tolstoy's works with too equal a respect: indeed, one gathers that he finds the later works such as *Resurrection* and *The Kreutzer Sonata* even better than his great masterpieces. He does this because he interprets them as iconic, in terms of "emblematic realism": Tolstoy's emblematic imagination is iconic he says (Ibid., p. 202).

Of course, Tolstoy changed his mind from time to time and it is clear that he wrote his later works in a different spirit from the earlier works and that which prompted the masterpieces. The crisis recorded in *A Confession* was, says Gustafson, Tolstoy's turning point: "The source of his depression, he came to see, was his own failure to participate in true life and true love" (Ibid., 161).

> Tolstoy the artist also underwent a crisis of values. His former major works . . . seemed to him to be unclear, poorly written, even wrong in their views. (Ibid., 161)

But the "unclarity" itself may have been an advantage, for once the creative impulse came to be subdued to his particular interpretation of Christianity it tended to become propaganda rather than art, and a propaganda that served his own rationalization of his problems. This involved, of course, his attitude to earthly and especially to sexual love:

> Love for is not love of . . . this exaltation of exclusive love . . . which Tolstoy believed modern culture, especially modern literature, and especially novels, indulged in and which, as he examined and condemned in *Anna Karenina* . . . "being-in-love", passionate or erotic love, is a most pernicious form of love because the love is evoked by the object and therefore one needs the object to have the love. . . . (Ibid., 182)

Thus there arises the "need to possess or control the object. . . ."—this impulse is avoided by moving on to a love that reaches beyond even physical reality: "Tolstoy wants to rescue the world from its enslavement to physical reality."

This may explain much about Tolstoy from his attitude toward Napoleon to his attitude toward consciousness, which latter he saw as the "divine eternal principle which I can participate in." But for most of us there is only "physical reality," while we hope to find transcendence through love of an object. The protest that the need for an object inevitably provokes the impulse to control the object derives from Tolstoy's own conflict between idealism and disgust. We might even protest that it was only because he was so traumatically deprived of his mother as object that Tolstoy set off on his quest for an ideal transcending spiritual reality which all the experiences of life are inferior to and to be subdued. Though I have no wish to deny or disqualify spiritual yearnings, I prefer a realism about human nature which, as might be based on philosophical anthropology, finds that our quest of meaning needs to be based on what we know of ourselves and of the truth of human emotional and psychic life, and an acceptance of our humanity as we are. And that is the position of the true artist.

I would argue that Tolstoy's great works are great art because they appeal to this kind of realism and because they are dramas which are enacted in the realm of a recognition and acceptance of human truth. Anna herself is for the most part portrayed in the light of this truth, and we suffer with her. To Gustafson she is a figure in a Christian exemplum or sermon: her chief failing is her self-deception, when she contemplates her position:

> She begins to lose sight of who she is or where she is going. Turned into the joy of her body, she comes to a crisis of faith, a necessary decision about identity and vocation. (Ibid., 307)

And in this she fails, out of self-deception and out of the failure to face her own reality. So, Gustafson tends to interpret the symbolism in rather crude terms that suit his Christian pattern: about the phantoms that haunt her dreams he says,

> The red hand bag is the container of her desires. . . . The old woman concerned with the temperature and her spread legs filling and fouling the whole place embodies and reveals Anna's animal self: the stoker-conductor bundled up against the storm, gnawing at the wall, and shouting in her ear, is the voice of her gnawing conscience, her divine self whose call to clear vision she will not hear. The arrival of the train at a station is Anna's coming and climax, the aim and end of her journey the fulfilment of her erotic need. And the storm, of course, is the passion to which she yields for the first time, but not yet as an active desire or decision. (Ibid., p. 309)

Gustafson does not mention the traumatic sight that Tolstoy endured when he saw the body of Anna Pirogova, his neighbor's mistress, an experience which set off the novel *Anna Karenina*. Nor does he say much that is illuminating about the mysterious little peasant about whom both Anna and Vronsky dream—a figure obviously closely related to the maxim Vengeance Is Mine. . . . Instead, he produces again a crude interpretation based on his own Christian view, a central feature of which is a distaste for sexual love:

> both Anna and Vronsky dream of a peasant with a dishevelled beard, bent over while doing something and speaking unintelligible words in French. This recurrent dream is of a violent mishap which is an ill omen: the mangled crushed body which foretells something. It is the only recurrent dream in Tolstoy's fiction. (Anna believes her position will be unravelled *(razvjazhet)* while Vronsky fears that his feeling for Anna is "tying *(privazyaet)* him to her more and more") Something iron (suggests a railroad—in Russian "iron road", *zheleznzja dovoga*). Anna's dream is an image of her conscience reacting in panic to her pregnancy . . . (and she) foresees that her death will be her punishment . . . the peasant is "doing something terrible in the iron over her. . . ." The peasant is "an image of Vronsky grown cold to her . . ." each instance of the recurrent dream captures a moment of inner assessment of some failing or flaw in the relationship which is threatening or destructive to the character. . . . (Ibid.)

This is only partially true: as will appear, I believe that the little peasant and the figures in the dreams arise in Tolstoy's unconscious, out of his fearful association of sexual love and pregnancy with some dreadful doom, and behind it the father glimpsed in sexual activity, in the primal scene, "doing something terrible with the iron." Tolstoy cannot control this image, or understand it or place it: it is by no means an appropriate image of a menacing conscience, troubling a Christian believer.

Gustafson is harsh on Anna herself: but the appeal of the book as a work of art arises from the author's sympathy with Anna, and the way he involves the reader's sympathy. It is true that he admits that "Anna is not punished by Tolstoy for her sexual fulfilment." But he goes on:

> In a fuller sense, Anna's story is a moral tragedy of self-enclosure. . . . Her story embodies and reveals the meaning of Tolstoy's words. . . . "When we are in God, i.e. in truth, then we are all together; when we are in the Devil, i.e. falsehood, then we are all separate." (Jubilee edition, 1890, 51:23)

But if the novel were a dramatization along these lines, how tedious it would be! It would read like a nineteenth-century moral temperance tract. Anna, besides self-deception, also experiences moments of vivid truth, and tries to find a way of dealing with her situation, from a recognition of her responsibilities. At one extreme she is torn in two, dreaming of having two husbands: at the other extreme she is utterly repentant to Karenin. It is true that at times "she hides from her own truth," but if that were all, we would not love and respect her as we do, or grieve for her in her tragedy.

What Gustafson does not tell us (like Mandelker over Dolly) is what Anna could do, what she might have done, to escape from her predicament. She has become trapped in a loveless marriage, in which the husband by his cold formalism and unresponsiveness, by his untenderness and his absorption in his world of bureaucratic "duty," fails to find the woman in his life and her potentialities for love. Anna declares, "He does not even know what love is." But Gustafson says that "The Karenin she creates in her dramatic rendering is the Karenin she needs"—which is most unfair, for Tolstoy shows him to be cold, mechanical, and incapable of finding the mysterious and passionate woman he is married to, or her needs. In spite of herself Anna is taken over by the impulse to fulfill herself in the way for which her soul yearns: and she argues that God has made her a woman with such yearning. She struggles against this fate, and becomes confused, duplicitous, and dismayed, but what could she have done? Should she have lived a life of renunciation, in the acceptance of a dead marriage? Should she have retreated into repentance and renunciation? As with Antony and Cleopatra, in Shakespeare's play, we hover between dismay at the lovers' rejection of their responsibilities and joy at their transcending magnificence—which leaves us enriched by a sense of the value of human choice and by the gravity of our ethical decisions, both of which elevate us to a high state of significance, in the pursuit of love and meaning.

Gustafson offers, too, a far too Christian interpretation of *War and Peace:*

> the war closes with a scene of the Christian love of enemy which is imaged in the sharing of God, set to the harmonious song of all together, and placed in an expanse of nature emblematic of that life which is eternal growth of love toward the all in all. (Gustafson, p. 283)

Does "love" triumph, throughout all the horror of the Napoleonic wars? Gustafson does not discuss the domestication of Natasha, which seems to be, as will appear, a sad reduction of this dynamic and beautiful creature to a kind of enslavement in Tolstoy's ideas of wifely potentiality. This is not a question of showing or not showing the pursuit of happiness or the exclusivity of object-love: Gustafson is harshly against self-fulfillment. Anna's final vision of life, he says, is

> the inevitable conclusion to be drawn from life understood as individual self-fulfilment. The pursuit of happiness for yourself alone, regardless of others, *which in the end is what the fantasy of romance entails,* inexorably leads to a world of struggle and strife. . . . Ibid., 130; (my italics)

But what of an impulse to reduce the woman in a married relationship to a role subservient to the man—by which I mean not only the established social pattern of the time, in a male-dominated society, but to the unconscious desires of the male author to keep women under control? This problem of Natasha will be examined later: it remains a problem, even if we accept the interpretation of Gustafson, that Tolstoy was seeking to explore Christian love in an emblematic realism. And as for Anna Karenina, what of the principle put forward in the Gospels—judge not that ye be not judged? (One interesting point one critic makes is that Tolstoy took the vengeance motto from Schopenhauer—who was in any case psychopathologically hostile to women—and in his first use of it he got the quotation wrong.)

It is true that Gustafson does produce a unifying picture of Tolstoy's overall quest: an obsessional preoccupation with the search for a purity of merging with the whole of reality which he saw as God:

> his early rules for behaviour, his lifelong habit of weight-lifting, his obsession with reworking his manuscripts, his tendency in his diaries to return to the same set of ideas just to write them out more precisely, his repeated moments of repentance followed by firm resolve for right action, his self-instructing message of "death, humility, silence" written on his finger-nail, his attempt to acquire the practice of perpetual prayer in order to reform himself, his theological belief in salvation through "effort"—all stem from the great need to find all from the self, to discover, nurture and reveal the perfection already within. . . . (Ibid., p. 6)

Doing battle with the major forces of intellectual and spiritual life in nineteenth-century Russia, Tolstoy thus stands alone, a stranger in his native land, says Gustafson.

> His task was to create an image and idea of life as understood in the Eastern Christian tradition but freed from what he believed were ecclesiastical misreadings, of dogmas and from what he felt was the pompous and meaningless jargon of most philosophical and theological discourse. . . . (Ibid., p. 456)

But in the course of this enterprise Tolstoy operated as an artist, trying at best to look openly at human experience, and to inquire into what men and women aspire to, what they are like, and what they can find of love and meaning. Later he fell into the pattern of bringing his creative work into the service of his overall propagandist will. In *War and Peace* and *Anna Karenina* something else took over, some creative, open, Socratic inquiring power that enabled him to depict human experience truly, without his Christian thumb in the scales, except for a few lapses, and it is this Tolstoy that I wish to celebrate.

* * *

To make an adequate criticism of a literary artist one has to attend to the words on the page, phenomenologically, as manifestations of the meanings of consciousness. Psychoanalysis here can be a valuable aid, because it is primarily a phenomenological discipline, by which the meanings of symptoms, actions, sexual activity, relationships, and cultural utterances may be studied, and because it seeks to include unconscious motives. To bring together insights from psychoanalysis and from the traditional modes of seeking out meanings of traditional literary criticism (in, say, the mode of William Empson's *Seven Types of Ambiguity,* 1949) is my chosen discipline, and it is this exacting discipline that much written in the name of "literary theory," "feminism," and "Marxist analysis" fails to do. The Christian critic, Gustafson, writes his best comments when he is attending to the local text in this way: yet I would suppose that in his overall estimation I would find it impossible to concur.

One critic (H. Kohut*) speaks of Tolstoy's "amoral" approach to his work. One can see what he means: the novelist cannot moralize or make his narrative accord to a moral pattern, certainly not the moral pattern of his explicit beliefs. If he had tried to do so the characters would have become mere instrumental puppets, moved about with no volition of their own, to enact a play that has already decided its moral outcome or "upshot": Gustafson seems to seek to reduce Tolstoy's art to such illustrative fables. We know that life is not like that: we know that people are complex and confused, as we are, and that their rational, ordered existence is continually in conflict with unconscious factors, with impulses that get out of hand—so that they are duplicitous or act against their best inclinations. And we know that if art is to deal with life, it must reflect this. Anna Karenina herself, for instance, as we shall see, is a self-contradictory character who declares herself straightforward at a moment at which she becomes aware of her duplicitousness and capacity for self-deception.

Yet, fundamentally, as we are aware all the time in reading him, Tolstoy displays an intense moral concern, which, while it is driven by a religious preoccupation with what it can mean to love, is imbued with deep sympathy and understanding of those who fail in this. This deep artistic concern, as we shall see, is a different driving force from the startling beliefs he held, about women and sexuality, at the conscious level, and even from his religious beliefs.

The artist's concern is at a deeper level—of a preoccupation with authenticity: are the characters being true to their deepest interests, and to their deepest concerns to be of integrity, true to the best impulses of their being? Here, of course, arise the problems of the tragedy, for with Anna Karenina the deepest impulses of her being are to love and be loved, when she is married to a man she discovers she does not love, and who offers her no possi-

---

*H. Kohut, *The Search for the Self,* ed. Ornstein (1980).

bility of loving her, and in spite of her best judgment forms an
adulterous liaison with a man who is overwhelmed by his love for
her, and whom she comes to love with every atom of her being.
Given this response from her deepest sense of what is authentic
for her, what else can she do but enter into a relationship that
makes all her other relationships—to her husband, to "society,"
to her closest friends, to her son—subject to an increasing inauthenticity? In this, the greatest complexities come from her inability to deal with her relationship with her son by Karenin, Seriohza,
whom she loves deeply. And while in a sense she acts out Tolstoy's
theories of the corrupting effects of sexual love outside marriage,
the actual story as it unfolds does not conform to a moralizing
fable that bears out Tolstoy's misogynist and deeply pessimistic
beliefs. In his original drafts, as Judith Armstrong points out,
Anna was unattractive, with a narrow, low forehead, and a short
turned-up nose. Her dress was bold and provocative, her voice
loud. In the same early draft Karenin was depicted as sensitive,
generous, and cultivated and not responsible for any contributing
factor to his wife's blatant flirtatiousness. Vronsky is portrayed as
a victim rather than as a seducer, unwillingly decoyed from his
firm and honorable intention of marrying Kitty into a shameful
affair with a married woman (Armstrong 1988, 44). In response
to a critic's complaint that he was cruel to give Anna Karenina
the end he did, Tolstoy replied that his heroes and heroines sometimes came to do things he would not have wished them to do,
and that what they actually did was simply what they would do in
life (*Tolstovski Yezhegodnik, 1912* [1912], 58; quoted by S. P. By-
chkov, *L.N. Tolstoy* [1954], 294; and also quoted by Theodore
Redpath, *Tolstoy* [1960]). In this Tolstoy admits that in writing the
author submits to some force that seems to speak "through"
him—and this, I believe, is the voice of authenticity, the deepest
awareness of what human beings ultimately want.

However, it is important to note that at times even Tolstoy's
genius was capable of serious falsification in his art. Whereas we
sense the truth, in the "upshot" of *War and Peace* and *Anna Karenina*, what shall we say of *The Kreutzer Sonata*? It feels convincing:
the technique is naturalistic, the sexual matters are dealt with in
terms of their real names, and the church and state clamped down
on the book—surely here must be truth! But, as Karl Stern says,
"the entire *Kreutzer Sonata* is pathological material presented by
a wily craftsman" (Stern, *The Flight from Woman*, p. 176)—it is a
sermon or pamphlet dressed up in narrative form. The critical

problem thus becomes one of distinguishing between the living truth of a creative perception, and those moments, and those works, in which a dynamic of falsity overcomes the artistic veracity.

2

The Man

It must come as a great shock to any student of literature to find that the author of *Anna Karenina* and *War and Peace* so savagely behaved in his treatment of the wife who loved him and who so dutifully served his literary interests: became, indeed, deeply disturbed in his treatment of women and eccentric in his attitudes to women.

Here it will be argued that the problems which Tolstoy had with women may be traced to his first experiences of woman, which were those of his mother. These were disastrous: Tolstoy's mother died when he was an infant, and the ensuing torment haunted him all his life. Several critics have recognized this source of Tolstoy's problems with women, but I hope to extend our insights here in the light of such studies of the predicament of the infant as those of D. W. Winnicott and John Bowlby, who have linked the infant's interaction with the mother and with the individual's whole capacity to "find" the reality of the world and of other people.

Tolstoy's personality is discussed with insight by Ruth Crego Benson in her short study *Women in Tolstoy: The Ideal and the Erotic*, 1973. She offers some very illuminating comments on Tolstoy's loss of his mother in infancy and quotations about this from his diaries and from other writings. She points out that his ideal literary heroines are modeled in part on the idealized image he held of his mother.

She died when he was only a baby. Yet the image he formed of her was "extraordinarily vivid and penetrated his imagination until the day he died" (Ibid., p. 4). And, of course, this image dominated his view of women.

As Benson points out, Tolstoy's mother remained for him "a holy idea."

> "When I was struggling with overwhelming temptations, I prayed to her spirit, begging her to aid me, and those prayers always helped me." (Jubilee edition, 34:354, quoted by Benson, p. 8)

34

So, Tolstoy's mother became associated with his guilt, and was enlisted by him in his attempts to maintain purity: by implication a sexual "fall" would seem to be an offense to mother and to her memory. A bereaved infant seeks in his agony of loss to devise an idealized image of the mother-woman, so intense that any tendency to meet women as normal mixed human beings, capable of sensual encounter, must seem to be a dreadful offense, not least because of the incest taboo. It may even seem to an infant that his own sensual hunger, because of the hungry fantasies that accompany such hunger, has threatened or has actually killed the mother. So, the mother image becomes the focus of a dreadful preoccupation with purity and holiness.

Mother became, for Tolstoy, God:

> "When I repeated the prayers which my baby lips had first lisped with my beloved mother, my love for her and my love for God mingled strangely into one feeling." (Ibid., 1:44, quoted by Benson, 8)

This is surely a later reconstruction of the situation, since no child of under one and a half years is really capable of repeating prayers alongside his mother, with any sense of their meaning. It is merely a way of putting the intense need in the baby-self to retain a radiant image of the mother, lost at the moment of developing the powers of speech and of the apprehension of reality, as a focus of being. Tolstoy had to compensate for the loss of the real woman (married to a real father) and so missed out on the normal processes of coming to terms with adult ambivalence, and the dim apprehensions of adult sexuality which enable the normal child to gain a sense that there is some experience that is special to his parents which gives them satisfactions, in which he has no part. This in turn colored Tolstoy's attitudes toward sexuality at large.

> "I don't remember my mother at all. I was one and a half years old when she died. It somehow happened that not a single portrait of her remained; *so that I can't picture her as a physical being.* In a way, I'm glad of that, because in my concept of her *there is only her spiritual image and everything that I knew about her is wonderful.* . . ."* (Ibid., 34:349, Benson, p. 8, my italics)

---

*Cf. "In his nurse's arms little Leo, twenty-three months old, screamed in terror at the sight of the livid mask whose eyes, full of tears, were fixed upon him with unbearable tenderness. He did not recognize his mother. He hated this strange woman. The nurse took him back to his bedroom where he grew calm again amidst his toys." Countess Marya Nikolayevna Tolstoy died on 4 August 1830, Henri Troyat, *Tolstoy*, 24.

There are other references to this intense idealization of the mother as we have seen. Tolstoy grew up dominated by an "ideal of perfection" and by a sense of a kind of love, and by a kind of relationship with the whole of creation, by which all earthly relationships and love became impossible to satisfy him.

If a man so becomes possessed by a holy image of his mother, he inevitably faces difficulties over love with any other woman. Out of this dilemma must have arisen the intense difficulties Tolstoy encountered over human sexuality, which resulted in his fanatical theories, about saving the world by persuading people to renounce sex altogether. One of the problems is that of attaching such idealization to the image of women that any sexual approach to her seems defiling and degrading because it smacks of incest. As Freud said,

> It sounds not only disagreeable but also paradoxical, yet it must nevertheless be said that anyone who is to be really free and happy in love must have surmounted his respect for women and have come to terms with the idea of incest with his mother or sister. Anyone who subjects himself to a serious self-examination on the subject of this requirement will be sure to find that he regards the sexual act basically as something degrading, which defiles and pollutes not only the body. The origin of this low opinion, which he will certainly not willingly acknowledge, must be looked for in the period of his youth in which the sensual current in him was already strongly developed but its satisfaction with an object outside the family was almost as completely prohibited as it was with an incestuous one. (Freud, "Universal Tendency to Debasement," in *Standard Edition*, 11:186*)

Tolstoy continued to be obsessed with a feeling that the sexual act was awful. In March 1909 at the age of eighty he was still possessed by a sense that it was ignoble and degrading. Henri Troyat says:

> Lying between cool sheets in his bed, he felt himself powerless, in spite of his eighty years, to prevent a return of sexual desire, and the thought horrified him. On 15 March he was preparing to breathe his last, and on 16 March he wrote in his diary:
>
>> It would be a hundred times easier to struggle against physical desire if carnal relations and the feelings that lead to them were

---

*I found this pertinent quotation in *Freud's Women* by John Forrester and Lisa Appingnesi (1992), 408. These authors say "One must commit incest in one's heart if one is to be able to love another woman freely."

not made to look poetical; if marriage were not presented as an admirable institution that makes people happy, whereas in at least nine thousand nine hundred and ninety-nine cases out of ten thousand, if not in all, it ruins their entire lives; if, from childhood to adulthood, people were persuaded that the sexual act (merely imagining a loved person in that posture is enough!) is an ignoble and bestial one that is meaningless unless it is uppermost in the minds of both partners that they are going to assume the heavy and complex responsibility of bearing a child and raising it to the best of their ability as a result of their intercourse. (Troyat 1968, 623)

This view of sexual relations is surely psychopathological, and it underlies Tolstoy's attitudes to marriage and to the family, which, as we shall see, became increasingly extreme. Mary Evans quotes a passage by Tolstoy from Tikhar Polner's *Tolstoy and His Wife* in which he comments on marriage in 1899: the language itself reveals the strange vibration of loathing:

The chief cause of unhappiness in married life is that people have been taught to think that marriage means happiness. The incentive for marriage is sex attraction, which takes the form of promises and hopes of happiness—a view supported by public opinion and by literature. But marriage cannot cause happiness. Instead, it always means torture, with which man has to pay for satisfying his sex urge. These tortures are lack of freedom, servility, revulsion, all sorts of moral and physical defects in one's mate, which one is forced to endure, such as temper, stupidity, dishonesty, vanity, drunkenness, laziness, greed, cupidity and immorality—all defects that it is much more difficult to endure in others than in oneself and which make one suffer as if they were one's own—and such physical imperfections as ugliness, slovenliness, odours, diseases, insanity and many others that are even more unbearable . . . the more happiness people expect of marriage, the more they suffer . . . Escape from torture is not in expecting happiness, but in anticipating the worst, and being prepared to bear it. If a man expects everything mentioned in the opening of *A Thousand and One Nights*, if a man expects drunkenness, stench, and revolting diseases, then he may overlook such minor defects as stubbornness, duplicity, and even drunkenness, cease suffering, and be happy in the realisation that worse possible things—insanity, cancer, and whatever else is mentioned in *A Thousand and One Nights*—are absent. Such a state of mind will make a man really appreciate everything good? (Polner 1946, 187)

Yet, as Mary Evans points out, Tolstoy's own wife Sonya shines as a model example of a faithful, bourgeois wife—however much her author-husband, whom she served devotedly, ill-treated and abused her. The last act of his life was to take flight from her, leaving a note behind in which he said,

> My departure will be bitter news for you and I am sorry, but please understand and believe when I say that I could not have done anything else. My position in the house has become unbearable. In addition to everything else, I can no longer live in the luxurious surroundings in which I have been living, and I am doing what old men of my age should do: I am leaving mundane affairs so I can spend the remaining days of my life in peace and solitude. If you learn where I am, please understand and do not come after me. Your arrival would only make our situation more difficult without altering my decision. I am grateful to you for the forty eight years of honest life you have spent with me, and I ask you to forgive me for everything I have done to you, just as I am forgiving you from the bottom of my heart for anything you might have done to me. I hope you will accept the new position in which my departure places you and you will not harbour any ill-will for me. If you wish to communicate with me, speak to Alexandra. She will know where I am and will forward anything important. She cannot tell where I am because I have her promise not to reveal my whereabouts to anyone. (Ibid., 210)

Ten days later he was dead. Her support was fundamental to his existence: but this mixture of rejection, apology, and repentance, and further rejection was typical. Evans says that "Up to and including the very moment of his death, Tolstoy was convinced that Sonya did nothing except thwart his will and, most fundamental, his understanding" (Evans, *Reflecting on Anna Karenina* 1982, 45).

Neither the feminist critics nor the Christian critics satisfactorily tackle these deep problems of horror over sexual love, in relation to Tolstoy's own behavior in marriage, to his theories about sex, the family, and love, in his theological works: nor do they offer any satisfactory account of how they influence his exploration of these themes in his creative work.

As Ruth Crego Benson points out, Tolstoy was body-haunted, obsessed equally by sexual desire and by the guilt of sexual satisfaction. It is possible, I suppose, that he actually *feared* sexual satisfaction (as did a patient of Winnicott's) because it *undermined the ideal image of women that kept him alive:* it destroyed the vision that hunger provoked in him, and left him destitute. So, he believed that "sexual relations debilitate and exhaust a person, debilitating him precisely in the most essentially human function, the function of the intellect" (Tolstoy, *Church and State and Other Essays*

[1891], 163, Benson, 3). Because he felt vulnerable, and since women humiliated him, they became scapegoats for the self-hatred that followed his sexual indulgences, and for his guilt and self-reproach. His yearning was for a mother as to a child, and so he could not stomach the adult woman:

> If only I could be little again and snuggle up to my mother *as I imagined her to myself!* Yes, yes, the mother whom I called to *when I could not speak,* my highest image of pure love; not cold, divine love, but earthly, warm, motherly. That is what my battered soul is longing for. . . . (*Dnevnik,* [1900], quoted by Janko Lavrin in *Tolstoy, an Approach* [1946], p. 18, Benson, p. 5; my italics)

He was brought up largely by a woman of remarkable moral qualities, Tatyana Alexandrovna Ergolsky, for whom he had "fits of rapturously tender love." And in deference to his memories of his mother, he devised a sense of the "sacred ideal" of womanhood such as his mother had been. As Benson says, this is reflected in its intensity in Levin's memory of his mother:

> Levin scarcely remembered his mother. The thought of her was sacred to him and in his imagination his future wife was to be a repetition of that enchanting and sacred ideal of womanhood which his mother had been. (Benson, p. 8)

By contrast with this idealization of women as they ought to be, Tolstoy developed a view of women in general as egocentric and emotionally erratic, and as creatures whose erotic influences were a constant threat to man's best impulses. He set out his own rules of conduct thus:

> Regard the society of women as an inevitable evil of social life, and avoid them as much as possible. Because from whom do we actually learn voluptuousness, effeminacy, frivolity in everything and a multitude of other vices, if not from women? . . . in this stage of corruption and vice they are worse than we are. (Jubilee edition, 46:32–33, Benson, 9)

Tolstoy declared that women are in all respects "morally [man's] inferior"—so he became implacably hostile to them, as Gorky found. To him, women were motivated by an egocentric and devilish self-interest. Naturally, he opposed women's liberation movements and he admitted in his diary in 1898 that for seventy years his "opinion about women has fallen lower and lower, and it's still falling even lower." Women's place was in the home, and she was biologically and emotionally marked for that role.

At first he believed that marriage, sanctioned by law and by a higher moral order, made marital intercourse a creative act. By contrast, romantic passion was debasing, unworthy, and destructive of domestic harmony. But later he lost his faith in marriage and began to delineate what Benson calls "sexuality's wasteland" in his last works.

As Benson says, "a barely concealed hysteria" provides the tone of the stories, "The Devil" and "Father Sergin" as well as in *The Kreutzer Sonata*. Tolstoy had quarreled with his wife while her infatuation with Sergius Ivanovitch Taneyev had disgusted him. In each of these works, the main male characters' lives and careers are ruined by events that revolve around a woman. The women not only act as the incidental catalysts of disaster: "they are endorsed with demonic powers" (Benson, 119). Tolstoy wrote in his diary:

> woman . . . is the tool of the devil. She is usually stupid, but the devil lends her his brain when she works for him. Thanks to this, she has accomplished miracles of intellect, perspective, and constancy— in order to do something vile. (Jubilee edition, 53:208, Benson, 120)

Kitty, we remember, saw something bewitching and devilish *(besovskoe)* about Anna Karenina's beauty and charm. And Benson suggests that Anna's exposed shoulders and bosom and their ivory color conjure up the image of Ellen Kuragin, whose sexuality encaptures Pierre Bezuhov in *War and Peace:* "Anna's charisma is more potent, however, because its source is not only the sensuality of her body, but of her spirit as well" (Benson, 80–81). There are many passages in both of the great novels in which Tolstoy pours scorn on the bodily exposure indulged in at the time by society women, and one senses both his guilt, his repudiation of these "wiles," to which society gives a sanction, and his fascination with this kind of display.

In the end, in *The Kreutzer Sonata* and in the two late stories already referred to, Tolstoy presents sexual solutions only as utterly impracticable or as productive of misery. He is sure that the sexuality that women represent, project, and provoke are the source of man's downfall.

> Because of them, careers are destroyed, character is corrupted, sexual desire flares out of control (Benson, 137)

In *War and Peace* and *Anna Karenina* Tolstoy is still willing to represent marriage as an effective and acceptable way to organize sex for the purpose of bearing children. But later he dismissed this possibility, and felt a profound fear, distrust, a contempt for sexuality, and intimacy of any kind. The possibility of reaching this position is there, of course, in the story of Anna Karenina and Vronsky who seem to be trapped in their own sexuality. We may even, indeed, feel some sympathy for the feminist argument, discussed in Mandelker, that Anna's predicament arises because she is trapped in a typical bourgeois marriage from which the only escape is adultery or death: the romantic illusion, which Anna picks up perhaps from the novel she is reading in the train, is but itself a fatal delusion. But even in an early work such as *Family Happiness* there was a deterioration of romantic illusion. In the later novel, *The Kreutzer Sonata*, any possibility of overcoming deterioration between partners appears as delusion or hallucination. The message of this late work, says Benson, is "the inevitable failure of woman relationships and the inescapable recognition of human alienation" (Ibid., 138). Of *The Kreutzer Sonata* she says it

> penetrates beyond a tragic view of experience ... its orgiastic tone and its insistent self-contempt invite us to celebrate, with the penitents, their capacity for evil and their *pride of guilt*. (Ibid.; my italics)

This is a trenchant criticism and it is impossible not to agree with this perceptive woman critic that

> his power was tragically flawed by his consistently limited and distorted view of the nature of sex, of women, and, therefore, of the men who were his chief concern. (Ibid.)

Yet, enigmatically, only because of these distorted views do we have the great tragic work *Anna Karenina*. It is true that Anna and Vronsky represent the "ambition, vanity and, above all, lust" of a promiscuous and degenerate society, and they were conceived by a man who regarded eros as debasing and self-destructive. Yet one only has to recall the sympathy both evoke in us, and the anguished bewilderment of their progress—together with the sense that they are seized with an urgent need to live, and to live life as it calls to be lived, to recognize how much greater is the art than the attitudes that prompted it—generated as they were by the disastrous death of Tolstoy's mother and the bereavement that left him baffled and bewildered about women, love, and sexuality.

* * *

Karl Stern says that "Psychoanalytical studies have shown that the two-year-old child does experience grief at the loss of the mother."

> Moreover, the child looks at the death of the mother frequently as though it were a case of leaving, of wilful abandonment, and this is associated with resentment. In other words, the original ambivalence (love-hate) which the child harbours towards the mother may be deepened to a degree which leaves no resolution, in the case of the mother's death. I have loved you, you have abandoned me, and therefore I hate you. (Stern 1966, 187)

John Bowlby, at the end of his volume on *Loss* (Volume 3 of *Attachment and Loss*), says he found there were good grounds for attributing a germinal capacity for mourning to young children at least from sixteen months onward.

> This implies that . . . they have the ability to retain an image of their absent mother, to distinguish mother from foster-mother and to know well whom they prefer. . . . (Bowlby, *Loss, Sadness and Depression*, 437)

He adds that if the cognitive psychologists are right in believing that a child of less than seventeen months has only the most limited capacity for symbolic functioning the term *mourning* may be inappropriate. This would surely square with the observations of Winnicott, about transitional object phenomena and disillusionment: for the child's mother to die when he was eighteen months is surely likely to confuse him seriously in his distress, as the (psychic) weaning process and all that it entails for consciousness.

It is not difficult for the present-day medical researcher to recognize that things that happen to a child in early infancy may influence its whole life. This is beginning to be recognized in physical medicine, and it may be assumed to be true of psychological problems. During the first weeks and months of life the infant is striving to put together a self and its world, and catastrophes at this stage can lead to severe damage to the reality sense, to the sense of identity, and to the capacity to love and to find meaning. The adult finds it difficult or impossible to escape from the consequent distortions of the reality sense because it has grown into his psychic tissue. So, I suggest that the catastrophe of the loss of his mother at the age of eighteen months, when she had in any case been nine months' pregnant, was crucially formative in Tolstoy's attitude to women and to everything associated with them: sex, love, hunger, guilt, childbirth, natural feeding, care and nurturing, and (since she had died) death: and, indeed, mortality. To enlarge this problem, we can take a hint from Jungian psychology, which sees a link between our attitudes to women and to Mother Earth: for in our consciousness, just as we emerged into life from women, that in union with women we shall find meaning, and finally that when we are buried in the earth, we are returning to our Mother. Our experience of the mother colors our whole experience of, and attitude to, nature and the world: and, so, ultimately, to the problem of the meaning of existence.

Tolstoy was much taken by the philosophy of Arthur Schopenhauer, and it would seem that this writer's extreme views of women and sex were felt to be especially palatable to him. He had a photograph of the philosopher over his desk (Edwards 1981, 142). In his philosophy, to his Teutonic mind, says Stern, "the universe seemed a huge dark vortex of insatiable forces which surely devour us unless the spirit is able to reduce them to a void" (Stern, 1965, 110).

The dire influence of Schopenhauer prompts a psychoanalytical diagnosis. Schopenhauer's mother, says Stern, was married to a much older man, in a marriage without love. Eventually the father was drowned and there was a suggestion of suicide. Heinrich Schopenhauer's widow became a celebrated literary blue-stocking: Feuerbach declared that she "had no heart or soul" (Stern, 1965, 117). She sounds very much like the schizophrenic-generating mother often described in psychoanalytic writings. She was, says Stern, "under a violent phallic drive": to her son she was "competitive and castrating"—she opposed her son's ambition to play the flute, and made a sarcastic remark about the title of his first great philosophical work. Eventually he made a final break with his mother after he disapproved of a lasting friendship of hers.

So, suggests Stern, Schopenhauer came to be so possessed by hate that to him (Mother) *nature could not possibly be ennobled.* The flesh cannot be spiritualized:

> No blessing can ever come from motherhood, for conception and birth serve only one purpose—the perpetuation of a curse. (Stern, 120)

With this view of nature and motherhood it is clear that it follows that sex is the *evil lying at the very center of nature:*

It follows that the genitals are the real focus of the brain, that representative of perception and as such, of the other side of the world, the world as idea. The genitals are the life-preserving principle, ensuring time its eternal life. In this capacity they were revered by the Greeks in the phallus, by the Hindus in the lingam, which are thus symbols of the affirmation of the will. Knowledge on the other hand, makes possible the annulment of the will, redemption through freedom, conquest and annihilation of the world. (Schopenhauer in *The World as Will and Idea*, quoted in ibid., 110)

To Schopenhauer sexual intercourse was a criminal act, says Stern:

The act through which the will affirms itself and through which man comes into being is an act of which all are ashamed in their innermost heart, which they, therefore, carefully conceal; yes, if they are caught at it, they are frightened, as if they were caught in a crime. It is an act which, in sombre reflection, one usually recalls with repugnance, in a more exalted mood even with abhorrence. . . . A strange sadness and remorse follow the performance of the act, a remorse which is most keenly felt after the first time, and generally is the clearer the nobler the character of the person. (Ibid., 111)

To the normal person, such a pronouncement will surely be startling. Did one experience "sadness and remorse" most keenly "after the first time"? And as for degrees of "clearness" about it, how does one judge the "nobleness" of the women with whom one has sexual intercourse—assuming that one does have such a number, from which to devise a scale? The mere assertion (implying promiscuity and a number of "conquests," some of which are "noble") betrays a strange and distorted view, of which the writer is unaware. Many people, surely, find the love of which the act is the culmination and of which it is the expression, enough to make one's recollections afterward a memory of a happy glow? And as for "abhorrence"! Surely only after the most desperate act of sex that is unmodified or blessed by love does one feel "abhorrence" and "repugnance"? And to postulate that the secrecy that normally accompanies sexual lovemaking is a sign that one regards it a "crime" is to misread those aspects of shame that according to the phenomenological analysis of Erwin Straus,* protect the creative being in sexual giving. Surely, we must find the views of Schopenhauer on women and sex to be extreme, and psychopathological?

---

*"Shame as a Historiological Problem," in *Phenomenological Psychology* (1966).

But, of course, these twisted views of Schopenhauer's influenced Tolstoy. In his play, *The Power of Darkness* (1887), for instance, sexual passion is a malignant force that drives men into foul baseness and precipitates unspeakable violence. This view partly explains why, after their mutual seduction, Vronsky and Anna are made to experience such shame—indeed, feel that they have committed a crime, and are murderers. It explains why Levin and Kitty experience that strange humiliation and dismay, during the first four weeks of their honeymoon. This interpretation of experience is not, of course, only based on Schopenhauer. Tolstoy himself obviously had strangely ambivalent feelings about sexual relations, as we see from Sonya's diaries: he felt increasingly that he should abstain, yet could not abstain and was overcome by "animal" lust, and then, after taking her (it would seem often without much consideration of her mood), would suffer terrible remorse. This problem was complicated by his seeming abhorrence of her desire, and by strange feelings of disgust, at making love to a pregnant woman or to a woman with a baby at her breast—feelings that perhaps can be explained in terms of the damage to his consciousness on losing his mother through childbirth.

His behavior over sexual relations with his wife was incredibly perverse, as Anne Edwards makes clear in her biography of Sonya, *Sonya: The Life of Countess Tolstoy* (1981):

> Since Masha's birth (which had almost killed her), she had been reluctant to become pregnant again. Her arguments for employing some kind of birth control (namely her husband's withdrawal before orgasm*) shocked and repelled Tolstoy. More than once they had quarrelled violently about this subject. Sonya saw that if she wanted to avoid becoming pregnant, she must forego sexual relations with her husband. It appeared that this difficult renunciation would be far more painful for her than for Tolstoy. He, in fact, had recently described marriage as "domesticated prostitution". Sexual restraint while she was pregnant no longer seemed enough to assuage her guilt; he had begun to believe that total abstention was necessary to achieve salvation. (Edwards 1981, 225)

---

*I cannot believe that it is this method that Anna expounds to Dolly in *Anna Karenina*, since later she tells Vronsky to his dismay that she will not have any more children. Sonya went on becoming pregnant long after Tolstoy had finished *Anna Karenina*, so Tolstoy obviously did not follow the advice he supposed Anna gave Dolly and must have supposed it wrong and immoral.

In July 1884 Tolstoy became restless and angry after a quarrel with his wife and insisted upon his "husbandly right." She had given birth only three weeks before, and refused him. He went down and wrote a furious remark in his diary, and returned to persist in his demands, and she yielded. Immediately after she began to hemorrhage and in the morning the midwife had to be called. The latter rebuked Tolstoy for his brutality and for his schoolboy haste. He was told not to have relations with his wife for a month, and she was ordered not to walk or go out driving or to get upset. Tolstoy was filled with concern and guilt. But soon he was writing in his diary, "Cohabitation with a woman alien in spirit, i.e. with her, is terribly disgusting."

A few years later he became obsessed with the idea that to follow Christ he had to refrain entirely from sexual activity. Husband and wife must sleep in separate rooms.

> If this did not remove temptation and a child was conceived, under no circumstances should an evil be compounded by the husband and wife having intercourse while the child was at the breast. (Ibid., 302)

Soon, he only had sexual intercourse with Sonya when he was impelled by lust and could not restrain himself. So, she spurned his physical advances, and in the conflict over this strange loveless behavior began to show signs of mental disturbance. It is not too exaggerated, surely, to say that over the problem of sexual relations with his wife Tolstoy behaved in a quite psychopathological way, and placed an intolerable strain on her mental and physical health. (It is also highly indicative that when there were some negative reviews of his novel *War and Peace*, which Sonya was transcribing by heroic labor, Tolstoy "was cold to her in bed": Ibid., 157.) Most indicative, however, of the origins of his problem is his belief from quite early on that "enjoyment of sexual relations with a *nursing woman* was the lowest form of bestiality" (Ibid., 121, my italics).

Yet it was extraordinary that Tolstoy despite his depreciation of women, was able to understand women, and to create such women in his novels as Natasha, Anna, Kitty, and Dolly. Of course, some of the feminists reject his images of women, but those with no ax to grind can see them as deeply penetrating, realistic, and sympathetic. This ambivalence became evident in Tolstoy's attitude to his wife. He was provoked into hate by trivialities on the one hand:

In me there often raged a terrible hatred of her. Sometimes I watched her pouring out her tea, swinging her leg, lifting a spoon to her mouth, and hated her for those things as though they were the worst possible crimes. (Quoted in Stern, 187)

Yet on the other he wrote admiringly and gratefully of her.

While I write, I hear the voice of my wife, whom I love more than all the world. I have lived thirty-four years without knowing that it was possible to love and be so happy. Why does such a being as she love me? (From a letter to a cousin, quoted in Stern, 187)

As Stern comments, "Nothing could prove more clearly . . . that the voice of hate has nothing to do with objective reality . . . (but) erupts out of the strata of pre-objective experience." And with Tolstoy the whole problem arose just at the moment when he was, as an infant, just becoming capable of moving beyond "pre-objective experience."

Many of Tolstoy's conscious attitudes to women, however, came to be reinforced by his reading of Schopenhauer, whose attitudes were full of abominable hate and contempt. (We should remember, when examining this philosopher-genius's attitudes here, that he had an equally atrocious hatred of the Jews, which, finding its way into Nazism, generated the Holocaust: indeed, as Stern remarks, "one can trace a direct descent from the irredeemable nonsense of Schopenhauer's 'will' to that incomprehensible phase of madness in this century that nearly succeeded in destroying the world" (Ibid., p. 122).)

Schopenhauer wrote:

For, as Nature has endowed the lion with claw and fang, elephant and boar with tusks, the bull with horns and the jelly fish with obscuring liquid—in the same way she has endowed woman with deceit, for her protection and defence. . . . (*Parerga and Para lipomena*, quoted in ibid., 112)

Tolstoy would seem to have taken a clue from this, when he makes Anna Karenina fall so easily into lying and deceit, when Karenin first challenges her interest in Vronsky. By the way, we should note here what Stern calls "the wealth of imagery referring to the phallic and the oral-sadistic":

all the power which (Nature) has given to Man in the form of physical strength and reason, she has lent to woman, under the guise of that gift (of deceit). Deceit is inherent to woman, almost as much to the stupid as the clever. To use it on any occasion comes as naturally to her as it comes to those animals to use their weapons, and she considers it as her right. Hence an entirely honest woman without deceit is probably impossible. . . . (*Parerga* &c quoted by Stern, 112)

The view of "nature" in this passage, which he parallels with a passage from the Marquis de Sade, Stern suggests, equates the evil dangerous image of nature with an orally sadistic mother, *the mother ever ready to destroy and devour,* a link which he reports to be often found in clinical practice in psychotherapy: behind it is often found the *vagina dentata,* the threatening toothed vagina of the castrating mother or woman. Schopenhauer's violently castrating mother made his philosophy attractive to a Tolstoy who had in him a dynamic of hatred directed against the mother who, rejecting him by dying, left him with a phantom of a destructive and murderous woman, and yet a woman murdered by sex.

Yet the strange truth is that Tolstoy also gave us in his greatest novel a penetrating rendering of the *participation mystique* between mother and infant—so excellent that Karl Stern quotes it in his chapter on "womanhood"!

He says that "Levin and Kitty represent perfect examples of the father and mother's relationship to the child."

> All this illustrates how the father develops an inner relationship to the baby properly when the baby just begins to come out of that primaeval world which he shares with the mother, from that *participation mystique.* . . . (Ibid., 34)

This is interesting because it was just as he was coming out of this *participation* that Tolstoy suffered the catastrophic blow of the loss of his mother.

The passages Stern quotes are Kitty's feeling that her baby needs her, and dashes to him.

> In her heart she knew that he not only recognized Agafia Mihailovna, but comprehended a whole lot of things that nobody ever knew, and that she was only just beginning to find out, thanks to him, for Agafia Mihailovna, for the nurse, for his grandfather, and even for his father, Mitia was only a weak little creature who demanded material attention, but for her he was already a human being, with a whole history of moral relations. (*Anna Karenina,* quoted in ibid., 33)

When Levin sees the baby being bathed they experiment to see whether Mitia recognizes people.

Levin bent over the bath, and the child seemed to know him. The cook was then called; she, too, bent over him and the child frowned and screwed up its face. . . .

Kitty declares that she has been warned that Levin said he had no feeling for the child. He declares that he was disappointed "not exactly in him, but in my feeling for him . . . there was only this feeling of pity, disgust. . . ."

> Kitty listened to him as she put on her rings, that she had taken off before bathing the baby. "There was more fear and pity than satisfaction. I never knew until today, during the storm, how I loved him." Kitty's face grew radiant. (Ibid., 34)

Perhaps only a man who had suffered such a traumatic loss of his mother as Tolstoy, with the consequent confusion of relationship and reality, could write such passages in a novel. They are very modern, and exemplify processes to which such thinkers as F. J. J. Buytendijk and Winnicott have attended. The former said that smiling was "the miming of mind"—the first moments of recognition in a baby convey a highly significant stage, in the processes of the I-Thou: for the sudden glint in the eye of the baby announces that its mind has entered into the human world, of encounter and of the recognition of one being by another—an intensely moving moment. The woman is equipped with the capacity to feel an interest in an infant, and to respond to it, *before* this stage is reached: this is her special gift, without which we would all be mad (although, as we have seen, some feminists call it protofascistic even to believe in such a capacity!). But for the man, as Stern observes, it is usual for him to take an interest after this stage is reached.

To enable women to perform this role of bringing a baby into being, they have a capacity which Stern describes as "transrational," to avoid the pejorative flavor of the word irrational. It is a form of *knowledge* or *awareness* that is not only independent of reason "but goes *beyond* it." For women "being and idea are indivisibly one," while love, as a natural gift, is a characteristic of all womanhood.

It could be that an individual who has been severely wounded in this very sphere—as Tolstoy was by losing his mother at the very moment of psychic need, just at the point of weaning—turns against women and tends to deny any moral capacity in them at all, vilifying them as morally inferior and deceitful: yet, at the same time, as well as creating a visionary, spiritual, unearthly woman, being able to see the reality of women's gift to being and sanity, in their motherly role.

* * *

I was fascinated to discover a study of Tolstoy which began with a chapter "Tolstoy's Dead Mother" and opened with a reference to Winnicott's *Playing and Reality:* this was Judith M. Armstrong's *Unsaid Anna Karenina* (1988). Armstrong invokes much from the study of literary theory and of psychoanalysis, but I find her use of literary theory confusing and it is difficult for me to invoke her psychoanalytical position, since she does not appear to be able to take on board the radical criticisms and reconsiderations of Freud made by more recent object-relations psychoanalysis and by existentialist psychotherapy. Whenever she invokes Derrida or Lacan or Laplanche, I feel, she becomes obscure (and at times ridiculous, as by talking at one point (Armstrong 1988, p. 23) about the *text's* "unconscious"). It seems to me that she is best when she makes simple old-fashioned literary analyses (e.g., Ibid., 89 on Anna Karenina's narcissism, or in ibid., 30 on Tolstoy's problem with women). And she makes the convincing point that Anna represents an aspect of Tolstoy's own personality, and suggests that she dies because he could not resolve his own psychic conflicts.

She notes in her first chapter that unconscious memories of the experience of the lost mother affect Tolstoy's attitudes. His very creative effort itself, she suggests, was impelled by the high moral association of his mother's saintliness and purity. She pays particular attention to the potency of *Childhood*, which, although not autobiographical, combines visual clarity and the invitation to identification.

> Sleepy, and with drooping eyelids, he sits in his high chair drinking warm milk with sugar in it. He hears her sweet warm voice as she talks to someone, and screwing up his eyes, he makes the image of his mother button—small, no bigger than "a little boy reflected in the pupil of an eye". (Ibid., p. 11)

This latter she sees as an imaginative physical image of the desire ascribed by M. Wolfenstein "to the parentless child—the desire to take into himself something of the lost mother," in her article "The Image of the Lost Parent," in *The Psychoanalyic Study of the Child* (28:433). She also sees the warm sweetened milk as a recapitulation of the blissful time when the baby nursed at his mother's breast. She relates Winnicott's observation that the mother allows the child to believe that her breast is part of the infant to Wolfenstein's observation that "the loss of a parent is also an intolerable injury to their fantasied omnipotences" (Ibid., 539):

> Try as he might, he cannot revive the magical moment when his mother is caught in his own pupil, just as the real Tolstoy child was unable to regain the lost presence of his really dead mother, yet constantly recreated her in his imagination. (Armstrong, 13)

Tolstoy was as she points out, both consciously aware of the significance to him of his lost mother, and unconsciously driven by the loss. He wrote late in life:

> Felt dull and sad all day. Towards evening this state changed to one of deep emotion—a desire for tenderness, or love. I wanted, like a child, to cling to some loving, compassionate being, and weep with emotion, and be comforted . . . become like a little boy and cling to my mother, as I imagined her to myself. Yes, Mother, whom I never called that, because I could not talk then. Yes, her, my highest image of pure love; but not cold, divine love—earthly, warm, maternal love. Mother, hold me. All this is mad, but it is all true. (Tolstoy, quoted in ibid., 1, presumably a different translation of the previous passage, p. 16, quoted by Gustafson)

I find it difficult, however, to be fair to Armstrong, because she, too, like Mandelker, seems to confuse issues by seeking to preserve the dogmas of feminism and the abstractions of literary theory rather than make her own mind up about her response to art. For instance, she cannot accept Kitty or Dolly, because "they have to be classed as the classic objects of masculine desire," and consigns them to "negative semantic space," whatever that may mean. (Does it mean that they are unspeakable?) On the other hand, when she produces an insight of her own, she makes a valuable contribution as when she says, "What [Tolstoy] loves in Anna is his own sexuality" (Armstrong, 94)

There were two or three factors in Russian life which bore on Tolstoy's moral thinking at the time he was writing *Anna Karenina*. One was the behavior of the czar who took a mistress and brought her flagrantly into public life: Tolstoy obviously felt that upper-class Russian life was becoming decadent, sexually. Then, locally, he was much troubled by the predicament of Anna Stepanovna Pirogova, the mistress whom a local magistrate had brought to his farmhouse: Alexander Nilolaevitch Bibikov. Oddly, Bibikov was a liberal-minded illegitimate son of a landowner, a nihilist, and a supporter of various liberal groups. He was arrested after an attempt on the czar's life in 1866 and was still under police supervision.

His mistress was treated abusively by him, and Bibikov was flagrantly unfaithful to her. Tolstoy's wife Sonya liked her and disliked Bibikov. Later Bibikov hired a young and beautiful German girl with whom he began an affair. We may detect in Bivikov some of the elements of Oblonsky.

It was just at this moment that Tolstoy conceived the idea of a novel based on

> the character of a woman of high rank who had lost her balance . . . he would try to make this woman pitiable and blameless, and that no sooner had he imagined her clearly than he also visualized all the other female characters of the story. (From Sonya's *Journal*, Edwards, 189)

The Tolstoys were very much wrapped up in Bibikov's escapades. Tolstoy, however, found it difficult at first to get on with his projected story. Then in January 1872 Anna Pirogova threw herself under a train. Bibikov had told her he was planning to marry the young German governess. Tolstoy attended the postmortem examination, and the spectacle of this woman's mangled naked body, with its skull dissected, had a terrible effect on his mind. It was, says Edwards, "his most disturbing encounter with death." He wondered what could have driven her to such a terrible death. And the sight must have confirmed his feelings that sexual instinct was the most destructive and fatal element in human experience. From the description of Anna Karenina's corpse, with its sexual overtures (her beautiful head being undamaged, though the eyes are still staring), I conjecture that possibly what he saw was *the mother destroyed by sexual intercourse* as he felt his mother had been destroyed as an infant, by some "terrible force," at the moment when he hungered for her with all his being, at a time of weaning, so that it might seem that this very hunger for her breast might indeed have contributed to her death. What had killed her? Some "other" rival—the new fetus which had usurped her primary maternal preoccupation, or the father, in creating this new being, by the dangerous act of sex. I believe that it was as if the most terrible fantasies of his babyhood were now visible in the world, so this became a most evocative moment.

At any rate, at the very moment Tolstoy left the scene, he heard a locomotive steaming into the Yarenki station where the body lay, beside it the little red bag (? symbol of the womb) she had been carrying, the sight of which unnerved him. And there he saw

A dwarfed peasant, gray-bearded and swathed in woollen rags, muttered to himself as he worked at the rails (Edwards, 198).

This spectacle became a specter that haunted Tolstoy. Immediately, Tolstoy's nightmare returned, the one he had suffered at Arzamas, after finishing *War and Peace*. He had been reading Schopenhauer, and his nerves were at a breaking point. He wrote in his notebook:

I must be reborn in order to be content . . . and to be reborn is to die.

On his journey to Arzamas at 2:00 in the morning he was "overcome by despair, fear and terror, the like of which I have never experienced before." He awoke in a strange dark room of a house where he was a guest, "feeling that he had to escape from something terrible." He asked himself, "Who is it? What do I fear?" "Me," answered a voice he believed in his half-awake state to be death. "I am here!" he spent the night huddled in prayer, unable to quell his terror. On his way to the next town he was afraid to look back over his shoulder. "The nightmare," says Edwards, "did not fade with time: the pursuing phantom remained with him for most of his life" (Edwards, 186).

It is this death-figure, the little muttering peasant, who says, "Vengeance is mine; I will repay," and who pursues Vronsky and Anna, until it destroys both their lives. The remark that "I must be reborn . . . to be reborn is to die" reveals the predicament of one who suffers from deep (schizoid) problems of feeling a radical weakness of identity, a sense of not being adequately born because of being deprived of the mother, at a critical time. As H. Guntrip reports, schizoid suicide is an attempt to be born, in this fashion, by dying. And as he ended writing *War and Peace* Tolstoy was left with a terrible feeling that all his efforts to hold himself together by writing, by "imagining, remembering, fantasying" had failed to yield results. Circumstances bore down on him, leading to this profound existential crisis.

He had another vision of the threatening figure of death later, after the death of Nikolenka, his baby of ten months, from meningitis, in February 1875, and when Sonya, in May, was almost three months' pregnant again. His aunt, Pelagya, who was the closest he could get to his mother, was also ailing. He cried out to Sonya in the night, and said he had "lost his way."

> He . . . told her that the ghostly image he had encountered at Arzamas had returned . . . he felt he was being pursued by death . . . the thing that had pursued him seemed to be everywhere he turned, and suddenly he could not recall where the stairs were . . . "It is a bad omen," Sonya said. . . . (Edwards, 216)

As when his mother died, his grasp on reality was disturbed: and throughout *Anna Karenina*, which he was working on at the time, we have the record of people feeling they have "another self," or a "brutal force" in life, that operates against their own authentic existence, and prompts them to desperate acts—Anna, Vronsky, and Karenin. And at the crucial moments, often associated with sexual impulses and childbirth, appears the muttering little peasant, who threatens their existence. This menacing figure is very complex, and emerged in the first instance, I believe, from Tolstoy's fantasy life as an infant—one who was first of all deprived of his mother's preoccupation, when she became pregnant when he was only a few months old and then when she was taken from him in childbirth.

Of course, the torments and the subsequent existential crises here can be seen in theological terms, in relation to the progress of Tolstoy's beliefs. But his beliefs can also be seen to be rationalizations of problems that arose from his formative experiences as an infant, in the strange legacy in the "psychic tissue" of a man who, as a baby, suffered severely from his mother's too-early next pregnancy, her withdrawal of "primary maternal preoccupation," experienced as the loss of the focus of his world, and his path to find reality, when she died.

Not long after this ghostly experience, Tolstoy's Aunt Pelagya died (December 1875)—even as she cried out "I don't want to die!"

> from the moment of her death an intangible wall was flung between Tolstoy and his wife, a wall that Sonya would try to tear down for the rest of their lives. Aunt Pelagya was Tolstoy's last link to his mother, the mother he had never truly known . . . he finally accepted that his mother was dead and that there was no-one who could keep her spirit alive for him. . . . With her loss he entered in earnest into a solitary combat with death. . . . (Ibid., 217)

Of course, what I have written in these last few pages opens up a vast area of complex phenomenological realities in Tolstoy's psyche: he was finishing *Anna Karenina* in 1875, but he claimed that he thought it now repulsive and was becoming absorbed by religious and spiritual issues which his wife found confusing and repellent: he was retreating into a new spiritual turmoil.

*   *   *

One of the most astonishing and revealing episodes related in Anne Edwards's book on the life of *Sonya* is Tolstoy's dream about a *porcelain doll* (Edwards, 109–12). Sonya and Tolstoy wrote an eight-page letter to Tanya the next day: Sonya began the letter, but Tolstoy took over and told, in a seriocomic tone, how he dreamed that Sonya had come into their bedroom while he was asleep.

We have noted that Oblonsky has a dream about women as little decanters. Here is a record of the underlying problem Tolstoy had, of needing to try to retain an image of his dead mother, this figure remaining in his mind, as a certain image or icon of women. Significantly, Sonya was pregnant at the time, and Tolstoy, as Edwards says, is trying to transform her into an untouchable: "a porcelain doll can by its nature have no responsiveness or desires." Surely, this is a highly significant piece of phenomenological symbolism.

I heard her opening the door, breathing and getting undressed all in my sleep. I heard her coming out from behind the screen and walking toward the bed. I opened my eyes and I saw Sonya, not the Sonya whom we know, but a Sonya made of china! . . . Do you know those little china dolls, with cold, bare shoulders and neck, and arms folded in front but made of the same piece of china as the body, with hair painted black and big artificial waves, with the black paint faded on top, and with protruding china eyes also painted black at the edges and set too widely apart, and a bodice with firm pleats, also of china and made out of one piece? Sonya was just like that—I touched her hand—it was smooth, pleasant to touch, cold and made of china. . . . I said, "Are you made of china?" She replied without opening her mouth (her mouth remained folded at the corners and daubed with bright crimson): "Yes, I am." A chill ran down my spine, and I looked at her legs. They too were china, and (you can imagine my horror) they stood on a china base made from the same piece as she was, representing the ground and painted green like the grass. Near her left leg a little above the back of the knee was a china support painted brown and probably representing a tree stump. It too was made from the same piece of china as she was. I realized that without this support she wouldn't have been able to stand up, and I became so sad, as you can imagine—you who loved her. I still couldn't believe my eyes and began to call her; she couldn't move without the support and the base beneath her, and she could only rock a little bit on her base so as to fall toward me. I heard the china bottom bumping against the floor. I began to touch her—she was all smooth china, pleasant to touch and cold. I tried to raise her arm—I couldn't. I tried to put my finger, or at least my nail, between her elbow and her side—I couldn't either. . . . I began to examine her bodice—all of one piece with her body, top and bottom . . . one piece of pleat of her bodice had been broken off at the bottom, and you could see something brown. The paint on the top of her head had peeled off a bit, and the white was showing. The paint had come off her lips in one place, and a piece of her shoulder had broken away. But everything was so true to life that you could tell it was the same Sonya of ours. The bodice I knew, embroidered with lace, and the black bun of hair at the back—only made of china—and the lovely delicate hands and the big eyes and lips—they were all exactly alike, only they were china—even the dimple on the chin and the shoulder bones in front. I was in a terrible state; I didn't know what to say or do or think; she would have been glad to help me, but what could a china creature do? The half-closed eyes, and the eyelashes and the eyebrows—from a distance they all looked real. She didn't look at me, but through me, at her bed. She obviously wanted to go to bed, and she kept rocking back and forth. I was at my wit's end, and took hold of her and tried to carry her over to the bed. My fingers made no impression on her cold china body and, what surprised me even more, she had become as light as a glass phial. And suddenly she seemed to shrink away, and she grew tiny, tinier than the palm of my hand, although she still looked exactly the same. I took hold of a pillow, stood her up in one corner, pummeled another corner with my fist, and laid her down there; then I took her nightcap, folded it into four, and covered her with it up to the chin. She lay there, looking exactly the same. I put out the candle and laid her down to sleep under my beard. Suddenly I heard her voice from the corner of the pillow: "Lyova, why have I become china?" I didn't know what to reply. Again she said: "Does it matter that I'm china?" I didn't want to upset her, and said that it didn't. I felt her again in the darkness—she was still cold, still china. Yet her belly was the same as when she was alive, protruding upward like a cone, and rather unnatural for a china doll. I had a strange feeling. I suddenly felt glad that she was like that, and I ceased to be surprised—it all seemed natural to me. I took her out, transferred her from one hand to the other, and put her down again by my head. She was quite happy. We went to sleep. In the morning I got up and went out without looking at her. I was so afraid of all that happened the previous night. When I came back for lunch she was just the same

again as she had always been. I didn't remind her of the previous
night, being afraid to upset her and Auntie. I haven't told anyone
about it except you. I thought it was all over, but during these past
days, whenever we are alone, the same thing has happened again. She
suddenly becomes a little china doll. When she is with others, everything is normal. She isn't dismayed by this, nor am I. To be frank,
however strange it is, I'm glad about it, and despite the fact that she
is made of china, we've very happy.

I'm only writing to you about all this, Tanya dear, so that you can
. . . find out from the doctors via Papa what it all means and whether
it is bad for the future child. We're alone just now, and she is sitting
by my necktie, and I can feel her sharp little nose digging into my
neck. Yesterday she was left alone. I went into the room and saw Dora
dragging her into a corner and playing with her, and almost breaking
her. I gave Dora a thrashing and put Sonya into my waistcoat pocket
and took her off to the study. However, I've now ordered a wooden
box with a clasp (it was delivered today from Tula), covered on the
outside with Morocco and the inside with crimson velvet, with a place
made for her so that her elbows, head, and back can fit exactly into
it, and she can't get broken. I'm covering it on top with suede as well.
Edwards, 199 ff.

In this story Tolstoy obviously intimates that Sonya's pregnancy
has transformed her into an untouchable—a porcelain doll that
by its nature can have no responsive desires. In the dream she is
the re-created image of the mother that the child Tolstoy has tried
to hold on to: but also dead—an icon. From another perspective
she is dehumanized and in the end is put away in a box. It is
indeed uncannily disturbing. Once again the Tolstoys, unable to
speak of their deepest emotions, were using the written word to
communicate.

Although Tanya thought the story rather odd and unsettling,
she gave it to her father as Tolstoy had asked. Dr. Behrs apparently did not perceive the complex sexual revelations in the little
tale, and he wrote to Sonya, "Your Lyova wrote such a fantastic
piece for Tanya that even a German would never have thought of
it. Amazing how fertile his imagination is. Sometimes it manifests
itself in very strange forms—he managed to write eight pages
about the metamorphosis of a woman into a china doll!"

The porcelain image is surely the ideal mother-woman figure
Tolstoy created. It is significant that the china figure "seemed to
shrink away"—as the image of the mother than Tolstoy tries to
cling to as a child must have shrunk away. The "horror" comes
because Tolstoy is looking at his dead mother (and it is because
the wife Sonya "becomes" the dead mother when she becomes

pregnant that intercourse with her is rejected as "bestial"). At the end, he puts the little doll in its coffin. The confusion between the doll and the real wife is uncanny: no wonder Tanya found it "rather odd and unsettling"!

*　　*　　*

We have looked at the origins of Tolstoy's tendency to idealize women—as Levin idealizes Kitty, or Pierre Natasha. Of his mother he wrote fifty years later that he yearned for "the mother whom I called to when I could not speak, my highest image of pure love." Of Tatyana Ergolsky he wrote how her influence "consisted first of all in teaching me from childhood the spiritual delight of love. She did not teach me that by words, but she filled me with love by virtue of her whole being" (both quoted in Benson, 6–7). Women were, of course, somewhat idealized in nineteenth-century Russian culture, although, as is clear from many novels, they were also brutally treated. Natasha and Kitty are both idealized, while Anna Karenina is a visionary woman, one of the most remarkable women ever created in fiction—beautiful, deprived, mysterious, passionate, bewildered, cruel, and tragic: a remarkable achieve-. ment for a man who had such a terror of, hatred of, and contempt for women. Anna Karenina is also a witch—but also represents those witchlike elements that Ann Ulanov and Barry Ulanov declare to be significant in the dynamic of the female soul, if women are to realize their full potentialities. (See Ulanov and Ulanov, *The Witch and the Clown* [1987].) For Tolstoy also wrote that "women are generally so bad that the difference between a good and a bad woman scarcely exists" (Benson, p. 4). Yet we can see how and why for Tolstoy, such a woman would be fraught with danger—and haunted, because she finds and realizes her sexual passion—her most dangerous and unmotherly feature.

It is likely that childbirth, to a man whose mother died in childbirth at the age of one and a half, seems to be the most terrible thing in the world—and this realization makes Tolstoy able to write the powerful and disturbing scene of Kitty giving birth, and of course Anna's puerperal fever (based on autobiographical material as it was; see Edwards, 195). There is also the terrible scene in *War and Peace* of the little princess's death in childbirth. But if childbirth is dangerous, then sexual intercourse is also the most threatening activity, since it always bears the risk of causing childbirth, as the child gradually learns as he grows up. Feeling this horror, by infantile logic, Tolstoy is perplexed by the agonies of wondering how sexual intercourse and childbirth can be modified and made less dangerous. Marriage, for a time, he believed to be a good method of bringing sexuality within the compass of religious meaning, and making it socially acceptable (or, speaking in psychological terms, *safe*). But later, no doubt under the promptings of the phantom woman who haunted him, and inspired by the mysogynist philosophy of Schopenhauer, he found it to be a matter of being imprisoned, and liable to lead to murder (as in *The Kreutzer Sonata*): impossible to control.

There is an infant logic, often examined in psychoanalytic literature, by which sex is like eating, and so has the accompanying dangers—as when food is eaten it disappears. Sex, which the child becomes dimly aware of, as an energy between adults, becomes to him something filled with danger, and even hurtful or murderous. This connection, especially in a person traumatized as an infant as Tolstoy was, explains the association of sex and murder that we often find in his work. It is this strange connection that makes Tolstoy write of the shame that overcomes Anna when she is first seduced, and the quite clear delineation of that adulterous act as an act of murder on the part of Vronsky:

> He felt what a murderer must feel when he looks at the body he has robbed of life. The body he had robbed of life was their love, the first stage of their love. There was something frightful and revolting in the recollection of what had been paid for by this terrible price of shame. Shame at her spiritual nakedness crushed her and infected him. But in spite of the murderer's horror before the body of his victim, that body must be hacked to pieces and hidden, and the murderer must make use of what he has obtained by his crime.
>
> And, as with fury and passion the murderer throws himself upon the body and drags it and hacks at it, so he covered her face and shoulders with kisses. (*Anna Karenina*, 165)

This is a remarkable passage, and suggests something behind it more like an infantile fantasy of adult sex rather than the feelings of an adult couple even after an act of love that is felt to be adulterous and shameful. There was, of course, a Christian horror of adultery, and both lovers have sinned: but the references to being "robbed of life" and "hacked to pieces" suggests a deeper revulsion which is associated with sadistic fantasies and with a morbid fear of sex. It is a most disturbing moment in the novel, not least because the act of love is presented as an act that leads to death (although Anna later argues that Vronsky brought her to life as Karenin could not). It suggests that Tolstoy himself, in the act of sex, was tormented by a feeling of committing murder, and so of deep and humiliating shame. "The body he had robbed of life was their love"—what can this mean, other than a perplexity arising from infantile fantasies and puzzlements about sex? (There are several case histories of men who fear that to give in to sex is likely to lead to their death: and, indeed, there is a symbolism in orgasm that makes it seem a little death.)

And here, I believe, we must invoke once more the concept of the primal scene. As an infant, Tolstoy was faced with the horror, that his mother died in childbirth as a consequence of the murderous act of sex. Several elements in his work suggest that he may have overseen or overheard parental sex, which as an infant he could not understand, and which he could only conceive of as painful and murderous. This is of course conjecture but this seems the only way to explain his sadistic and murderous visions. (Cf. the terrible wife-murder in *The Kreutzer Sonata*.)

By the same infantile logic, whenever there is a hint of passionate love in the air, in Tolstoy's novels, there is a hint of the haunting presence of the primal scene, with all its murderous menace— leading here in the end to Anna's terrible death. We need to remember that the whole novel *Anna Karenina* was sparked off by his witnessing the body of the woman who threw herself under a train out of sexual jealousy after being supplanted by her partner's new mistress.

So, as Anna contemplates her situation, just after meeting Vronsky, trying to pretend that nothing has happened, she goes into a nightmare state ("What is that on the arm of the seat, a fur cloak or an animal? And what am I doing here? Am I myself or someone else?") and half-sees the peasant of her haunted dreams ("The peasant with the long waist starting gnawing at something on the wall. . . .") and

> after this there was a terrible screech and clatter, *as though someone were being torn to pieces;* then a red light blinded her eyes, and at last a wall rose up and blotted everything out. . . . (Ibid., 116; my italics)

We recognize this, on a second reading, as a premonition of her death: but it is also a rendering of that strange state of suspended animation such as Dickens makes Oliver Twist have, when he becomes aware of the presence of Fagin—which Stephen Marcus associates with the half-wake state in which the infant Dickens became aware of the primal scene.* As soon as sexual passion

*Stephen Marcus, *Dickens: From Pickwick to Dombey* (1965).

begins to develop in his novel, Tolstoy has his character go into a state of the kind experienced by an infant confronted with the primal scene. Anna is beginning to become aware of her love for Vronsky: her sexual instinct is taking over and urging her toward passion—and so, in Tolstoy's view, toward death: yet she is inevitably drawn to it: "All this, far from seeming dreadful, was rather pleasant."

In Tolstoy's view, giving oneself up to sexual passion was like giving oneself up to being "torn to pieces," because to himself as a confused infant, this is what he dreaded, when he overheard parental sexual activity, if we conjecture that he did. There is also, in this novel, the curious symbolism of light, as here "a red light blinded her eyes." When Anna kills herself, the candle goes out. This, too, I believe, we may associate with the curious state of the infant who is awakened by parental sex, and becomes curious to see what he is forbidden to see, and this becomes linked in Tolstoy's mind with the damage done to his view of reality when his mother died. So, too, throughout *Anna Karenina,* the peasant fumbling in his sack, who appears in dreams both to Anna and Vronsky, is an actor in the primal scene—the father, become peasantlike, in his sexual activity, muttering that it is necessary to beat the iron while engaged in bewildering activities (with a matted beard) that seem to have no sense to the infant. Anna, we may remember, also dreams that a servant interpreted her dream as meaning she would die in childbirth. And the last glimpse of Anna's corpse that we are given, is as of someone who has been killed by sex:

> her mangled body, still warm with recent life, stretched out on a table shamelessly exposed to the gaze of all. The head, which had escaped hurt, with its heavy plaits and the curls about the temples, was thrown back, and the lovely face with its half-open red lips had frozen into a strange expression—pitiful on the lips and horrible in the fixed open eyes—as though she were repeating that fearful threat—that he would be sorry for it—that she had uttered during their last quarrel. (*Anna Karenina,* 814)

This is extremely disturbing, because it is the figure of a woman as conceived by a horrified infant, a mother who has been murdered by sexual intercourse. It is the culmination of the strange epigraph of the novel (Vengeance Is Mine: I Will Repay): and also the expression of her insane impulse to be revenged on Vronsky, all at once. Vronsky tries to remember her as she was when he first met her at the railway station, "mysterious, exquisite, loving, seeking and bestowing happiness," and not "cruel and vindictive" as he remembered her at the last. In a sense Vronsky is Tolstoy looking at his dead mother and trying to remember her as "bestowing happiness" rather than as killed by sexual intercourse: an image that must have been merged in Tolstoy's mind with the appalling spectacle of the mangled body of Anna Pirogova. But there is no doubt that he writes this terrible scene out of a feeling that sexual intercourse must in the end destroy the woman who gives way to passion, unless some means is found to modify this dreadful impulse. And this belief arose in him as an infant, when his mother died, as a consequence of being sexually possessed by the father, in terrible scenes that he witnessed, half-asleep, but could not understand, and conceived of them as vengeful, sadistic, and murderous:

> all the time he was rummaging, he kept muttering very quickly, in French, you know, rolling his r's: *il faut le battre, le fer; le broyer, le pétrir.* . . .

Note that this nightmare is associated with a prediction that she will die in childbirth—and that immediately after, she feels her fetus quicken ("the stirring of the new life within her"). The threat of death is inextricably linked with the stirring of new life.

Vronsky, too, has had this dream, only a page or so before: his *participation mystique* with Anna makes him share even her dreams, because they are locked in passion.

> "The peasant-beater—a dirty little man with a matted beard—was stooping down doing something, and all of a sudden he began muttering strange words in French." (Ibid., p. 380)

A chill of horror runs down his spine. Surely in this we recognize Tolstoy's own unconscious reminiscences of the primal scene—that he attributes to both his adulterous lovers?

The terrible fear of sexual intercourse as dangerous also explains that extraordinary paragraph about Levin and Kitty's honeymoon. On the "positive" side of the book, the characters most closely identified with Tolstoy and his wife, Levin and Kitty, are made almost as guilty after their first experience of sexual intercourse, despite the fact that theirs is blessed and hallowed by marriage:

> Altogether their honeymoon—the month after their wedding—from which tradition gave Levin to expect so much, was not merely not a

time of sweetness but remained in the memories of both as the bitter-est and most humiliating period of their lives. They both tried in later life to blot out from their memories all the ugly, shameful incidents of that morbid period, when both were rarely in a normal frame of mind, rarely quite themselves.

It was only in the third month of the marriage that life began to run more smoothly for them. (Ibid., 509)

Levin is obviously close to Tolstoy himself: the incident in which he and Kitty declare their love by chalked letters is taken from Tolstoy's own experience. So, we may take the terms he uses to describe their early sexual relationship as referring to his own experience: "bitterest," "humiliating," "ugly," "shameful," and "morbid"! These are extraordinary words for the first days of such a deep early love—and must surely strike one as describing something utterly different from one's own experience. How many of us would use such bitter adjectives about our first com-mitted sexual encounter?

It becomes apparent, when one studies this passage, and the passage where at last Vronsky and Anna have had their first adul-terous union, that Tolstoy's feelings about sexual love are intensely complex, full of dread and apprehension, of doom. And if we explore his life, his philosophies, his diaries, and those of his wife, we find that around the subjects of love, women, and sex his views and fears border on insanity. He was not only an extremely guilty man, as some psychoanalytic observers have noted (Kohut, e.g.) but possessed by attitudes and behavior that are clearly psycho-pathological. And it is most indicative that many of these crazy beliefs, that made him horribly cruel to his wife, revolve around the experiences of pregnancy, birth, and giving suck, as we shall see: about which all one can say is that, phenomenologically, such problems are only what one would expect of a man traumatized by the loss of his mother as an infant in childbirth, who has idealized women so much in consequence that he can only find sexuality dangerous and deathly.

Tolstoy's behavior to his wife in real life was deeply deranged: and we may detect from accounts of it the same unconscious ele-ments emerging from the disaster of his infancy—his loss of his mother. I will explore this subject in further detail through one episode, as reported in *Sonya: The Life of Countess Tolstoy* by Anne Edwards (1981). There was conflict between Tolstoy and his wife, with their first child, because Sonya was having great trouble feed-ing the baby. She had unbearable pain in her breasts: she had open fissures on her seriously inflamed breasts. But Tolstoy was adamantly opposed to the employment of a wet nurse, and considered it obscene and immoral for a woman not to nurse her own child. Warned by the doctor that his wife was in a dangerously weakened condition, Tolstoy accused Dr. Shmigaro of improprieties in his examination of his wife and of fostering corruption by depriving her of the "only means which might have kept her from coquetry." Sonya tried to accord to her husband's wishes, but wrote in her diary:

> I have a great longing to rest, to enjoy the open fields, and I feel like a prisoner in jail. I am waiting anxiously for my husband's return [with the wet nurse]. . . . I love him with all my heart, with a good, steady love, though with a slight feeling of inferiority. I'm going now to sacrifice myself to the child. . . . (Anne Edwards, 120)

Later she wrote:

> It is revolting not to nurse one's own child—who says it isn't? But what can be done against a bodily defect? I instinctively feel he is unjust to me. Why should he go on torturing me like this? . . . and just as he would like to wash me off the face of the earth, because I am suffering and am now taking care of the child, so I don't want to see him because he goes on writing and doesn't suffer. . . . *What a weakness on his part to be unable to be patient until I am better.* I suffer and endure ten times as much as he. (Ibid., 122; my italics)

Anne Edwards says that Tolstoy read these agonized words a short time later, and "feeling a strong (but fleeting) guilt," wrote an apology directly below them (the Tolstoys used to both keep diaries and read one another's diaries as a means of communication). But I believe that it was the sentence I have italicized that really penetrated Tolstoy's mind—for, clearly, he was totally wrapped up in a false solution to the problem—which was a defense against weaknesses of his own. For a moment, like a patient under psychotherapy, confronted with his weaknesses and false solutions, Tolstoy saw the truth: he wrote:

> Sonya, forgive me, I now realise my fault, and I know how great it is. *There are days when one seems to be guided not by one's own will, but by some irresistible outside power.* That's why I treated you so badly . . . I always knew I had many faults, but thought that I at least had a tiny spark of feeling and generosity within me. And yet I could be cruel and unkind—and to whom? to the one being who alone loves me—Sonya. I know that one doesn't forgive and forget such things; but I know

you better now, and realise more fully all my meanness. Sonya, my darling, I was unkind and revolting and—*but there is a good man within me who sometimes falls asleep.* Love him, Sonya, and don't blame him. (Edwards, 122; my italics)

But only an hour after writing this Tolstoy walked into their bedroom and found Sonya handing the baby to a wet nurse. In a rage, he tore open her diary and crossed out the apology with a large bold X. She wrote a record below, that he had crossed out these lines of kindness and remorse, before she had even had time to read them!

Tolstoy was obviously often driven by irrational impulses, as Edwards declares. But if his actions do not fit any reasonable logic, what logic do they follow?

One aspect of Tolstoy's behavior at this time perhaps gives another clue. His antipathy to sexual intercourse deepened into a belief that any sexual act not directed at procreation was immoral: marital chastity was the ideal state.

A man can only come to such a conclusion—we may say such a *lustful* man, as Tolstoy had showed himself to be—if he has concluded that sex is intensely destructive and dangerous. Tolstoy no doubt found some confirmation in the religious attitudes of his time, and as Gustafson indicates he employed the notion of Christian love—love of God—to denounce human sexual love as too dependent on an object and so liable to lead to the attempt to control the other—thereby leading to grief and alienation. But his own gloss on this whole question is deeply imbued with particular preoccupations and fanatic principles—even to the extent of insisting that people should give up sex altogether, in order to serve God. Such fanatic impulses suggest a psychopathological horror of love, sex, marriage, procreation, and even breastfeeding. This we may surely trace to the way his own whole relationship with the world of reality had been disturbed, just at the moment when his mother was engaged in what Winnicott calls the necessary "disillusionment" of her infant, as she introduces him to reality. It was as though a failure at the time of weaning had destroyed his world.

The experience of dealing with his wife's problem in feeding her baby would have raised in Tolstoy appalling problems left in him by his own weaning. His insane insistence that his wife *must* feed her baby obviously arises from his own experience of having his own relationship with the world disturbed by the sudden loss of his mother, just at the moment when needed to complete the process of weaning, and the process of finding himself in a real world.

We may find illuminations of the origins of such psychological problems in Tolstoy by turning to those who have studied the original processes by which an infant develops a grasp of his own reality, of the reality of the world and of others—bearing in mind that Tolstoy as an infant was in the process of developing those capacities when his world was shattered by his mother's too-soon pregnancy and death. As Winnicott says, "the good-enough mother . . . starts off with an almost complete adaptation to her infant's needs, and as time proceeds she adapts less and less completely, gradually, according to the infant's growing ability to deal with her failure" (Winnicott, *Playing and Reality*, p. 10).

> The infant's means of dealing with this maternal failure include the following:
>
>   1. The infant's experience, often repeated, that there is a time-limit to frustration. At first, naturally, this time-limit must be short.
>   2. Growing sense of progress.
>   3. The beginnings of mental activity.
>   4. Employment of auto-erotic satisfactions.
>   5. Remembering, reliving, fantasying, dreaming: the integration of past, present and future. . . . (Ibid.)

"*If all goes well* the infant can actually come to gain from the experience of frustration, since incomplete adaptation to need makes objects real, *that is to say hated as well as loved.*" (my italics)

The "object that behaves perfectly becomes no better than a hallucination." The implication of these remarks is that only by a gradual process of experiencing "maternal failure" does the child come to find reality at all. And this may be especially applied to the finding of the reality of persons. At the beginning, "adaptation needs to be almost exact":

> and unless this is so it is not possible for the infant to begin to develop a capacity to experience a relationship to external reality, or even to form a conception of external reality. (Ibid., 11)

The mother, at the beginning, by an almost 100-percent adaptation affords the infant the opportunity for the *illusion* that her breast is part of the infant. It is, as it were, under the baby's magical control.

The mother's eventual task is to disillusion the infant, but she has no hope of success unless at first she has been able to give sufficient opportunity for illusion. . . .

A subjective phenomenon develops in the baby, which we call the mother's breast [In a footnote Winnicott explains that in this he includes "the whole technique of mothering]. . . . The mother places the actual breast just there where the infant is ready to create, and at the right moment. (Ibid., 11)

From birth, the human being is concerned with the problem of the relationship between what is objectively perceived and what is subjectively conceived of:

at some theoretical point early in the development of every human individual an infant in a certain setting provided by the mother is capable of conceiving of the idea of something that would meet the growing need that arises out of instinctual tension. The infant cannot be said to know at first what is to be created. At this point in time the mother presents herself. . . . The mother's adaptation to the infant's needs, when good enough, gives the infant the *illusion* that there is an external reality that corresponds to the infant's own capacity to create. In other words, there is an overlap between what the mother supplies and what the infant conceives of. . . . Psychologically the infant takes from a breast that is part of the infant, and the mother gives milk to an infant that is part of herself. (Ibid.)

The mother's next task, having provided the opportunity for illusion is *disillusionment*.

This is preliminary to the task of weaning, and it also continues as one of the tasks of parents and educators. In other words, this matter of *illusion* is one that belongs inherently to human beings and that no individual finally solves for himself or herself. (Ibid., 13)

The mere termination of breast-feeding is not a weaning. What Winnicott is talking about is the whole complex process whereby an individual finds that he is not part of his mother, but a creature in himself in relation to reality and to real persons.

Here Winnicott brings in transitional object phenomena: the first possession which symbolizes the child's grasp of his experience of the mother and himself, by which he moves toward possession of his language and culture.

It is related both to the external object (mother's breast) and to internal objects (magically introjected breast) but is distinct from each. (Ibid. 14)

If the disillusioning process is interrupted, as by the loss of the mother, then the individual will be left in a state of confusion, seeking to complete the process of finding self and world and self and other, which is exactly what happened to Tolstoy—all of whose creative efforts can be seen to emerge, out of the need to work on these processes of "remembering, reliving, fantasying, dreaming." His novels, for example, are full of moments of "reliving," as with the fragments of autobiographical experience, remembering the experience of battle, and reports on people's dreams. And at the heart of his creative pursuits are the problems of death, love, women, and the meaning of life. We may say that the impulse to be a tragic artist originated in the breakdown of the weaning process—but also that the terrible doubts over confusions, about self and otherness, and of the effects of fate, the "irresistible force" that seems to impinge on life, may be traced to this source, too.

Tolstoy was insufficiently "disillusioned" by his mother, and so suffered serious disruption of his capacity to recognize the reality of the self and the world. When he was a small boy he thought he could fly.

> He had thought that if he held his knees together tightly with his arms and threw himself down from a great height, he would be able to soar like a bird. Alone in the nursery one evening, he decided to put his plan into execution. Crawling out a window and balancing himself on the ledge, he grasped his knees close to his body and sprang forward into the night; he landed, miraculously without one broken bone, but with a slight concussion, in the courtyard below. (Edwards, 103)

Tolstoy uses this autobiographical experience in *War and Peace*, when Prince Andrey overhears Sonya and Natasha talking:

> Sonya made some reluctant reply.
> "No, do look what a moon! . . . Oh, how lovely it is! Do come here. Darling, precious, do come here. There, do you see? One has only to squat on one's heels like this—see—and to hold one's knees—as tight, as tight as one can—give a great spring and one would fly away . . . like this—see!"
> "Mind, you'll fall." (*War and Peace*, 522)

Tolstoy, himself, as we shall see, showed from time to time a strange inability to appreciate the reality of others. For instance at one stage he attacked and seriously injured a young girl who did not pay him undivided attention (he later married her daughter). Yet, while he showed such deficiency, in his art he penetrates reality with acute imaginative vision. Such a man remains an extraordinary enigma—but his enigmatic characteristics are such as might emerge from a childhood disaster such as I have dwelt on.

3

War and Peace

I approach Tolstoy's war novel with some trepidation: what can one say about a novel of such immense scope? I return to reading it every year or so: yet there are parts of it I can read only with difficulty. It is the most satisfying novel I know, and a great relief from the triviality of most present-day writing. Yet I am always greatly disappointed by the end, in which Tolstoy turns his propaganda machine on his heroine, while giving us a lecture on history and war, whose prosiness seems a dry and barren end to the great drama. Yet reading the novel overall is a great experience—one that leaves one with a blank feeling—of what can one possibly read after this, with any satisfaction?

Is it still possible to say something illuminating about this work? I propose to examine it in the light of my conclusions about Tolstoy's writing, especially his problem with women. I have suggested that the murder that is at the center of the propaganda novel *The Kreutzer Sonata* is Tolstoy's fantasy of the sexual act, as envisaged in the primal scene: the culmination of a dread of women in act of intensely relished murder. I have suggested, too, that the image of the little peasant who haunts *Anna Karenina* is a fantasy of the father in the primal scene fantasy, who has killed the mother. I have suggested that Tolstoy was haunted all his life by his infant fantasies, of the mother being killed by sex—the sex that led to the pregnancy that took her away psychically, from her baby, and then killed her. Sex, women, pregnancy, and childbirth haunted him with the most terrible dreads.

In defense against the loss of his mother and of all the deprivation associated with it, Tolstoy idealized women, as pure and perfect: thus because it is impossible to think of sex with one's mother, he could never embrace the whole reality of femininity, including women's sexual needs. This meant, too, that he found it difficult to embrace the reality of the world—although, as by writing *War and Peace*, he endeavored in his writing to find and encompass

70

that reality, on a massive scale. He began writing two years after his marriage in 1862. He first intended to deal with the Constitutional Conspiracy which came to a head with the accession of Nicholas I to the throne in 1825. While studying the events of this period he found himself carried back to the time amid which his characters had grown up: the Napoleonic wars. So he put aside *The Decembrists* and set out on the gigantic *War and Peace*. The attraction of the Napoleonic wars was surely the tremendous threat they posed to his own country, as a symbol of the worst thing that could ever happen, and of the possible breakdown of all reality.

So, one has to appreciate the vast scale of the undertaking of a novel of such scope, and at the same time to note the weaknesses that came from the same sources of deprivation and need.

Foremost, one has to say, *War and Peace* is about death, and in the light of the contemplation of mass slaughter, in the context of a futile war, it presses the existential problem to the absolute extremes. The main characters—Pierre Bezuhov and Prince Andrey Bolkonsky—and, to a lesser extent, Denisov, Dolohov, and Nikolai Rostov, are carried along on tidal waves of mortal combat, as, indeed, is little Petya Rostov, whose death is one of the most poignant episodes in the novel. In the face of death and suffering the question continually returns, "What do men live by?"

The Rostovs are a delightful family and one follows their fortunes with a deeply involved sympathy: they embody Tolstoy's preoccupation with "the family." Close to them is Pierre Bezuhov, who, like Levin in *Anna Karenina*, embodies many of Tolstoy's own characteristics, and his strange combination of näiveté and perplexity, together with his also engaging mixture of delinquency and tenderness. All this makes him a fascinating character, and his notorious wandering adventures in the Battle of Borodino and the Siege of Moscow represent a literary conception of remarkable originality, employed to explore the horrors of war and the breakdown of civilized community in a particularly original and acute way. Like Tolstoy, Bezuhov never ceases to inquire into his own nature and predicament, to ponder the things that are happening to him, and to place them in the eternal scheme of things—to always attend to the ultimate existential questions, in the face of death: he strives to find answers to the question What do men live by? and confronts problems of philosophy and religion with courageous honesty. Prince Andrey Bolkonsky, who is yet another manifestation of Tolstoy's own complex and immense personality, does this too, from another point of view, with as little success: and, indeed, it is the failure of both of these sensitive and intelligent men to solve the problem of life that makes *War and Peace* such a great novel: their partial solutions are great triumphs of human endeavor, even so.

Reading this novel is always traumatic: indeed, one may even say that it is unbearable, and in my own several and frequent readings, I have found there are episodes that I find it hard to read again. To write an analysis of these passages has been deeply disturbing. One has to open oneself to the experience of *War and Peace* with some care, as it sears one as does no other work of literature (except perhaps *King Lear*). The episodes I cannot always bear include the worst of the terrible battle scenes at Austerlitz and Borodino: the executions in which Pierre Bezuhov is involved when he is arrested as an incendiary, and the death of Platon Karataev on the march of the prisoners. The death of Petya Rostov is also deeply disturbing as I have said. In these incidents we experience the essence of Tolstoy's achievement of tragedy.

Against these harrowing moments we find set the achievement of love. Much of *War and Peace* is devoted to what in contrast to the many preoccupations with women and being, one may call false male solutions, from the early episodes in which Pierre sinks into delinquency and drunken quasi-criminal acts, to the great battles, and the vice that takes place around Pierre's wife Ellen and her set. The central thread of positive values by which we know these manifestations to be false is Pierre's relationship with Natasha Rostov: a love that grows and develops sub specie aeternitatis and has the same gravity and absolute quality that Tolstoy's love for his own wife displayed—and to which he was so often catastrophically treacherous. Tolstoy's women in *War and Peace* are done with a deep appreciation of the special qualities of women as human beings, and so of their particular capacity to menace civilization if they prove to be unreliable (which is no more than to say when they prove to be human and frail). Admittedly, toward the end of the novel, this appreciation becomes propaganda, as we shall see, for Tolstoy's particular concept of the good wife, and in this we find his impulse to control women. But in his perception of those special and mysterious, strong and beautiful, qualities that women bring to life, though it is irradiated by idealism, is nonetheless true: for women bring to civilization those qualities that are expressed in cultural concepts of the angel—the capacity for sympathy and understanding, feeling and care, devoted love, and inspiration. They are the custodians of being, while those men who can admit the qualities of being may be said to be admitting feminine qualities in their makeup. Women can, of course, also bring treachery, falsification, the capacity to manipulate, and corruption. But overall *War and Peace* is a remarkable tribute to women, even imbued as it is with penetrating realism—and from the hand of one who, as his life progressed, found himself in increasing dread of women, and intensely contemptuous of, and hostile to, them.

There is a sense in which *War and Peace* could be retitled *False Male Doing and Its Consolation and Resolution by Female Element Being.* One aspect of the novel is the recognition of the female capacities of men, especially under dire stress (take e.g., the moment when the doctor kisses Andrey on the lips after he has examined his [second] wound and has realized it is fatal).

Prince Andrey speaks the passage that could be taken as a motto for the novel (speaks it to Pierre, who looks at him "with eyes full of scared sympathy," and speaks it just before the battle in which he is fatally wounded):

> War is not a polite recreation, but the vilest thing in life, and we ought to understand that and not play at war. We ought to accept it sternly and solemnly as a fearful necessity. . . . The military is the most honoured calling. And what is war, what is needed for success in war, what are the morals of the military world? The object of warfare is murder; the means employed in warfare—spying, treachery . . . the ruin of a country, the plundering of its inhabitants . . . tricking and lying, which are called military strategy . . . in spite of all that, it is the highest class, respected by every one . . . they slaughter and mutilate tends of thousands of men, and then offer up thanksgiving services for the number of men they have killed . . . supposing that the more men have been slaughtered the greater the achievement. . . . (*War and Peace,* 979)*

Pierre realizes that this is their last meeting, and Andrey goes to sleep ("before a battle one needs to get a good sleep") thinking of Natasha, her spiritual force, and Anatole Kuragin's exploitation of her: this is but one of the many occasions when the inspiration to men's spiritual yearnings that Natasha provides is set against the huge foreboding threat of massive battles and of other historical disasters in Russian history. In the end, as I shall argue, this inspiring woman is made into a hausfrau deliberately stripped

---

*Page numbers in the discussion of this novel refer to the Heinemann edition, translated by Constance Garnett (1930).

of her charm, vitality, and capacity to inspire, to serve Tolstoy's propaganda campaign to keep women under control, alas. But until this happens she is an exceptional and inspiring creation.

* * *

One theme of the opening pages of *War and Peace* is that of Prince Andrey's problems with his wife, the little princess.

In Tolstoy's novels there do seem to be unresolved enigmas which express unconsciously problems he could not solve for himself. The little peasant with a matted beard is one such enigma in *Anna Karenina,* together with the motto: Vengeance Is Mine—I Will Repay, as we shall see.

In *War and Peace* there is a parallel enigma behind the marriage of Prince Andrey Bolkonsky, and thus behind his involvement in the plot. Bolkonsky, like Pierre Bezuhov, is seen by many critics to be an aspect of Tolstoy himself: Pierre and Andrey, as it were, act out dramatically the experiences of the complex Tolstoy in events in war and peace. Both embody Tolstoy's curiosity about the nature of reality, and both exhibit his philosophical torment, in trying to come to terms with it and with its meaning. Both have tormented problems in their relation to women, and both center on Natasha as a high source of idealized love—only to be let down by her disastrous lapse with Kuragin.

Andrey's original dissatisfaction with his wife is never explained or analyzed. And in the end she seems to cast over Andrey a reproof, that he has done something to her that has led to her death. This becomes most clear much later in the book:

> Near the altar of the church at Bleak Hills was a little chapel over the tomb of the little princess, and in the chapel had been placed a marble monument brought from Italy, representing an angel with its wings parted about to take flight for heaven. The angel had the upper lip lifted as though about to smile, and one day Prince Andrey and Princess Marya, as they came out of the chapel, confessed to one another that, strange to say, the face of the angel reminded them of the face of the little princess. But what was stranger, though this Prince Andrey did not confess to his sister, was that in the expression the sculptor had chanced to put into the angelic face, Prince Andrey read the same words of reproach which he had read then on the face of his dead wife: "Ah, why have you done this to me? . . ." (456)

Behind the symbolism of this we may, I believe, detect the long struggle of Tolstoy as a child to hold together an image of his lost mother, one that was as pure as an angel, and one that might well bear the expression "Why have you done this to me?"

The little princess's death comes as a severe shock, near the beginning of the book. Of course, young women did die in childhood more commonly than nowadays: but the significance of the death is underpinned by Prince Andrey's gloomy discontent over his marriage, into which we are given no insights. The little princess is very charming.

> As is always the case with perfectly charming women, her defect—the shortness of the lip and the half-opened mouth—seemed her peculiar, her characteristic beauty. Every one took delight in watching the pretty creature full of life and gaiety, so soon to be a mother, and so lightly bearing her burden. (7)

Men watching her feel they are "becoming like her" and this makes them feel they are being "particularly successful this evening."

Her husband, she declares, is deserting her: "Tell me what this nasty war is for," she asks: she says this at the moment Pierre makes his first entrance in the novel. (8).

When Prince Andrey comes in, he is described as a "very handsome young man, of medium height, with clear, clean-cut features."

> Everything in his appearance, from his weary, bored expression to his slow, measured step, formed the most striking contrast to his lively little wife. . . . Of all the wearisome faces the face of his pretty wife seemed to bore him most. With a grimace that distorted his handsome face he turned away from her. . . . (14)

His wife speaks to him and he scowls and turns away: Pierre takes hold of his arm whereupon his face twists into a grimace of annoyance at anyone touching him—but when he sees Pierre's smiling face he gives him a smile that is unexpectedly sweet and pleasant.

Later, it would seem as if Prince Andrey has become cold to his wife *because she is pregnant*, though Tolstoy does not quite fill this out (he must have known from his own experience that some men do have considerable problems with a pregnant wife). He declares to Pierre that "the life I lead here, this life is—not to my taste." When his wife declares that she is frightened, he asks coolly, with "frigid courtesy," "I still don't understand what you are afraid of," she replies,

> "No, Andrey, I say you are so changed, so changed. . . ."

There is some embarrassment in her discussing her condition before Pierre, but as she goes on the couple almost quarrel, and Prince Andrey's patience becomes nearly exhausted. She cries,

> "I have long waited to say to you, Andrey, why are you so changed to me? What have I done to you? You go away to the war, you don't feel for me. Why is it?" (28)

He wasn't like this, she says, six months ago: now he treats her like a child. The princess is in tears and Pierre finds it hard to bear. She becomes angry and accuses her husband of thinking of nothing but himself.

> She glanced from under her brows with lovely eyes at her husband, and her face wore the timorous, deprecating look of a dog when it faintly but rapidly wags its tail in penitence. (p. 29)

This exchange gives us a clue to the whole undertaking of this novel, which is, as I have said, about feminine preoccupation with being on the one hand, and false male doing on the other—war, that is in part a denial of the tenderness of feminine creativity, peace, the future, and meaningful living. Faced with the commitment to the pregnant future, Prince Andrey goes off to war, and in this he represents one impulse in Tolstoy's men, to deny the feminine aspect of his own personality: and the reason is the unconscious fear of tenderness and of pregnancy as death.

One might even say, I believe, that it is *surrender* that is feared—surrender to the processes of life—of which war is the opposite, a surrender to death. Prince Andrey is hostile to his wife out of a fear of dependence on her—and one can see how the dangers of dependence were appalling to Tolstoy, who lost his mother in infancy.

To our surprise, and with no explanation, Prince Andrey warns Pierre Bezuhov not to marry;

> "Never, never marry, my dear fellow; that's my advice to you. . . ."

The way the Prince goes on is even more perplexing:

> "don't marry till you have faced the fact that you have done all you're capable of doing, and until you cease to love the woman you have chosen, till you see her plainly, or else you will make a cruel mistake that can never be set right. Marry when you're old and good for

nothing. . . . Or else everything good and lofty in you will be done for. . . ." (30)

Andrey's objections to marriage seem to be that "everything is frittered away in trifles" and that one stands in marriage, "on the same level with the court lackey and the idiot." This is Tolstoy propaganda, put in Andrey's mouth: we have seen nothing in the behavior of Andrey's wife that would justify such pathological hatred: he goes on:

> "My wife . . . is an excellent woman. She is one of those rare women with whom one can feel quite secure of one's honour; but, my God! what wouldn't I give now not to be married!" (Ibid.)

"It seemed" says Tolstoy, "that the more lifeless he was at ordinary times, the more energetic he became at such moments of *morbid irritability*" (my italics).

Revealingly, Prince Andrey compares himself with Bonaparte:

> he was working his way up, going step by step straight to his aim, he was free. . . . But tie yourself up with a woman, like a chained convict, you lose all freedom. And all the hope and strength there is in you is only a drag on you, torturing you with regret. Drawing rooms, gossip, balls, vanity, frivolity—that's the enchanted circle I can't get out of. I am setting off now to the war. . . ." (30–31)

And he speaks of "this imbecile society without which my wife can't exist, and these women. . . . Egoism, vanity, silliness, triviality in everything—that's what women are when they show themselves as they really are."

> "looking at them in society, one fancies there's something in them, but there's nothing, nothing, nothing. . . ." (31)

Tolstoy, as we know, believed this, at least in one part of his character: "How can he say that?" asks Pierre of himself, as if to speak from that side of Tolstoy that worshiped Sonya.

> "It seems absurd to me," said Pierre, "that *you, you* consider *yourself* a failure, your life wrecked. . . ." (Ibid.)

But Prince Andrey has said nothing about himself being a failure or having his life wrecked: it is almost as if we are listening to an internal dialogue in Tolstoy himself. Why ever should Andrey say, "I am a man whose day is done" (Ibid.)? It is at this point that Andrey gets a promise out of Pierre that he will not go off to join Anatole Kuragin and his decadent companions—a promise he immediately breaks.

Pierre shrugs his shoulders and says "What would you have? . . . Women, my dear fellow, women": to which Andrey replies "Ladies, that's another matter, but Kuragin's women, women and wine, I can't understand." The argument is not unlike the discussions in *Anna Karenina* between Levin and Oblonsky. But they arise out of Tolstoy's own ambivalence—unable to escape his capacity for lust, unable to escape his swings from idolizing women to despising them and attempting (with his wife) to put women under control. (Lurking behind such moments lies the truth that to take recourse to prostitutes, which is what Pierre means by "women," is itself a mode of behavior to which men who are afraid of relationship, love, and commitment are prone: and Tolstoy himself must have known this from experience.)

The actual death of the little princess is superbly vivid: as one might expect from an author who lost his mother in childbirth when he was a baby, the scene is realized with particular intensity and meaning. There is an underlying sense that Prince Andrey has caused her death, by sexual relations with her: Tolstoy, as we know, was obsessed with the dangers of sexual love:

> The glittering eyes, staring in childish terror and excitement, rested on him with no change in their expression. "I love you all, I have done no one any harm; why am I suffering? help me," her face seemed to say. (401)

She stares at her husband with "a face of inquiry, of childish reproach":

> "I hoped for help from you, and nothing, nothing, you too!" her eyes said. (Ibid.)

When Prince Andrey, after hearing her terrible scream, goes into the room,

> She was lying dead . . . there was the same expression still on the charming childish face with the little lip covered with fine dark hair. "I love you all, and have done no harm to any one, and what have you done to me?" said her charming, piteous, dead face. . . . (402)

And her face still asks this when they bury her:

"Ah, what have you done to me?" it still seemed to say; and Prince Andrey felt that something was being torn out of his soul, that he was guilty of *a crime he could never set right nor forget*. . . . (402; my italics)

The repetition and the intensity suggest that Tolstoy never forgot being presented to his dying mother, nor his efforts to reconstitute her image: nor his sense that she was the victim of a terrible crime that could never be righted—a crime that all human beings were impelled to commit, by lust, as he was impelled, as all men are. His father was guilty of this crime, and he was also guilty, in resorting to sex, which was to him unconsciously a resort to impurity toward the mother. When the old prince kisses the little princess's dead face, it even says to him, "Ah, what have you done to me, and why" ("And the old man turned angrily away, when he caught sight of the face"). The unspoken answer is, "We have exposed you to sexual love, and it is that which has killed you." Women, sexual love, and death are the themes of this great novel.

* * *

The opening words of the novel indicate one feature of *War and Peace:* to the social gatherings of the Russian ruling class, Napoleon and war are remote problems, the dreadfulness of which are not apparent to most of those present, certainly not to the women:

"Well, prince, Genoa and Lucca are now no more that private estates of the Bonaparte family. No, I warn you, that if you do not tell me we are at war, if you again allow yourself to palliate all the infamies and atrocities of this Antichrist (upon my word, I believe he is), I don't know you in future, you are no longer my friend, no longer my faithful slave, as you say. . . ." (1)

This is Anna Pavlovna Scherer, a confidential maid of honor to the empress. She is talking to Prince Vassily, father of Ellen and Anatole Kuragin. In her drawing room are Lisa, Princess Volkonsky, Elena (Ellen), Pierre Bezuhov, Prince Ippolit, and Prince Andrey.

The conversation is trivial and desultory. Some of the company are trying to arrange favors for members of their families—appointments in the forces and so forth. The one serious topic is Bonaparte, and there is some conflict, over Napoleon's execution of the duc d'Enghien and of his relationship to the French Revolution. Some of the guests, especially Pierre Bezuhov, admire Napoleon, and it is evident that Russian high society is divided on this issue. They are even to some extent compromised since their culture is much influenced by France, and the language they use for civilized intercourse is French, too.

Prince Andrey and Pierre Bezuhov are sympathetic friends, although they are obviously very different characters (even though they are both alter egos of Tolstoy himself). Bezuhov asks Andrey why he is going to the war:

> "What for? I don't know. Because I have to. Besides I'm going. . . ." he stopped. "I'm going because the life I lead here, this life is—not to my taste." (26)

He is going to war because, he says, he cannot tolerate the woman-dominated socialite circles of Moscow life: I have suggested that perhaps he is going to war because he cannot bear his wife's pregnancy. To go to war therefore has in it I suggest an element of *false male doing,* in the attempt to escape a society that seems too trivial to endure, under the influence of "society" women, in the realm of peace.

We might here perhaps invoke further a fascinating insight from Winnicott, the psychoanalyst, on male and female characteristics. One possibly relevant essay is that on "This Feminism" in *Home Is Where One Starts From* (London: Penguin, 1986). He says:

> The awkward fact remains, for men and women, that each was once dependent on a woman, and somehow a hatred of this has to be transformed into a kind of gratitude if full maturity of the personality is to be reached. (Winnicott 1986, 193)

He goes on to consider why "males seek danger." Women go through the risk of childbirth: there is a danger inherent in the woman's natural function.

> Men envy women this danger; moreover, they feel guilty because they cause pregnancies and then sit pretty and watch women going through it all, not only the childbirth, but the whole confinement and the terribly restricting responsibilities of infant care. *So they take risks too,* and they will always do so. . . . (Ibid.)

Winnicott relates this problem to war:

> The awful thing about war is that so often those men who survive have to admit they found maturity, including sexual maturity, in the course of taking the risk of dying. (Ibid.)

Though Winnicott does not mention it, over 90 percent of crime is also done by men. It seems to me a valuable insight that risk-taking is an inclination to which men take resort, in order, unconsciously, to compete with the fate of women. We can apply this directly to *War and Peace:* the death-defying antics of men in drunken escapades, the men in battles, the ventures of Prince Andrey and Paul Bezuhov, the wild risk-taking of Petya are set in the wider pattern against the calm devotion of the women in family life, and such terrible developments as the death of the little princess, to emphasize the differences between the sexes, and between war and peace.

Andrey and Pierre share the capacity for "dreaming and philosophising," while Pierre as we have seen is amazed that Andrey considers himself a failure. Andrey wants to escape from "Egoism, vanity, silliness, triviality in everything"—and both of these men, in the course of the book, press themselves into the suffering of war, as it were, in order to find an existential gravity, in which the problem of the meaning of life can be found. Both in the event find it through their relationship with Natasha Rostov—though she is only a child when the novel opens.

There is a sense from that opening that Russia is reluctantly at war. A parallel episode to the opening sequence occurs later in section 3 of part 9, about 1812. The czar has made a treaty with Napoleon at Tilsit, but in June Napoleon decides to march on Moscow, and his troops begin to cross the Niemen. This is a characteristic moment in the novel.

On the Russian side there is no general plan of action, there was a commander in chief for each of the three armies, and no commander overall.

> Every effort of the men who surrounded the Tsar seemed to be devoted to making their sovereign spend his time pleasantly and forget the impending war. (*War and Peace,* 766)

A ball is organized in the house of Count Bennigsen at Vilna, and takes place on the very day Napoleon's troops cross the Niemen in their assault toward Moscow. Countess Bezuhov is there, and Boris Drubetskoy. Everything is going surprisingly well when a staff general, Balashov, comes in and begins to tell his news to the czar.

Boris hears the czar exclaim "To enter Russia with no declaration of war!" There follows a sequence during which Balashov is treated to a disdainful egoistic performance by Napoleon himself, on an emissary's mission to protest to the French.

Prince Andrey is going to war, this second time, in anger against Anatole Kuragin who has attempted to seduce the woman to whom he is affianced—Natasha (a characteristic risk-taking venture): "he began dreaming of the happy moment of satisfied hate when he would meet Kuragin. He knew he was with the Army." It is at this point that Prince Andrey reflects that life seems to be a series of senseless phenomena following one another without any connection. In their going to war men are impelled by the dynamics of hate and even by a feeling of meaninglessness, even as they are caught up in patriotism and fervor for the czar: they may well seem to be driven by unconscious motives such as Winnicott diagnoses.

The reader's impression from all such scenes is one of a ruling class which has no sense of purpose and no coherent reason for fighting Napoleon. They decide it is unfashionable to speak French, but their culture is much influenced by France, and they admire many of Napoleon's reforms. They are continually caught out, and everything seems to blunder along until the retreat from Moscow seems to save them from Napoleon's army, as if by happy coincidence.

But within these great historical events, the reasons why individuals behave as they do seem to be highly subjective and wilfull: Prince Andrey's impulse to go into battle seems to be the wilfull impulse to get himself killed, because of his betrayal by Natasha Rostov, since with this all meaning seems to have gone out of his life. Pierre, too, seems lost, existentially speaking, without his being able to develop his relationship with Natasha. He wanders into the battlefield out of existential curiosity, prompted by the unconscious impulse to take risks.

Between the triviality and corruption of Russian socialite life and the inhuman horrors of war, their yearning love for Natasha in both men seems to be the one gleam of hope, that promises to make life meaningful, and to raise it on to another, spiritual, plane. Both have had difficulties with women: Andrey because he seemed unable to tolerate his wife's pregnancy; Pierre because he allows himself to drift into a false marriage. Andrey finds love fulfilled with Natasha in a sexless situation in which she is devoted to nursing him. And, as we shall see, when at last Pierre marries Natasha, her charm and her civilized gifts are abandoned, the fire is gone, and she becomes a plump, child-bound, overpossessive Russian mother-figure, devoted only to "the family," and her capacity for inspiration is forfeited. Neither men really solve the problem of women, that is, as I would see it, men's problem with women. Yet both are inspired, in their search for ultimate meaning, by their image of Napoleon. Interestingly, and pertinently in relation to Tolstoy's problems, it is only when he is dying and beyond any peril of sexual relations with Natasha that Andrey finds transcendent love by her inspiration, while Pierre, once he is married to Natasha, is made to subject her to severe control—or, rather, Tolstoy, with his thumb in the scales, reduces her to that condition.

* * *

Politically, *War and Peace* seems to offer very little, except to delineate the confusion and alternation between hope and cynicism, in the leading protagonists, Andrew Bolkonsky and Pierre Bezuhov. We see war emerging from an impersonal historical process, in which the leading figures seem to be impotent and egocentric: the consequences deadly and anarchic, but seemingly beyond control. What difference would politics have made to the Napoleonic wars? Men are inspired by love, and undergo spiritual refinement by suffering: they aspire to develop an adequate sense of the meaning of life, but end up absorbed by the arrival of their offspring—at least this is true of Pierre. Occasionally, they fall into what might be called a false existential solution, like Pierre's Masonic episode. But there is little that is illuminating on the political front, and it is difficult to link developments there with the other major themes in the novel.

From time to time individuals seem to find hope in some new solution, as when Pierre addresses the Freemasons on possible new developments, which they dismiss as "illuminism." When Prince Andrey is elected to the Committee on Army Regulations he becomes full of hope:

> He experienced now in Petersburg a sensation akin to what he had known on the eve of a battle, when he was fretted by restless curiosity and irresistibly attracted to those higher spheres, where the future was in preparation, that future on which hung the fate of millions. From the angry irritability of the elder generation, from the curiosity of the uninitiated and the reserve of the initiated, from the hurry and anxious absorption of every one, from the multiplicity of committees and commissions—he was learning of new ones every day—he felt that now, in the year 1809, there was in preparation here in Petersburg some vast political contest, and the commander-in-chief in it was a

mysterious personage whom he did not know, but imagined to be a man of genius—Speransky. (529)

—Speransky, however, turns out to be another empty hope. It is interesting to note how Tolstoy accounts for the different spheres of Russian society in which Prince Andrey had influence:

> The returning party welcomed him warmly, and sought him out, in the first place, because he had the reputation of being clever and very well read, and secondly because he had already gained the reputation of being a liberal by the emancipation of his serfs. The party of the dissatisfied older generation welcomed him simply as the son of his father, and reckoned on his sympathy in their disapproval of the reforms. The feminine world, *society*, received him cordially because he was a wealthy match of high rank, and a person almost new, encircled by a halo of romance from his narrow escape from death and the tragic loss of his young wife. (Ibid.)

—All the promise for which Prince Andrey is hailed seems to be based on false premises.

Pierre Bezuhov has tried to put into practice some philanthropic ideas he has developed on the basis of Masonic principles. These come across the cynicism of Prince Andrey, and there is a revealing exchange between them.

Andrey is anxious to convey to Pierre his new view of things:

> "I only know of two very real ills in life, remorse and sickness. There is no good except the absence of those ills. To live for myself, to avoid these two evils: that's the sum of my wisdom now."
>
> "And love for your neighbour, and self-sacrifice?" began Pierre. . . . (470ff)

Pierre goes on to say that he is now trying to live for others. Prince Andrey says with him it is quite the reverse: "I live only for myself."

Pierre protests that trying to give the peasants education and social services provides an enjoyment that is the only happiness in life. Prince Andrey agrees at least that he too is building a house as Pierre is building hospitals, but he scoffs at Pierre's ambitions to provide for the spiritual needs of the peasants and to lighten their burdens. Pierre exclaims,

> "Oh, this is awful, awful! . . . I don't understand how one can live with such ideas. . . ."

At last he comes out with the principles of freemasonry: "our holy brotherhood is the only thing that has real meaning in life." Prince Andrey retorts,

> "Why is it I alone don't see what you see! You see on earth the dominion of good and truth, but I don't see it." (479)

Does he believe in a future life? Pierre asks. Pierre propounds a theory that nothing disappears in the universe: "I always shall be and always have been, and . . . in that world there is truth." Andrey takes a much more atheistic view, and it is evident this is rooted in the loss of his wife:

> "when one goes hand-in-hand with some one, and all at once that some one slips away *yonder into nowhere,* and you are left facing that abyss and looking down into it. And I have looked into it. . . ."

> "Well, that's it then! You know there is a *yonder* and there is *some one. Yonder* is the future life; *some one* is God." (480)

Pierre goes on to talk about God, as they are entranced by a sunset.

"if only it were so," says Andrey, and he sees in the sunset sky a glimpse of eternity just as he had on the field of Austerlitz when he was wounded:

> "and something that had long been slumbering, something better that had been in him, suddenly awoke with a joyful, youthful feeling in his soul. . . . there began . . . a new life in his inner world. (481)

Both in Pierre and Prince Andrey and in their relationship, in which each is concerned with the well-being of the other, Tolstoy traces his own philosophical impulses—tormented by the problem of death (as he was by the loss of his mother) he tries to find grounds for feeling that life has a meaning, though such hopes are often dashed. And by straining at the problem, all his leading characters seem to penetrate beyond it, to find that the sense of meaning evaporates, leaving sometimes only a glow of immediate contentment, sometimes a sense of emptiness. Can the solution be in giving out to others, in being beneficent, or in serving one's country? Can it be found in love for women, and in particular for one especial woman, Natasha Rostov? This theme underlies all the dealings with politics and social issues throughout the novel. In the end, as with Levin in *Anna Karenina,* the greatest

satisfaction for the protagonist comes from entering into, by identification, the simple philosophy of resignation of the illiterate
peasant, as Pierre identifies with Platon Karataev: in what, as we
shall see, the existentialist psychotherapist calls "engagement."

Whatever historical errors Tolstoy makes, and whatever errors
of political interpretation, his theme is one that reaches down into
human consciousness, and explores the problems of authenticity
and love, the unconscious factors which so many commentators
on political and historical matters ignore. He shows that men tend
to act as a swarm, in battle, following what they feel is an aim and
purpose, and when it leads to chaos, rewrite events to make a
pattern, afterward. In reality, men are vulnerable, and are aware
of their insubstantial selves, even in the heat of battle, and often
become aware of their families and of the women they love, when
isolated in some vast enterprise. As an artist, he allows his heroes
to be baffled and bewildered in their quest for ultimate meanings,
and to find solace in the most unexpected experiences—the sky
over a battlefield, a comet, or their experience of the stoic courage
of an ordinary lower-class outcast, such as Platon Karataev. In
such a creature Tolstoy delineates a version of human love that
offers hope and promise, which is capable of contributing a refining power to the sensibility, as well as the idealizing love of women.

*   *   *

The existential conflict in the novel culminates in the life and
death of Andrey Bolkonsky and in the survival of Pierre Bezuhov.

The central theme is the focus of the love of these two men for
one exceptional woman. The one moment when the impact of
the feminine on these men's souls goes disastrously wrong is
around the episode in which Natasha is deceived by Anatole Kuragin: in this disturbing episode the full horror of decadence is
explored. Natasha nearly dies, Bolkonsky is emotionally wounded
and disillusioned, and Pierre made to suffer terribly—for he has
the same kind of impulse to idealize women as his creator, and
this idealization is badly affected.

Ironically, the first impulse for the attempted seduction comes
from the kind of macho delinquency in which Pierre himself has
taken part earlier: Pierre has been a companion of Prince Anatole
Kuragin, who sets out to seduce Natasha: "Pierre remembered
that all the usual gambling set were to meet at Anatole Kuragin's
that evening, after which there usually followed a drinking-bout,
winding up with one of Pierre's favourite entertainments" (32–
33). These "favourite entertainments" are not specified, but we

can imagine them to be like Vronsky's—watching women dressed as Eve, displaying themselves in some public show, with perhaps a visit to the brothel to follow. Pierre also remembers that he has promised Andrey Bolkonsky not to go to Kuragin's. Bolkonsky has said to him, "You are dear to me just because you are the one live person in all our society. You're lucky. Choose what you will, that's all the same. You'll always be right, but there's one thing: give up going about with the Kuragins and leading this sort of life. It's not the right thing for you at all; all this riotous living and dissipation and all. . . ." At this time Pierre was living at the house of Kuragin's father, and they were proposing to marry Anatole to Prince Andrey's sister to reform him!

But Pierre immediately reneges on his solemn promise to Prince Andrey:

> the idea at once occurred to him that his promise was of no consequence, since he had already promised Prince Anatole to go before making the promise to Andrey. Finally he reflected that all such promises were merely relative matters, having no sort of precise significance, *especially if one considered that tomorrow one might be dead* or something so extraordinary might happen that the distinction between honourable and dishonourable would have ceased to exist. Such reflections often occurred to Pierre, completely nullifying all his resolutions and intentions. He went to Kuragin's. . . . (33; my italics)

Tolstoy thus puts into Pierre some of his own characteristics and dramatizes a conflict within himself between what might be called his Andrey characteristics and his Pierre characteristics. The impulse here seems clearly to follow a tendency toward false solution, arising from a deep existential dread: tomorrow we die, so distinctions between honorable and dishonorable cease to exist, and a reckless nihilism takes over. Tolstoy was like this himself, in his gambling, and in his resort to brothels—which made him so guilty that, like Levin in *Anna Karenina*, he feels bound to show his diary giving details of these debaucheries to his wife before they get married.

In the episode that follows, Pierre joins in the gambling and exploits of drunken daring, with Dolohov and Kuragin, and they end up tying a bear to the back of a policeman, and dropping him into the Moika river. These antics are seen as atrocious by Moscow society: at the Rostovs' they report to one another that Pierre has been banished to Moscow while Dolohov has been degraded to the rank of a common soldier. Yet "the ladies could not help laughing at it themselves" (41): the antic enlivens Moscow gossip, and is all part of the decadence of that society.

At this moment Natasha is still a child of thirteen: "*Quelle delicieuse enfant!*" exclaims a guest.

> The dark-eyed little girl, plain, but full of life, with her wide mouth, her childish bare shoulders, which shrugged and panted in her bodice from her rapid motion, her black hair brushed back, her slender bare arms and little legs in lace-edged long drawers and open slippers, was at that charming stage when the girl is no longer a child, while the child is not yet a young girl. (43)

Such is the huge time-scale of the novel that we are to see this little girl grow up and become the mother of three children. In the room also are Boris, Nikolay, a curly-headed youth, the count's eldest son, Sonya, the count's niece, and little Petya, all of whom are to play parts in the great drama.

Bezuhov inherits his father's estates although he is illegitimate. And he marries Ellen Kuragin, Anatole's sister, of which marriage more later. Natasha grows up to become an enchanting girl, and men begin to fall in love with her: Denisov, for example, declares at one stage "The little witch, she can do anything with me!" and he actually asks for her hand. Her mother tells him,

> "my daughter is so young, and I should have thought that as my son's friend you would have come first to me. In that case you would not have forced me to make this refusal. . . ." (p. 426)

Our fascination with Natasha is enhanced by many glimpses of her lively and energetic youthfulness, and even by the account of her prowess and courage in the hunting scenes.

> Natasha, without taking breath, gave vent to her delight and excitement in a shriek so shrill that it set everyone's ears tingling. In that shriek she expressed just what the others were expressing by talking all at once. And her shriek was so strange that she must have been ashamed of that wild scream, and the other must have been surprised at it at any other time. (p. 635)

We follow Natasha with great tenderness, from her appearance as a little girl, through adolescence, and her delightfully playful relationship with her mother, and her tearful and bewildered betrothal to Prince Andrey. At the end of the hunting scene, she emerges as a natural Russian dancer:

Where, how, when had this young countess, educated by a French emigree, sucked in with the Russian air she breathed the spirit of that dance? . . . the spirit, the motions were those inimitable, unteachable, Russian gestures the uncle had hoped for from her. . . . She danced the dance well. . . . (642)

Natasha is, one might say, the embodiment of life's mystery, and of the feminine element of being, seen against the somber background of war-torn early nineteenth-century Russia. And she is the darling of the delightful Rostov family, which is so united by love (she is very close to her brothers as well as to her father and mother) and by its traditions of honor and courtesy.

* * *

Significant in the courtship of Prince Andrey Bolkonsky is the moment when, unintentionally, he overhears Natasha and Sonya talking out of a window in the night. A number of Tolstoyean themes are brought together—the pathetic fallacy of human feelings in relationship to nature and the landscape; illogicality, and the impulse to deny reality. Prince Andrey is thirty-one, and already a widower, and catches glimpses of the possibility of making a new start in life.

He becomes aware of an ancient oak tree:

With its huge, uncouth, gnarled arms and fingers sprawling unsymmetrically, it stood an aged, angry and scornful monster among the smiling birches. Only the few dead-looking, evergreen firs dotted about the forest, and this oak, refused to yield to the spell of spring, and would see neither spring nor sunshine. (p. 519)

The oak seems to him to reject all "faith in . . . hopes and deceptions." Prince Andrey concludes that he and the oak are right: "our life is over." But as he drives one day along the road to the Rostovs' house at Otradnoe, he hears merry girlish cries, and sees a slim and pretty girl: "What is she thinking about, and why is she so happy?" he wonders. He glances at Natasha, "continually laughing and full of gaiety" and asks himself the same thing, "What is she so glad about?"

He is annoyed with himself for staying but because the night is so hot he throws open the shutters, and his eyes rest on the spring sky. He hears the voices of girls singing a musical phrase. He hears the rustle of Natasha's garments and her breathing. She cries "Do you know such an exquisite night has never, never been before?"

She then enacts a moment in Tolstoy's young life: or at least talks of it—talks of the moment when he threw himself off a roof, in defiance of reality:

> "One only has to squat on one's heels like this—see—and to hold one's knees—as tight, as tight as one can—give a great spring and one would fly away. . . . Like this—see!"
> "Mind, you'll fall." (522)

Prince Andrey is aware of some serendipity in the moment: "As though it were on purpose."

> All at once there stirred within his soul such a wholly unexpected medley of youthful hopes and ideas, running counter to the whole tenor of his life, that he made haste to fall asleep, feeling incapable of seeing clearly into his own state of mind. (523)

That happened in the spring: Andrey returns in June. He sees the same tree:

> The old oak, utterly transformed, draped in a tent of sappy dark green, basked faintly, undulating in the rays of the evening sun. (Ibid.)

And there comes upon him "an irrational, spring feeling of joy and renewal":

> All the best moments of his life rose to his memory at once. Austerlitz, with that lofty sky, and the dead, reproachful face of his wife, and Pierre on the ferry, and the girl, thrilled by the beauty of the night, and that night and morn—it all rushed at once into his mind. (524)

He decides that life is not over at thirty-one: everyone must know this:

> "Pierre and that girl, who wanted to fly away into the sky; everyone must know me so that my life may not be spent only on myself; they must not live so apart from my life, it must be reflected in all of them and they must all share my life with me!" (Ibid.)

He has a spiritual or reflective crisis, in which various ideas enter his mind to change the whole current of his life: ideas connected with Pierre, with glory, with the girl at the window, with the oak, with women's beauty, and love. (Gustafson is interesting on the symbolism of the sky in Tolstoy and how it symbolizes Heaven. Natasha for Andrey is the girl who wants to fly into the sky; see Gustafson, *Leo Tolstoy*, pp. 63ff.)

After dancing with her at a ball Prince Andrey falls in love with her. He is haunted by the moment when he heard her gay talk to Sonya that night as, lonely in his widowhood, he was gazing out of a nearby window. He becomes betrothed to her, but has to arrange, at the insistence of his father, to defer the marriage for a year. He says to Pierre,

> "I should never have believed it if anyone had told me I could love like this. . . . It is utterly different from the feeling I once had. The whole world is split into two halves for me: one—she, and there all is happiness, hope and light; the other half—all where she is not, there all is dejection and darkness. . . ."
> "Darkness and gloom," repeated Pierre, "yes, yes, I understand that. . . ." (*War and Peace*, p. 591)

But to Prince Andrey's father the match is not a brilliant one from the point of view of birth, fortune, or distinction. Prince Andrey is older than Natasha, who is still very young. Andrey's hesitance puts a considerable strain on Natasha: she frequently bursts into the tears of "an offended child, who does not know why it is being punished," and she is tortured both by the elaborate politeness with which Prince Andrey approaches the problem, and by the prospect of the year's delay on which Andrey insists, to placate his father, who is opposed to the match. She barely understands why this has to be, and is in a strangely tense and unreal state as the arrangement is made, without any formal announcement. The betrothal is awkward and strained from the beginning, because of Andrey's caution, his overrespect for his father, and because of Natasha's immaturity and inexperience.

It is significant that Prince Andrey urges Natasha, if she is ever in difficulties while he is away, to confide in Pierre, who has been very close to Andrey throughout the progress of his betrothal. It is also significant that Princess Marya does not approve of the match. In his dealings with his son and Princess Marya, however, Andrey is strictly rational, dealing with them "with an exaggerated logicality, as it were punishing some one for that secret, illogical element working within him."

The betrothal to Natasha is strange. Andrey is so much older than she, and there is a sense that she is persuaded into the relationship and persuaded into believing herself to be in love:

> "You know that from the very day when you first came to Otradnoe, I have loved you," she said, *firmly persuaded that she was speaking the truth.* (597; my italics)

On Andrey's part, there is some ambiguity:

> Prince Andrey held her hands, looked into her eyes, and could find
> no trace of his former love for her in his heart. Some sudden reaction
> seemed to have taken place in his soul, there was none of the poetic
> and mysterious charm of desire left in it; instead of that there was
> pity for her feminine and childish weakness, terror at her devotion
> and trustfulness, an irksome, yet sweet, sense of duty, bringing him
> to her for ever. The actual feeling, though not so joyous and poetical
> as the former feeling, was more serious and deeper. (Ibid.)

"Can this be I, the baby-girl (as everyone used to call me?)" thinks
Natasha. The Bolkonsky family seems to lack the warmth and
spontaneity of the Rostovs. Natasha is startled by being told that
Prince Andrey's son is not to live with them. Natasha wonders
about him being a widower. Princess Marya regards Prince Andrey's desire to marry again as "short-sighted." So this betrothal
is not at all promising, and Tolstoy delineates with great subtlety
the essential flaws in it—Natasha's unreadiness and the degree to
which she deceives herself as to its rightness; Andrey's hesitating
coolness and withdrawal; the effects of the opposition of his family; and the fact that the Rostovs, although a charming and lively
family, offer no advantages of finance or consequence where marriage is concerned.

* * *

Prince Andrey's courtship of Natasha is thus strangely marked
by uncertainty. Moreover, there is also a strange opposition between his love for Natasha and Pierre's: there is no hostility between Pierre and Andrey on the issue, but Pierre feels deeply
about his friend's interest in her, as though it were a rival claim.

The problems emerge eminently before the formal betrothal,
when Natasha has a feeling of awe and turns pale in a panic of
expectation every time she is left for a moment alone with Andrey.
She feels that he wants to tell her something but cannot bring
himself up to the point.

Natasha, we need to remember, is only just sixteen. At the recent ball she is described as standing with "her thin arms hanging
at her sides, and her scarcely outlined bosom heaving regularly."
So, she is not much more than a child. Of Andrey, she tells her
mother:

> "Only I'm afraid with him, I'm always afraid with him. What does that
> mean? Does it mean that it's the real thing? Mamma, are you asleep?"
> "No, my darling. I'm afraid of him myself," answered her mother.
> (589)

When she asks her mother whether it matters that Andrey is a widower, her parent advises her to pray to God: "marriages are made in heaven."

Prince Andrey is at that very moment talking to Pierre. The latter has seen Natasha turn from a woman who seemed "positively plain" to a "beautiful creature" as Andrey spoke to her and he thinks:

> "Something very serious is happening between them. . . ." and a feeling at once of gladness and of bitterness made him agitated. . . . (p. 586)

Later, Prince Andrey tells Pierre that he is in love with Natasha and determined to marry her.

> "I have never lived till now, but I cannot live without her. . . ."

Pierre replies, "That girl is a treasure. . . ."

> "My dear fellow, don't, I entreat you, be too wise, don't doubt, marry, marry, marry. . . . She loves you, I know it. . . ." (591)

His friend seemed to be an utterly different, new man. "What had become of his ennui, his contempt of life, his disillusionment?"

But Andrey goes away, somewhat unwillingly, telling Natasha that she is quite free to change her mind about her betrothal, urging her, if she is in difficulties, to be sure to talk to Pierre. Pierre himself is deeply disturbed by the relationship between Andrey and Natasha, although he outwardly approves of it. We feel there is a lack of spontaneity in the betrothal and are unsure about its authenticity. Tolstoy delineates these problems beautifully: he was in his early years aware of his own desire to act in accordance with conventional behavior: *comme il faut*, and he was aware of what might be forfeited, by such formality.

* * *

Natasha Rostov is clearly no character delineated in a moral fable to enact the significance of Christian love: she lives, in the work of an artist devoted to the portrayal of human truth.

The home life of the Rostovs is an essential part of the background of the book, as is especially Natasha's childishness at first. We follow Natasha from being a very young girl growing up in this remarkable family, and thus the threat to her future becomes intensely poignant. The incidents of family life are superbly conveyed to us. Pierre has known Natasha since she was a child:

> Natasha walked into the drawing room, and going straight up to Pierre, laughing and blushing, she said, "Mamma told me to ask you to dance."
> "I'm afraid of muddling the figures," said Pierre, "but if you will be my teacher. . . ." and he gave his fat hand to the slim little girl, putting his arm low down to reach her level. (78)

While the musicians are tuning up, they sit down together:

> Natasha was perfectly happy; she was dancing with a grown-up person, with a man who had just come from abroad. She was sitting in view of every one and talking to him like a grown-up person. She had in her hand a fan, which some lady had given her to hold, and taking the most modish pose (God knows where and when she had learnt it) fanning herself and smiling all over her face, she talked to her partner. "What a girl! Just look at her, look at her!" said the old countess, crossing the big hall and pointing to Natasha. Natasha coloured and laughed.
> "Why, what do you mean, mamma? Why should you laugh? Is there anything strange about it?" (79)

Natasha quite naturally falls into the part of being a grown woman: but in a moment, when her father begins to dance, she is a child again.

Natasha is thirteen at the beginning of the book: she is gazing at Boris "as girls of thirteen gaze at the boy whom they have just kissed for the first time." Her glance sometimes strays to Pierre, and "at the look on the funny, excited little girl's face, he felt an impulse to laugh himself without knowing why" (p. 71).

The present-day reader will notice a number of things about upper-class childhood in Russia at the time which are in marked contrast with the situation in the present day. The children in Tolstoy's novels are very much part of the family: they all eat together and with the guests, and so are taught good manners and self-possession naturally from the beginning. They also dance with the company, and sing songs: there is no "youth culture" which has been separated off for commercial purposes, as in our time, with the inculcation of an unnatural hostility to the adult world. Of course, divisions between youth and age occurred in Tolstoy's time, as when Natasha comes under the influence of Anatole Kuragin, and turns even against Sonya: but this is an exceptional development, and is shown to be an exceptional consequence of a decadence in upper-class life.

They also make their own entertainment, and this in turn has a particular effect on their concept of time, generation, and history. This comes out especially in the striking episodes delineated at Christmas.

'Does it happen to you," said Natasha to her brother . . . "to feel that nothing will ever happen—nothing; that all that is good is past. . . .' (652)

They remember a Negro who appeared, the source of whom they never discovered.

"And do you remember how we were rolling eggs in the big hall, and all of a sudden two old women came in, and began whirling round on the carpet. Did that happen or not? Do you remember what fun it was?. . ."

Smiling with enjoyment, they went through their reminiscences; not the melancholy memories of old age, but the romantic memories of youth, those impressions of the remotest part in which dreamland melts into reality. . . . (653)

Natasha, Nikolay, and Sonya are present together with Dimmler, "who was not young," and the old countess in the background. They begin to talk about dreams, and metempsychosis. Natasha declares that "I know for certain that we were once angels somewhere beyond, and we have been here, and that's why we remember everything. . .". With the wild philosophy of youth, when told it is difficult for us to conceive of eternity she asks why it is hard:

"There will be today, and there will be tomorrow, and there will be for ever, and yesterday has been, and the day before. . . ." (654)

Natasha is in a slightly tense state, because she is wanting Prince Andrey, who is away for a year even as she is engaged to him. A few pages back she has said to herself,

"My God, my God, the same people, the same talk, papa holding his cup, and blowing it the same as always". . . .

—and she feels with horror an aversion rising up for all her family, because they were always the same. Yet when she sings, the whole family is entranced by her. Petya (now fourteen) rushes in to say the mummers have arrived, and her spell broken Natasha flies into a hysterical rage, sobbing and screaming at her brother, because his interruption has shattered the calm she has achieved over her tension.

Into this family situation, fraught with softness, tenderness, strength, tedium, tension, and dismay come the house-serfs dressed as mummers—bears, Turks, tavern-keepers, and ladies:

> awe-inspiring or comic figures, at first huddled shyly together in the vestibule, bringing in with them the freshness of the cold outside, and a feeling of gaiety . . . with more liveliness and unanimity, they started singing songs, and performing dances, and songs with dancing, and playing Christmas games. (656)

The family go off to devise costumes for themselves: Nikolay becomes an old lady in a crinoline, Petya a Turkish lady, Dimmler a clown, Natasha a hussar, and Sonya a Circassian with a burned cork mustache.

They feel that their disguises are so good that they must show them to somebody else, and decide to go to the Melynkovs four versts away. They are in a mood of holiday gaiety, and their excitement seems to take them on to a different plane, of fantasy and adventure. They recognize one another, but also become fascinated by one another's adopted persona. Trotting along in their sledges in the snow in the moonlight they become enchanted. The scene evokes the particular culture of Russia at this season, among all classes, a ritual culture which provided them, together with their servants, with a sense of something larger than themselves, to do with the natural world, time, and mystery. The Russian Orthodox Church played a role in this as did the folk culture that emphasized the ties to nature. It is significant that having recreated a manifestation of this culture, they feel bound to share it with others.

They find the Melynkovs also trying to keep themselves amused. Excited by the crowd of clowns, bears, hussars, and other figures the Melynkovs go off and robe themselves in disguises. They dance, and the old lady of the family recognizes no one, not even her own daughters. They all join in games, using a string, a ring, and a silver rouble.

They play those ritualistic games in which people try to forecast their sweethearts, and Nikolay falls in love with Sonya, seeing her anew in her cork mustache. With the assistance of the maids,

Natasha and Sonya try to see their sweethearts in a mirror. Sonya half-sees what she takes to be Prince Andrey "lying down"—an image to which she returns at the time later when he is really dying. But to Natasha this image, while Prince Andrey is away and she is pining for him, is terrifying.

> "I feel so frightened for him, and for me, and frightened for every-thing. . . ." cried Natasha . . . she got into bed and long after the candle had to be put out she lay with wide-open eyes motionless on the bed, staring into the frosty moonlight through the frozen window panes. (667)

This part of the novel ends in tension: the Rostovs are appalled by Nikolay's intention to marry Sonya: because she is poor and the family is in enough difficulty over money. Natasha resents Prince Andrey's absence. The old countess becomes ill because of the emotional strain.

But the Christmas episode has great enchantment, and endears us to the family, not least because it is the embodiment of a young, civilized, peaceful life, with all its hope and promise, and its capac-ity for rising above mundane existence into joy and enchantment, toward deep meanings, despite its hardships and poverty, at the heart of a country at war. It is an intensely Russian episode, con-veying the magic of traveling by sledge in a Russian winter and the warmth of family life and self-organized entertainment, in touch with folk-ritual and the associated church festivals. Another intensely Russian episode is the hunting scene, the one in which Natasha becomes so excited that she utters her remarkable scream. Here the chase of the old gray wolf, the fox, and hare hunts, the musical episodes afterward in the hunting lodge, the physical energy and satisfactions, and the rural food they con-sume—all convey the flavor of a particular Russian world, and the background of intense life against which the major actions are played out.

* * *

The threat to this propitious turn in Andrey's life comes from the very area of delinquency and corruption to which Pierre Be-zuhov gives himself at the beginning of the book—a sphere to which his wife belongs, and to which she contributes a particular corruption. Hers is the sphere of sophisticated society, to which in *Anna Karenina* Vronsky belongs. In that sphere is Anatole Kur-agin, who is a companion of Doholov:

He did not care a straw what people thought of him. . . . What he loved was dissipation and women; and as, according to his ideas, there was nothing dishonourable in these tastes, and as he was incapable of considering the effect on others of the gratification of his tastes, he believed himself in his heart to be an irreproachable man, felt a genuine contempt for scoundrels and mean persons, and with an untroubled conscience held his head high. (714)

In this episode, although Tolstoy takes a firm moral position, we do not feel that he is haunted by his obsession with the potential treachery of women. It is a delineation of the way in which an innocent can be exploited, and perhaps bears a close resemblance to the world of Jane Austen's novels. At one point Tolstoy suddenly steps forward and adds the pertinent comment:

Rakes, those masculine Magdalens, have a secret feeling of their own guiltlessness, just as have women Magdalens, founded on the same hope of forgiveness. (Ibid.)

Tolstoy's moral position over this incident is clear. When Dolohov warns him that there are dangers in his attempt to abduct Natasha, Kuragin replies with what seems to us, since we know her so well, a cruel remark of male dominance:

"You know I adore little girls," said Anatole: "they're all confusion in a minute. . . ."

This playboy view is endorsed, of course, by no less a person that Pierre's wife Ellen. She knows as Pierre does that Anatole is already married, having been forced to marry his daughter by a Polish landowner. When Natasha is disturbed by Kuragin's boldness and by the way he presses her arm as he helps her into her carriage, Ellen, seeming to Natasha "so unapproachable and dignified," is kind to her and "she felt almost in love with this handsome and good-natured woman."

Ellen, for her part, was genuine in her admiration of Natasha, and in her desire to make her enjoy herself. Anatole had begged her to throw him with Natasha, and it was with that object that she had come to the Rostovs'. The idea of throwing her brother and Natasha together amused her (718).

She tells Natasha that her brother "is madly, madly in love with you, my dear." Natasha blushes, and Ellen exclaims and declares

"If you do love someone, it is not a reason to cloister yourself. Even if you are betrothed, I am sure your betrothed would have preferred you to go into society rather than to languish in ennui."

Natasha reflects,

"So then she knows I am engaged. So then they with her husband, with Pierre, with that good Pierre, talked and laughed about it. So that it means nothing." And again under Ellen's influence what had struck her before as terrible seemed to her simple and natural. . . . "And why not enjoy myself," thought Natasha, gazing at Ellen with wide-open wondering eyes. (Ibid.)

The corrupting effect of Ellen's sophisticated casuistry is clear. Marya Dmitryevna says "I don't care to associate with Countess Bezuhov and I don't advise you to. . . ."—but it is too late. Ellen has the subtle corrupt power of the decadent society lady, such as that Fanny Price encounters in Jane Austen's *Mansfield Park* in the Crawfords. Pierre knows only too well what kind of woman his wife is: he says to her afterward

"Wherever you are, there is vice and wickedness. . . ." (747)

Kuragin and Ellen, of course, are immensely experienced and impelled by the kind of narcissistic motive that drives Vronsky in *Anna Karenina*. In the theater Kuragin simply looks at Natasha:

He looked her straight in the eyes, almost smiling, with a look of such warmth and admiration that it seemed strange to be so near him, to look at him like that, to be so certain that he admired her, and not to be acquainted with him. (707)

It is significant, of course, that this happens in the theater, since it is full of manic elements and imbued with the egoistic self-dramatization of the habitual seducer. The fantasy role that Kuragin acts out penetrates Natasha's innocent fascination and undermines her emotional life: it is beginning to bring about changes at what Leslie H. Farber calls "the first realm of will"—the level at which emotional changes come about that we cannot control but only recognize.*

Tolstoy interposes descriptions of the action on the stage, to create the unreality of the theatrical show, whose effect is to make

---

*"The Two Realms of Will," in *The Ways of the Will* 1964), 1–25.

Natasha feel that her reality sense is undermined. Anatole is introduced, and Natasha talks to him, feeling that to do so is improper. When he flirts with her, she feels that in his uncomprehended words there is some improper intention. Also,

> as she looked into his eyes, she felt with horror that, between him and her, there was not that barrier of modest reserve she had always been conscious of between herself and other men . . . she felt that they were close as she had never been with any man. . . . (*War and Peace*, 710)

She feels "harrassed and excited." After Kuragin has pressed her arm, she is appalled:

> "My God! I am ruined!" she said to herself. "How could I sink to such a depth? . . ." Everything seemed to her dark and dreadful. . . . (712)

But just as, when Pierre broke his promise to Prince Andrey, and felt that all his promises were meaningless because he might die at any moment, so Natasha loses her sense of honor and feels her reality-sense deeply disturbed: she becomes confused:

> "Am I spoilt for Prince Andrey, love or not?" she asked herself.

Nothing has happened, "yet some instinct told her that all the old purity of her love for Prince Andrey was lost." Tolstoy must have known well what the effect of a seducer's persuasions would be on a young girl (it seems from the biographers that he was briefed over such matters by his daughter Tanya, who told him tales of her youth while they were out riding).

To Natasha, Anatole seems to be "a handsome, daring man." He has the facility to look into her eyes without any moral barrier—an accomplished technique that the seducer develops out of his own perverted need. But Kuragin, as we learn in the next chapter, was in trouble with his gambling debts, and has a fancy for gypsy girls and actresses. He has been married but has abandoned his wife. And he is simply an adventurer, indifferent to the effect of his escapades:

> What might come of a flirtation—Anatole was incapable of considering, and had no notion, as he never had a notion of what would come of any of his actions. . . . (715)

It is poignant to find the enchanting Natasha believing that when Anatole exclaims "I tell you that I am mad, mad with love of you. . . ." that he is a genuine lover: and even more when she regards his love-letter, composed for him by Dolohov, as the expression of an honorable and sincere affection.

At an improvised ball she dances with Kuragin, who squeezes her waist and kisses her hand; at last "burning lips were pressed to her lips." Next day the ersatz love-letter arrives and she feels in it "echoes of all that it seemed to her she was feeling herself."

> "Since yesterday evening my fate is sealed: to be loved by you or to die. There is nothing else left for me," the letter began. Then he wrote that he knew her relations would never give her to him, to Anatole; that there were secret reasons for that which he could only reveal to her alone; but that if she loved him, she had but to utter the word *Yes*, and no human force could hinder their happiness. Love would conquer all. He would capture her and bear her away to the ends of the earth.
>
> "Yes, yes, I love him!" thought Natasha, reading the letter over for the twentieth time, and finding some special deep meaning in every word (725)

Tolstoy makes it quite clear that this letter is a spurious concoction that exploits all the clichés of romantic love, to deceive a young girl on behalf of a sensual adventurer. It marks a clash between the world of Ellen Bezuhov, of sophisticated decadence, and of the world of the Rostov family, where everything is governed by tradition and honor. It is perhaps difficult to the modern reader to appreciate the degree of assault being made here on normal patterns, by which a suitor would be required to address the parents of a girl first, before making an offer to her. Kuragin's attempt to exploit Natasha is deeply dishonorable. We know, of course, that Anatole is already married, has had many affairs, and is careless of the future: he has no intention of committing himself to Natasha for life, and he knows that she is already betrothed. Obviously, this cynical triumph over a young girl's feelings is going to provoke an earthquake in the Rostov household and a catastrophe in her emotional life, whatever the outcome.

* * *

It should be noted that Natasha is vulnerable to Kuragin's blandishments especially because of the strain on her of the postponed betrothal. She is aware that Prince Andrey is meeting considerable opposition from his father, and that it is in deference to the old man's objections that Andrey has delayed his marriage. As Nikolay Rostov believes, "if he cared for Natasha he could get on just as well without his crazy old father's consent" (610). Moreover, Natasha gathers that Andrey's sister, Princess Marya, does not like her and resents the marriage.

Indeed, she has been taken by Count Ilya Andreitch to call on Prince Nikolay Andreitch, at the gloomy house in Vosdvizhenka, and has been virtually insulted. Her father was in a nervous fidget, no doubt feeling that there is some disdain for the Rostovs there. The old prince was in a bad mood. Princess Marya dislikes Natasha from the first glance: "She thought her too fashionably dressed, too frivolously gay and vain": she is filled with unconscious envy. The old prince has shouted that he doesn't want to see them. Natasha feels offended and makes haste to get away. Although Marya forces herself to congratulate Natasha on her happiness, Natasha is aware that she is lying. When she gets home Natasha sits in her room, "crying like a child, choking and sobbing."

She tries to persuade herself that she loves Andrey enough to bear all this: "And what does it matter to me about his father and sister; I love no one but him, him, him. . . ." But the continuing absence of Prince Andrey continues to torment her and so she is in an especially vulnerable state: she has to try to preserve the fantasy of her betrothal to Prince Andrey, in his absence, and the fantasy of the theater, both on stage and among the "brilliant" audience, undermines and confuses the fantasy she is trying to preserve. Intoxicated by the extraordinary manifestations of the theater, and persuaded by Ellen to "enjoy herself," she falls into the persuasion of the fairy-tale atmosphere which Kuragin is trying to create.

One of the strange aspects of the effect of this fantasy on Natasha is that she confuses the two men:

> She was tormented by the insoluble question, Which did she love, Anatole or Prince Andrey? Prince Andrey, she did love—she remembered clearly how great her love was for him. But she loved Anatole too, of that there was no doubt. "Else could all that have happened?" she thought. . . . "What am I to do, if I love him and the other too?" she said to herself, and was unable to find an answer to those terrible questions. (722)

In this perhaps we have the germ of the predicament of Anna Karenina, who dreams of having two husbands, both called Alexei, and that she cannot decide between them. And, again, a woman who feels imprisoned by conventional modes, against which her deeper will rebels, under romantic persuasions. For one of the contributory factors, to her confusion, is the less than complete attention of Prince Andrey himself, to this young inexperienced girl, in deference to his irascible father, who does not consider this a satisfactory match, and who does not see the need for Prince Andrey to marry again at all.

* * *

In the structure of the novel, Natasha is the focus of that love, in the meeting and commitment of true selves, that is at the utter extreme from the manifestations of destructive hate in human life—as realized in war. It is Natasha as a creative spirit who saves Pierre Bezuhov from despair and destruction: for her to be deceived is a terrible blow both to Pierre and to the reader. To allow her to be seduced and ruined would have undermined the hopeful hold on existence that enabled Tolstoy to portray the ghastly ruin that war brings on individuals and society, and on civilization. At the explicit level we know that Tolstoy had a deep conviction that women are treacherous and that sexual love was a serious threat to civilized society. But here his worst convictions are held in check: he may have been throwing a desperate dice, contemplating Natasha as prey to Anatole Kuragin and Dolohov's complicity—she might have behaved, as does Anna Karenina, in a way he could not control, in which case we may well wonder how he could have held the novel together. As it is, Sonya becomes the instrument of salvation.

Sonya reads Anatole's concocted letter and perceives that he is "a deceiver and a villain," and she thinks at once of the effect on the family: "What will Nikolenka—dear, noble Nikolenka—do when he hears of it?" For a moment she supposes that Natasha felt insulted by the letter. But when the latter awakens, she is defiant:

"I can't help it! . . . I can't keep it secret from you any longer. . . . You know we love each other. . . ." (726)

Natasha shows herself totally overwhelmed by Kuragin's attentions:

"it is only now that I have felt such love. . . . As soon as I saw him, I felt that he was my sovereign and I was his slave. . . ." (727)

This enslavement through passion was, of course, fascinating to Tolstoy: in *Anna Karenina* he makes much of Vronsky's feeling of devoted enslavement, and of Anna's feeling that she is taken over by some force outside herself. Sonya feels "horror and aversion," while Natasha proclaims she has "no will" in the matter. Sonya weeps tears of shame and pity for her friend. "Why this secrecy?" she asks.

"Natasha, have you thought what the *secret reasons* can be?" But Natasha is appalled that Sonya doubts Anatole, and flies into a mood of irritation and despair. Later Sonya tells Natasha that she is afraid that she will be ruined. She replies,

> "Then I will be ruined, I will; I'll hasten to my ruin. It's not your business. It's not you, but I, will suffer for it. Leave me alone, leave me alone. I hate you!" (729)

Sonya sees Natasha signaling to an officer and realizes that she is going to run away with her lover. She has become "unlike herself." (Tolstoy was fascinated by the power which, it can seem, can take people over as by powerful passion: Anna is divided against herself and admits there is "another self in me, one I fear.") Sonya suspects that Natasha has refused Bolkonsky. In the end she decides to tell Marya Dmitryevna, who has such faith in Natasha, because she is "mindful of all the benefits she has received from the family" and because she loves Nikolay. The turning of the tide over the attempted seduction of Natasha is a crucial reassertion of the values of the aristocratic family, in its attempts in Russia to uphold honor and the integrity of the individual: even in the midst of war and the collapse of values in decadence (such as Countess Ellen is caught up in).

The attempt on Natasha is a characteristic planned escapade. Kuragin and Dolohov have raised twenty thousand roubles and have a plan to whisk Natasha off sixty versts to Kamenka where an unfrocked priest would perform a marriage service with two stooges as witnesses. It has become a prank on the par with the drunken feats in which Pierre Bezuhov takes part earlier in the novel. It has taken on its own momentum: Dolohov tries to warn Anatole that he is taking serious risks: "Do you suppose they'll let it rest? It will come out that you are married. Why, they will have you up on a criminal charge, you know."

Anatole responds that he is talking nonsense:

> And Anatole, with that peculiar partiality (common in persons of dull brain), for any conclusions to which they have been led by their own mental processes, repeated the argument he had repeated a hundred times over to Dolohov already. "If this marriage is invalid . . . then

it follows I'm not answerable for it. Well, and if it is valid, it won't matter." (733)

—and he dismisses the prospect of throwing away so much money on an adventure as also nonsense. Perhaps we remember this futile recklessness when we see Kuragin later having his leg amputated, and later when we learn he has died from his wound. And this futile death raises in our minds the solace men can set against their own mortality: we may compare the way Natasha and Bolkonsky find one another in love, as she nurses him as he dies by degrees from his wound: and the way Pierre and Natasha are brought together, after a long experience of terrible suffering on both sides, which concludes the suffering caused by Natasha's betrayal of Prince Andrey. Anatole, Andrey, and Pierre are each deeply involved with Natasha, and their suffering and (in two cases) their deaths are set against her especial vitality and capacity to experience joy and to create life. But Anatole's attitude, that she is exploitable ("Ah, what a foot, my dear boy, what a glance! A goddess! . . . Eh?"). One might almost say that there is a gruesome symbolism in Anatole's concept of Natasha in terms of "what a foot," seeing the woman in terms of a part object, and the way he asks to see his own leg once it is removed by the surgeons: in this are implicit the limitations of the exploitative narcissistic sensual view of relationships: giving way to the temptations of the mere flesh—which is mortal and likely to perish. Tolstoy is himself at home, of course, among the adventurers: he knows the kind of ancillaries such men depend on—the heavy drinking, furious driving individuals like Balaga, who is paid a thousand or two roubles every now and then, for spirited horsemanship. Tolstoy knows that such sexual adventures are exciting because of the very element of risk: Anatole at this moment wears a sable cap, a fur pelisse, and a silver belt. He poses as a romantic hero, and he and his conspirators toast their adventure, flinging the glasses on the floor afterward. They plan to wrap Natasha in a sable cloak when she emerges, and the abduction is planned down to the last detail, with whistle signals and fast-driven sledges, like a military operation. And in this, again, we recognize a symbolism in which war and peace are in conflict: for the essence of this escapade is "false male doing," of a soldier's escapade, and the way Kuragin gloats on the romantic possibilities of his coup resembles Napoleon's pleasure at witnessing the corpses on the battlefield. Both signal the excitement and satisfaction that belong to the death of love, in the pursuit of narcissistic adventure, and that risk that compensates men for being men.

The conspirators are met, of course, with defeat, but Dolohov snatches Kuragin out of the courtyard. Marya Dmitryevna has gotten the whole story out of the weeping Sonya. Natasha is locked in her room.

She is in a desperate state: she cries out "I shall die" (later she takes arsenic): she also cries "Why did you hinder everything? . . . Who asked you to?" Tolstoy was aware how rueful passion, once aroused in a woman, could provoke this anarchic state, with its self-destructive potentiality. Natasha sobs, in response to Marya's allegation that Anatole is a "scoundrel," "He's better than any of you," she cries,

> And she sobbed with a despair with which people only bewail a trouble they feel they have brought on themselves. (740)

Natasha does not sleep all night, and her lips are tightly shut and parched, her eyes staring: her illness is long-lasting.

It is significant to note the physical torment that a girl betrayed in such a way is depicted as having to endure. From today's chatter about sex and relationships one might suppose that such experiences are no longer found: yet one knows from personal experience that young people can be so tormented, by failures of relationships and infidelity. (St. Valentine's Day is still the worst day in the year for youthful suicides.) And such torment is known among adults, too—witness the recurrent terrible acts of violence, such as men gassing or shooting their children, or their wives' lovers. If we take the reality of emotion, such distress is still common, and is part of the everyday reality of human needs for satisfactory and meaningful relationships.

*   *   *

The subtle drama of Natasha's lapse requires that we recognize what an offense to the girl herself the attempted seduction is. This needs to be emphasized at a time when what is still called the novel—that is, the commercial product—positively celebrates perversions, unfaithfulness, and the most extreme antics of promiscuity and sensationalism, as though there were no values and no truth in the area of sexuality. Perhaps only the psychotherapist knows the truth in this realm.

We need to accept Tolstoy's realism about the emotional realities

involved, and their social bearing, and to appreciate the gravity
of his artist's view.

Here, the key figure is Pierre Bezuhov, who has himself known
the madnesses of reckless "bohemian" behavior. In the subsequent
chapter he passes Anatole Kuragin in Tverskoy Boulevard:

> Anatole was sitting in the classic pose of military dandies, the lower
> part of his face muffled in his beaver collar. . . . His face was fresh
> and rosy; his hat, with its white plume, was stuck on one side, showing
> his curled, pomaded hair, sprinkled with fine snow. (743)

Pierre is envious of Anatole: "Indeed," he exclaims, "he is the real
philosopher! . . . He sees nothing beyond the present moment of
pleasure: nothing worries him, and so he is always cheerful, satisfied, and serene. What would I not give to be just like him!" But
surely we ourselves would rather be like Pierre himself, and note
the difference between the self-satisfied narcissist, and the man
who is capable of finding the reality of others. Even as we recognize that there is something appealing about the complacent im-
moralist, like Oblonsky, there can be no doubt that they are
lesser men.

Pierre notices Natasha's "thin, pale, and ill-tempered face." "She
looked round at him, frowned, and with an expression of frigid
dignity walked out of the room." When he is told that Natasha
had attempted to elope with Anatole Kuragin, with whom Pierre's
wife had thrown her, he is "hardly able to believe his ears."

> That Prince Andrey's fiancée, so passionately loved by him, Natasha
> Rostov, hitherto so charming, should give up Bolkonsky for that fool
> Anatole, who was married already . . . and be so much in love with
> him as to consent to elope with him—that Pierre could not conceive
> and could not comprehend. . . . (Ibid)

"He could not reconcile the sweet impression he had in his soul
of Natasha, whom he had known from childhood, with this new
conception of her baseness, folly and cruelty. . . ." "'They are all
alike,'" he said to himself, reflecting that he was not the only man
whose unhappy fate it was to be bound to a low woman" (744).

This is a terrible moment, not only for Pierre, but also for
Tolstoy himself, who hovered on the brink of contempt for
women, even as he idealized them: only as an artist is he able
to allow women to be as they really are: as ambivalent as any
human being:

the more he felt for his friend, the greater was the contempt and even aversion with which he thought of Natasha. . . . He could not know that Natasha's heart was filled with despair, shame and humiliation. . . . (Ibid.)

Pierre is obliged to tell Natasha that Kuragin is already married: she becomes incapable of speaking, in her state of shock.

Pierre goes off to confront Anatole, with "glittering eyes. . . ." and with a "terrible look of rage and power": to his wife he declares, "wherever you are, there is vice and wickedness" and when he challenges Kuragin, his face becomes "distorted with fury":

> with his big hand he clutched Anatole by the collar of his uniform and proceeded to shake him from side to side, till Anatole's face showed a sufficient degree of terror. (747)

Pierre calls him a scoundrel and a blackguard and threatens him with a heavy paperweight. He forces Kuragin to hand over Natasha's letters, and urges him to silence. He goes on:

> "You must understand . . . you are ruining a whole life, simply because you want to amuse yourself. Amuse yourself with women like my wife . . . but to promise a girl to marry her . . . to deceive, to steal. . . . Surely you must see that it's as base as attacking an old man or a child! . . ." (748)

Anatole doesn't see it: he challenges Pierre to a duel, but Pierre takes back his words and pays Anatole to leave Moscow for Petersburg.

Natasha has taken arsenic, but has been given antidotes and is out of danger. Pierre goes to Prince Andrey, who is coldly dismissive, and who laughs unpleasantly about Natasha: he gives Pierre her letters and declares that he cannot forgive her:

> "that's all very noble, but I'm not equal to following in that gentleman's tracks . . . never speak to me of that. . . ."

Pierre detects behind Princess Marya's sympathy for her brother a relief that the marriage is broken off: she had a contempt and dislike for the Rostovs.

Pierre goes to see Natasha, who is now tormented by regret: she is wretched at the wrong she has done Bolkonsky. Natasha's whole body heaves as she tells Pierre she begs Andrey to forgive her. A feeling of pity floods Pierre's heart. He asks if she loved "that bad man" and Natasha says "Don't call him bad": "I don't know . . . I don't know. . . ." She begins crying again and Pierre is again overwhelmed with pity, tenderness, and love.

Natasha is surprised to hear such gentleness, tenderness, and sympathy in his voice. She cries out, "Don't speak to me like that; I'm not worth it!" But Pierre tries to persuade her that the whole of her life is still before her, and makes the astonishing declaration:

> "If I were not myself, but the handsomest, cleverest, best man in the world, and if I were free I would be on my knees this minute to beg for your hand and your love."
> For the first time for many days Natasha wept with tears of gratitude and softened feeling. . . . (755)

Pierre leaves, "restraining the tears of tenderness and happiness that made a lump in his throat." It is a turning point in his life, too. He looks up at the 1812 comet: with its white light.

> It seemed to Pierre that it was in full harmony with what was in his softened and emboldened heart, that had gained vigour to blossom into a new life. (756)

Natasha, even in her broken and humiliated condition, perhaps even because of her shame and confusion, has the power to inspire Pierre, toward a new phase of his life. As Gustafson says, "In between Natasha's sin and her repentance Pierre encounters the sky" (Gustafson, 77).—the sky being again the symbol of the eternal—of being sub specie aeternitatis.

* * *

Pierre has known Natasha since childhood and the Natasha who remains in his mind is the effervescent creature who graces the Rostov household with such vitality and charm. Perhaps one of the most striking moments is when Natasha, who is sixteen—some time before Prince Andrey falls in love with her—is contemplating her relationships with Boris: she seems to be in love with Boris as in the past, but wonders whether this, now four years ago, is a piece of childhood nonsense, or a current obligation.

She runs in to her mother's room bare-legged with her hair in curl papers. Her mother is saying her prayers and has got to the part when she asks whether "this couch" will be her bier.

> That couch was a high feather-bed with five pillows ... Natasha
> skipped in, sank into the feather-bed, rolled over towards the side,
> and begun snuggling up under the quilt, tucking herself up, bending
> her knees up to her chin, kicking out and giving a faintly audible
> giggle as she alternately hid her face under the quilt and peeped out
> at her mother. (*War and Peace*, 559ff)

These visits of Natasha to her mother at night are one of the
greater pleasures for mother and daughter. Natasha declares that
she wants to talk to her mother, and she does so in a playful and
oblique way: it is superbly done. The countess is impressed by her
daughter's "strikingly serious and concentrated expression."

> "Well, so what then?" she said.
> "You have completely turned his head, and what for? What do you
> want of him? You know you can't marry him."
> "Why not?" said Natasha, with no change in her attitude.
> "Because he's so young, because he's poor, because he's a relation
> ... because you don't care for him yourself."
> "How do you know that?"
> "I know. It's not right my darling."
> "But if I want to. . . ." said Natasha.
> "Leave off talking nonsense."
> "But if I want to. . . ."
> "Natasha, I am serious. . . ." (560)

Their conversation is inconclusive, but slipped into the exchange
are serious pronouncements: and the gravity of the exchange is
disguised in play:

> Natasha did not let her finish; she drew the countess's large hand to
> her, and kissed it on the upper side, and then on the palm, then
> turned it over again and began kissing it on the top joint of the finger,
> then on the space between the knuckles. . . . (Ibid.)

It is indeed extraordinary that a girl who enjoys such intimacy
with her mother is later going to risk herself as the victim of a
professional seducer. Her mother begins to tell her about a cousin
she was in love with. Natasha prattles on:

> "Not to be married, but—just so," she repeated.
> "How so, my dear?"
> "Oh, just *so*. I see it's very necessary I shouldn't marry him, but . . .
> just *so.*"
> "Just so, just so," repeated the countess, and, shaking all over, she
> went off in a good-natured, unexpected elderly laugh.

"Don't laugh, stop," cried Natasha, "you're shaking all the bed. You're awfully like me, just such another giggler. . . . Stop. . . ." (561)

The identification prompts further inquiry:

"What do you think? Were men as much in love with you? And he's very nice, very, very, very nice! Only not quite to my liking—he's so narrow, somehow, like a clock on the wall. . . ."

To which the countess replies, "What nonsense you talk!"

Bezuhov, says Natasha, in a flight of fancy about the color of people, is "blue, dark blue and red, and he's quadrangular."

Natasha hears the count coming and slips off to her own bed. In her own room she indulges in an orgy of self-love, as girls of sixteen do, speaking to herself of herself in the third person: "She is charming. . . ." and speaking of herself as she imagines some very clever man speaking: "extraordinarily clever and then pretty, extraordinarily pretty, graceful. . . ." And she falls asleep passing into "another still happier world of dreams, where everything was as easy and as beautiful as in reality, and was only better because it was all different."

The next day her mother has a talk with Boris and from that day he gives up visiting the Rostovs. The playful, dreamy exchange between the child-girl and her mother has brought out a reality, of her growth to a new state, and the playful intimacy has enabled her to accept this without pain. But it is this playful, serious, self-delighting Natasha who is foremost in our minds, as the embodiment of the feminine principle, in *War and Peace*.

* * *

As I have said, *War and Peace* presses hard at the problem of death, in an existential way, and explores the nature of love, as a way of finding meaning in the face of death. Incidentally, as an undercurrent, the question of mere sexual possession is shown to be incidental, to this problem: Anatole Kuragin's preoccupation with Natasha's charms, with her pretty little feet, narcissistic and bodily sensual, is devoid of that love which would seek to find her as a woman as being, is shown to be ultimately deathly. If his attempt to abduct her had gone as he planned, what would have been the outcome? A duel with one of her family, and the girl reduced to a state of ruin, after a brief experience of a fake marriage: probably Kuragin himself dead, and Natasha's emotional life blighted forever. As it is to our horror, after a few more chapters, we learn of his death from fatal amputation of his leg, on which he has jauntily strutted in his amorous posturing, but sees it at last in horror at its separate existence, covered with dry gore.

"O! Oooo!" he sobbed like a woman. . . .

Prince Andrey, whose body has been destroyed, and who is waiting for the end, is reunited with Natasha who kneels before him, asking for forgiveness. We can see the appeal of such a love to Tolstoy, tormented as he was by a dread of sexual love. The man is already dying and so is moved into a sphere beyond the fear of death: and Natasha, in her guilt and repentance, can be without thought of sexual commitment. In this love relationship Tolstoy can concentrate on love that transcends the bodily reality that he found so troublesome. What meaning can such a love have, and how can that meaning be asserted against the nothingness that threatens to take over, as the collapse of everything threatens to overwhelm everyone, toward the end of the Napoleonic war.

As Natasha goes to Andrey "an irresistable force drew her forward." When she comes to him he is "looking just as she had always seen him," with "his shining eyes, gazing passionately at her,"

> and especially the soft, childlike neck, showing above the lay-down collar of the nightshirt, gave him a peculiarly innocent, childlike look, such as she has never seen in him before. She ran up to him and with a swift, supple, youthful movement dropped on her knees.
> He smiled and held out his hand to her. (1157)

In the next chapter we return to Andrey's progress since his wound, and since he had seen the sufferings of the man he had not liked. He is in pain and his mind is not in its normal state.

> All the faculties of his soul were clearer and more active than ever, but they acted apart from his will. . . . (1159)

He watches the insects in his candle and reflects:

> "A new happiness was revealed to me, that could not be taken away from man. . . . Happiness beyond the reach of material forces, outside material, external influences on man, the happiness of the soul only, the happiness of love!" (1160)

He feels as though "a strange, ethereal edifice of delicate needles or splinters were being raised over his face, over the very middle of it."

> He felt that . . . he must studiously preserve his balance that this rising edifice might not fall to pieces. . . . (Ibid.)

At one point "thought and feeling floated to the surface again with extraordinary clearness and force":

> "Yes, love . . . but not that love that loves for something, to gain something, or because of something, but that love I felt for the first time, when dying, I saw my enemy and yet loved him. . . . (1161)

The sight of the suffering and dying Anatole has obviously been significant for Andrey. He reflects on the nature of love again:

> "Loving with human love, one may pass from love to hatred; but divine love cannot change. Nothing, not even death, can shatter it. It is the very nature of the soul. And how many people I have hated in my life. And of all people none have I loved and hated more than her." And he vividly pictured Natasha to himself. (Ibid.)

He feels he understands her sufferings, her shame, and her penitence, and sees the cruelty of his abandonment of her. He sees in a figure by the door "the white face and shining eyes of that very Natasha he had been dreaming of." Suddenly, the face of that very Natasha is before him.

> "You?" he said. "What happiness."

When she asks for his forgiveness, he declares, "I love thee more, better than before." From that time, Natasha never leaves Bolkonsky's side, and she displays great skill in nursing him.

Here we begin to understand the pressing personal need in Tolstoy, to explore the nature of love and the spiritual or meaningful quality it can give.

Given the complex composition of Tolstoy's psychological life, we can see how it translates into the myths of his novel. *War and Peace* gains its power over us because of the long spiritual journeys of Pierre Bezuhov and Andrey Bolkonsky. Both are in love with Natasha Rostov. Both are entrapped in unsatisfactory marriages, and yearn for a spiritual relationship. Both are adversely affected by the machinations of a sensual woman—Ellen Bezuhov, Pierre's wife: Andrey by her use of her brother to undermine Natasha. One might say that both of these existential heroes are violated by the influence of the wicked woman who is devoted to the indulgences of the flesh (much is made of Ellen's inclination to display her beautiful shoulders and bosom and the contrast between her beauty and her decadence).

The ordeals of war impinge on both men, and they go through intense suffering in the battles in which they become involved: both are intensely aware of what is happening to them. Andrey tends to become cold and cynical, and rejects his sister's religious inclinations. Pierre learns deeper and deeper sympathy, as he experiences at first hand the sufferings and ponders the deaths of common soldiers and down-and-outs. Andrey is twice wounded, the second time fatally: Pierre is nearly shot as an incendiary: he has taken the ultimate risk.

At the time of his lying wounded, even as he yearns for the Natasha who has wronged him by her impulse to infidelity, Andrey, rendered sexless and with a mortal wound, is faced with her, repentant and asking for forgiveness. I would conjecture that there is in this scene a fantasy in Tolstoy of his mother asking for forgiveness for having betrayed him with the father. In this encounter he can contemplate enjoying the spiritual rapture which his idealized mother inspired in him, not least because the relationship is now beyond sex.

The reunion of Andrey and Natasha has all the power of a reunion of Tolstoy with his dead mother, or, one might say, his union with the female principle, stripped of the dangers and temptations of its sexual component.

> Although with the renewal of affectionate relations between Prince Andrey and Natasha the idea did occur that in case he recovered their old engagement would be renewed, no one—least of all Natasha and Prince Andrey—spoke of this. The unsettled question of life and death hanging, not only over Prince Andrey, but over all Russia, shut off all other considerations. (1163)

The latter sentence gives the clue to the great scope of the novel *War and Peace:* it presses, with its colossal involvement in Napoleon's assault on Russia, the existential problem to its limits, of how to find meaning in the relationship between men and women, when women were the prime source of inspiration of the soul, but yet also a source of evil: the other evil of course, being the tendency of men to take to false male solutions, of universal hate and destruction. (We may also find in this progress something of Winnicott's insights into male risk-taking. Andrey and Pierre are pursued through the most terrible risks, and in suffering in these processes they learn to come to terms with women: both through Natasha. They learn to understand and embrace the female principle and to find it less of a threat, through love.)

Princess Marya is inclined to be hostile to Natasha, but when she sees her face with its expression of "boundless love for him . . . an expression of pity, of suffering of others, and of passionate desire to give herself up entirely to helping them" she relents:

> It was clear at that moment there was not one thought of self, of her own relation to him, in Natasha's heart. (*War and Peace*, 1230)

Princess Marya and Natasha hedge round the truth, of whether Prince Andrey will survive. They dare not mention it, but when Marya sees Natasha sob over the "whole truth," she knows. There has been a sudden change in Andrey's condition, and he is dying: she realizes that

> he had suddenly grown softer, and that that softening, that tenderness, was the sign of death. (1231)

Andrey seems to belong to another world:

> he understood something else that the living did not and could not understand, and that entirely absorbed him. (1232)

Prince Andrey knows that he is dying, that he was already half-dead:

> he experienced a sense of aloofness from everything earthly, and a strange and joyous lightening in his being. (1235)

He had experienced the dread of death, but after coming to himself after his wound, "as though set free from the cramping bondage of life, there had sprung up in his soul that flower of love, eternal, free, not dependent on this life, he had no more fear, and no more thought, of death."

Since Natasha has come to him, however, he has been troubled by an attachment to life.

> It was the sudden consciousness that life, in the shape of his love for Natasha, was still precious to him, and the last and vanquished onslaught of terror before the unknown. (1236)

"Can fate have brought us together so strangely only for me to die?" he thinks: "Can the truth of life have been revealed to me only for me to have spent my life in falsity. . . ." He says, "Natasha, I love you too much! More than everything in the world!" He falls asleep but wakes in a cold sweat of alarm:

> "Love? What is love?" he thought. "Love hinders death. Love is life. All, all that I understand, I understand only because I love. All is bound up in love alone. Love is God, and dying means for me a particle of love, to go back to the universal and eternal source of love." (1238)

He has a dream in which he is trying to shut a door behind which is "*It*",—death. He feels that death is an awakening—and since that awful moment the change has come that Natasha recognizes.

Marya and Natasha now wait for the end, realizing that Prince Andrey is slipping away. He dies and Natasha closes his eyes:

> She closed them, and did not kiss them, but hung over what was the newest memory of him. "Where has he gone? Where is he now?" (1240)

They weep from the "emotion of awe that filled their souls before the simple and solemn mystery of death that had been accomplished before their eyes."

Prince Andrey's has been a long agony and his death has made a profound mark on Natasha, as does the death of Petya, on the discovery of which she has to comfort her mother. It is indeed poignant that Natasha, who has been such a close and ebullient companion of Petya, should have to save her mother from despair and madness at this terrible news. The effect on Pierre is profound. When they meet again, Natasha is so changed by suffering that Pierre does not at first recognize her. He goes to visit Princess Marya:

> Pierre recollected that the princess had always had lady-companions of some sort with her, but who those companions were, and what they were like, he did not remember. "That is one of her companions," he thought, glancing at the lady in the black dress. . . . (1403)

He sees her as "a good, kind, friendly creature, who need be no hindrance to his talking freely to Princess Marya." But the latter, becoming embarrassed, asks, "You don't recognise her?"

Pierre glanced once more at the pale, thin face of her companion, with its black eyes and strange mouth. Something very near him, long forgotten and more than sweet, gazed at him out of those intent eyes. (Ibid.)

It is a deeply moving way of conveying the onset of the final moment of rediscovery of one another, between Pierre and Natasha, after so much suffering on both sides.

"But no, it cannot be," he thought. . . .
. . . at that moment Princess Marya said, "Natasha!"
And the face with the intent eyes—painfully, with effort, like a rusty door opening—smiled, and through that opened door there floated to Pierre a sudden, overwhelming rush of long-forgotten bliss. . . . It was Natasha, and he loved her. . . . (1404)

* * *

Prince Andrey Bolkonsky thinks, at the moment he confronts death, "Love? What is love?" . . . "Love hinders death. Love is life. . . . Love is God. . . ." To die, he reflects, means "a particle of love, to go back to the universal and eternal source of love." Tolstoy's leading characters have this kind of crisis, and reflect on parallel lines: Levin, Bezuhov, and Bolkonsky.

In a sense the questions that lie beyond this kind of musing are the child's questions—the kind of questions a child asks, say, at the age of eight or nine, but never gets answered: they are the great poetic-philosophical questions all the same, unanswerable as they are. One can understand why Tolstoy himself was so perplexed by such questions, not least under the influence of the "scientific view," that he contemplated suicide. And one can understand how he was impelled into these questions by his mother's death.

I would remind the reader at this point that Karl Stern argues in *The Flight from Woman* (1966), that a similar catastrophe in the life of Réné Descartes led him to devise a philosophy in which the universe itself was regarded as a rejecting mother, from which man was alienated, combined with devastating doubt—and this became the basis for both modern scientific advance, and the modern feeling in man of being alienated from the universe.

The flaws in Tolstoy's argument are evident: love does not hinder death, for instance. Nor in dying do we go back to the "universal and eternal source of love," unless we subscribe to Christian belief.

The truth of *War and Peace* lies in the portrayal of the way in which an emotional disaster can destroy a character's well-being, and deal a devastating blow to the attempt by individuals to make sense of their lives. We see Pierre Bezuhov desperate to escape from his confused and chaotic life, and to realize his rich capacities for love, sympathy, moral concern, and the pursuit of meaning. Natasha as a very young girl and young woman seems to have both the capacity to draw these out in Pierre, and to devote her life to such high aspirations. But her susceptibility to the attempt by Anatole Kuragin to seduce her and betray her makes her seem "like all the others," treacherous and capable of the coarsest and most stupid lapse, as is any human being.

Confronted with the reality of her lapse, she becomes seriously ill and only after lengthy treatment (but actually because of her youthful elasticity) does she begin to get well. However, she still cannot sing, or laugh: "Laughter and singing especially seemed like scoffing at her grief" (*War and Peace*, 826)

> An inner sentinel seemed to guard against every sort of pleasure. . . .
> As soon as she began to laugh or attempted to sing all by herself, tears choked her; tears of remorse; tears of regret for that time of pure happiness that could never return. . . . (Ibid.)

It is only with her brother Petya that she feels at ease: and of the guests who come to the house she is only glad to see one person: Pierre Bezuhov.

> No one could have been more tender, circumspect, and at the same time serious. . . .

Pierre, of course, is in love with Natasha, but he is married, and it seems to him that he is too old to think seriously of this young woman as a possible lover.

> Sometimes Natasha noticed some confusion or awkwardness in Pierre in her presence, especially when he was trying to do something for her pleasure or afraid something in the conversation might suggest to her painful reminiscences. (827)

She puts this down to his general kindliness and shyness, and she remembers his declaration of his attachment to her, when he said that had he been free he would have asked on his knees for her hand, as the "kind of meaningless nonsense one utters to console a weeping child." She feels between herself and Pierre the kind of moral barrier such as she did not feel between herself and

Kuragin. She cannot conceive that their relationship would blossom into "that tender, self-conscious, romantic friendship between a man and a woman of which she had known several instances."

Natasha goes through a carefully delineated religious crisis, in which, praying often, she feels that God is guiding her soul, and she prays to him to "have mercy on her, in horror at her own vileness." She knows she is pretty, but it gives her no pleasure. And her torment seems to her bound up with the torment that Russia itself is going through.

She prays for her brother and for Denisov, for Prince Andrey, and for the first time becomes aware of the shortcomings of her behavior toward her father, her mother, and Sonya: and she even prays for Anatole, as an enemy. She is deeply affected, in her torment, by a prayer for the czar, for his army, and for victory over the enemy:

"just weapons of brass in the hands that wage war in thy name, and gird them about with strength for the battle. . . ."

She is terribly inspired by these prayers, but

"she had no distinct idea what she was asking for in this prayer . . . she could not pray for the trampling of her enemies under foot . . . she felt in her heart a thrill of awe and horror at the punishment in store for men's sins . . . and prayed to God to forgive them all, and her too. . . ." (835)

Pierre himself is wound into another fantasy related to masonic theories about the number 666, Napoleon, and himself. In making these connections Tolstoy is perhaps exploring the pressure on the individual consciousness, of widespread political and military catastrophes, such as Napoleon's invasion of Russia. And he is reinforcing the parallel between Natasha's fate in relation to Pierre, and the fate of the nation. The march on Moscow, the losing of battles at Austerlitz and Borodino, and the retreat from Moscow disrupt the traditional life of everyone, so that at times they are threatened by the total breakdown of social order and community. Natasha relates this to her own sins and develops the capacity for a universal pity and forgiveness, as part of her recovery, when the dynamics of the hate of "false male doing" have been turned on her. Pierre has wandered into a seemingly hopeless situation, in which he is in a "wrong" marriage and a confused personal religious and political situation: the one positive feature in his life is his relationship with Natasha, that resembles that of Daniel Deronda to Gwendolen Harleth in George Eliot's *Daniel Deronda:* somewhere between an admirer and a spiritual and moral advisor—indispensable and inspiring at the same time. Pierre understands Natasha as nobody else does, and she relies on his sympathy to maintain her hold on life. But the life of each is menaced by the force of circumstances.

Pierre goes to the Rostovs and hears Natasha singing: he is "surprised and delighted." She asks him "is it wrong of me to sing?"

> "I shouldn't like to do anything you wouldn't like. I trust you in every-thing. You don't know how much you are to me, and what a great deal you have done for me!" (840)

She doesn't notice how much Pierre flushes at these words. She asks him about Prince Andrey and Pierre declares that he has nothing to forgive: he remembers his declaration about asking her on his knees, if he had been free, and the same words rise to his lips. She tells him, "Any one kinder, more generous than you, I have never known. . . ."

The moment is lost, by Petya's entrance, imploring Pierre to help him join up, and to overcome the distress this intention causes to his mother and father. But Pierre notices Natasha's eyes that are "unusually brilliant and eager" and "turned upon him with more than cordiality in them": he is reduced to embarrass-ment and hesitation, and they look at one another in dismay.

Natasha is clearly falling in love with Pierre, while he has always been in love with her. But the situation is impossible: he leaves without a word and he makes up his mind not to visit the Rostovs again. We are about halfway through the novel and it is clear that Pierre's future can only be with Natasha—but there are worlds of suffering each has to go through before they can be free to love one another as they deserve.

But we have already been given the state of Pierre's mind, vis-à-vis Natasha. He is in love with her and she is the foundation of his philosophy of being:

> Ever since the day when Pierre had looked up at the comet in the sky . . . and recalling Natasha's grateful look, had felt as though some new vista was opening before him, the haunting problem of the vanity and senselessness of all things earthly had ceased to torment him. That terrible question: Why? what for? which had till then haunted him in

the midst of every occupation, was not now replaced by any other question, nor by an answer to the old question; its place was filled by the image of *her*. If he heard or talked of trivialities, or read or was told of some instance of human baseness or folly, he was not cast down as of old; he did not ask himself why people troubled, when all was so brief and uncertain. But he thought of her as he had seen her last, and all his doubts vanished; not because she had answered the questions that haunted him, but because her image lifted him instantly into another bright realm of spiritual activity, in which there could be neither right nor wrong, into a region of beauty and love, which was worth living for. Whatever infamy he thought of, he said to himself, "Well, let so and so rob the state and the Tsar, while the state and the Tsar heap honours on him; but she smiled at me yesterday, and begged me to come, and I love her, and nobody will ever know it," he thought. (835)

He still, however, leads an aimless and idle life.

It is an interesting passage, this delineation of the rapture Pierre feels in his love for Natasha. It is not that she provides the basis for any philosophical or religious rejection of his obsession with "the vanity and senselessness of all things earthly." She doesn't provide the answers to the questions why? and what for? either in their old forms or any new forms. It is simply that her "image" fills the space where those questions lurked, and this gives him hope.

He is not cast down, either by triviality or by perceptions of baseness and folly, even though life is no less brief and uncertain. It is rather that the image of her love for him lifts his instantly into a new realm of spiritual activity: a region of beauty and love *where there is neither right nor wrong*, a strange state of affairs.

The parallel, of course, is the way Levin, in *Anna Karenina*, ceases to agitate about the brevity of life and about the intolerable burden of mortal life, to concentrate his attention on his newborn son, and on Kitty as his beloved mother. It is of course a portrayal that has a great deal of Tolstoy in it—whose recollection and construction of the ideal image of his mother's pure and spiritual reality could do so much to take him out of the world into a sphere where the "old questions" no longer mattered, and there was "neither right nor wrong." The rapture may be heavenly, but it is not yet a condition in which to relate to a real woman in an earthly marriage.

* * *

There is a strange sense that to the Russian society most threatened by war it was something of a game. I suppose it was always
more difficult to involve people at all levels of society, before the
concept of "total war" was arrived at: though by the end of the
Napoleonic wars the war had become virtually total, since civilians
were involved, at least after Smolensk was shelled.

But what Tolstoy calls "the life of the drawing-rooms" is singularly detached from serious concern over the reality of events:

> Between the year 1805 and 1812 we had made peace with Bonaparte
> and quarrelled with him again; we had made new constitutions and
> unmade them again, but the salons of Anna Pavlovna's and of Ellen
> were precisely as they had been . . . before. (890)

Anna Pavlovna's salon, in which the whole novel begins of course,
sees in Bonaparte's successes a malicious conspiracy, "the sole aim
of which was to give annoyance and anxiety to the court circle of
which Anna Pavlovna was the representative." The set gathered
about Ellen and talked about "the great nation" and the "great
man," and regretted the breach with France. Anna Pavlovna's set
refused to admit French people. In Ellen's salon reports of cruelty
and barbarous methods of warfare by the French were discred-
ited, and all sorts of reconciliatory efforts on the part of Napoleon
were discussed. They regarded the patriotic fervor of Moscow
with irony and witty, if circumspect, raillery.

If Tolstoy is right about these historical circumstances, it would
seem that there were sets whose fashion it was to be a kind of
third column in regard to the war. The appointment of Kutuzov
as supreme commander provokes some diplomatic squirming and
volte-faces, but meanwhile Napoleon has passed through Smolensk and is moving closer and closer to Moscow.

What one gets from Tolstoy, whether he is historically accurate
or not, is a sense of halfheartedness about the war, among the
Russian ruling class, whatever patriotic fervor was abroad, in the
army, and among the rich merchants and landowners.

* * *

In representing war Tolstoy creates a general picture of events
moving by themselves, by inexorable laws of human collective activity, in history: and of confusion at the local level, whereby individual men are caught up in violent events, and only afterward
reorganize and arrange the things that happened to them into
some coherent pattern.

At the very local level, however, Tolstoy depicts something else—the essential reluctance that individuals have, to take part in the insane manifestation of hate that war is. An instance is the experience of Nikolay Rostov when he is taking part in the advance on Ostrovna with his squadron of hussars. He is on a big sorrel horse with a white tail and mane, "a fine spirited beast of the Don breed," a Cossack horse. Because he had become inured to fear, he had not the slightest sense of being afraid. The cannons are firing, and the Uhlans gallop off through the infantry. Cannon-balls come whistling, but the sound has an inspiring and cheering effect on Rostov. He can see the Uhlans engaging with the French dragoons on gray horses and feels that if he were to charge the French with his hussars now, they could not hold their ground.

He sets off, as he would have done at a wolf hunt, without thinking or considering. With the same feeling with which he had dashed off to cut off a wolf's escape, Rostov gallops to cut off the broken ranks of the French dragoons. He picks out one of them and flies after him. The Frenchman sits crouched on his gray horse, urging it with his sword.

> In another instant Rostov's horse dashed up against the grey horse's hindquarters, almost knocking it over, and at the same second Rostov, not knowing why he did so, raised his sword, and aimed a blow at the Frenchman. (821)

The instant he did this all Rostov's eagerness suddenly vanished.

> The officer fell to the ground, not so much from the sword cut, for it had only just grazed his arm above the elbow, as from fright and the shock to his horse.

The French officer is hopping along the ground with one foot in his stirrup. He is screwing up his eyes and glanced up at Rostov with an expression of terror.

> His pale, mud-stained face—fair and young, with a dimple on the chin and clear blue eyes—was the most unwarlike, most good-natured face, more in place by a fireside than on the field of battle. Before Rostov could make up his mind what to do with him, the officer shouted "I surrender." (Ibid.)

The hussars gallop back with their prisoners. Rostov is "conscious of some disagreeable sensation, a kind of ache at his heart." A glimpse of something vague and confused seems to have come to

him, with the capture of the French officer and the blow he had
dealt him. Even though when he gets back, and receives a com-
mendation from his commanding officer (when he expected a
reprimand, since no order to charge had been given) he has an
"unpleasant vague feeling of moral nausea." He remembers how
his hand had paused even as he lifted it, when he perceived the
Frenchman's dimple in his chin.

> All that day, and the next Rostov's friends and comrades noticed that,
> without exactly being depressed or irritable, he was silent, dreamy
> and preoccupied.

He doesn't drink, tries to be alone, and seems absorbed in
thought. There was something he could not fathom, in the very
exploit for which he had won the St. George's Cross.

> "So they are even more frightened than we are," he thought. "Why,
> is this all that is meant by heroism? And did I do it for the sake of
> my country? And was he to blame with his dimple and his blue eyes?
> How frightened he was! He thought I was going to kill him. Why
> should I kill him? My hand trembled . . . I can't make it out, I can't
> make it out. . . ." (823)

He is unable to find any clear solution of the doubts that trouble
him: but he has allowed himself to ponder the essence of war,
which is of murder by men caught up in the rationalizations of
hate. Tolstoy's writing about war has the authentic flavor of coming from a man who has known war and the pity of war—and
knows of the multiple deceptions by which men are capable of
implicitly denying the horrors they have committed, and what
they know about themselves. His primary concern was with the
truth and falsity of war: W. B. Gallie makes this emphasis in his
essay on Tolstoy in *Philosophers of Peace and War* (1978). He quotes
from the closing paragraphs of *Sevastopol:*

> Perhaps what I am saying here is one of those evil truths which should
> never be uttered, but should be kept hidden unconscious in each
> man's soul, lest they prove hurtful. . . . For who is the villain, and who
> is the hero of my story? *All* . . . all are good, and all are evil. . . . The
> hero of my story, whom I love with all the energy of my soul, and
> whom I have tried to set forth in his full beauty is—The Truth.

* * *

The effects of military conflict are made especially vivid in *War
and Peace* by the way Tolstoy concentrates on the individual expe-

riences of Prince Andrey and members of the Rostov family. For
instance, Prince Andrey defends Captain Tuskin, whose battery
he has observed closely, just as Tuskin is about to be reprimanded
for abandoning two guns (his reckless and brave defense has in
fact been responsible for the successful action beyond anything
else): and Nikolay Rostov has been wounded in the arm, in a
somewhat confused engagement.

> "Who are they? Why are they here? What do they want? And when
> will it all end?" thought Rostov, looking at the shadowy figures that
> kept flitting before his eyes. The pain in his arm became ever more
> agonising. (*War and Peace*, 241)

Tolstoy does what no military man allows himself to do—follows
the processes of consciousness in men on the field of battle. In
general, the convention is to split off the individual inner life
from the deeds, as soldiers do, with their ironic way of talking,
out of fear of hurt and death. Tolstoy portrays all the inner fear,
even as he describes the death and injury to hundreds of men on
the battlefield and by this means the burden of suffering becomes
at times almost too much to bear. With Rostov

> He was heavy with sleep, crimson circles danced before his eyes, and
> the impression of these voices and these faces and the sense of his
> loneliness all blended with the misery of the pain. (241–42)

He dozes off for a minute, but in that brief interval he dreams
of innumerable things:

> He saw his mother and her large, white hand; he saw Sonya's thin
> shoulders, Natasha's eyes and her laugh, and Denisov with his voice
> and his whiskers. . . . All that . . . was inextricably mixed up with the
> soldier with the harsh voice. . . .

> "Nobody cares for me," thought Rostov. "No one to help me, no one
> to feel sorry for me. And I too was once at home, and strong and
> happy and loved," he sighed, and with the sigh unconsciously he
> moaned. (242)

"In pain, eh!" asks a soldier sitting near him by the fire.

> "Ah, what a lot of fellows done for today—awful!" Rostov did not hear
> the soldier. He gazed at the snowflakes whirling over the fire and
> thought of the Russian winter with his warm, brightly lighted home,

his cosy fur cloak, his swift sledge, his good health, and all the love and tenderness of his family. "And what did I come here for?" he wondered. (Ibid.)

In the battles there is endless confusion, mistakes, and chaos, followed by soldiers lying about what happened and what they did: the only constant is the perplexed misery of the combatants, and their memories of home.

* * *

Much of the military action in *War and Peace* takes place as if in a dream: when one penetrates to the consciousness of participants, this is what one finds. Nikolay Rostov's first charge is like this: he gallops toward the enemy and lifts his saber, making ready to deal a blow. He

felt as though he were in a dream being carried forward by supernatural swiftness and yet remaining at the same spot.

"What's the matter? I'm not moving? I've fallen, I'm killed. . . ." Rostov asked and answered himself all in one instant. He was alone in the middle of the field. . . . There was warm blood under him. (227)

His horse is fatally wounded and his arm is sprained.

"Hasn't something gone wrong with me? As such things happen, and what ought one to do in such cases?" he wondered as he was getting up. (Ibid.)

Some men came running up who are talking a foreign language. "Can they be the French?" Rostov wonders. Being so near them seems so awful to him he cannot believe his eyes.

"Who are they? What are they running for? Can it be to me? Can they be running to me? And what for? To kill me? *Me*, whom every one's so fond of?" He recalled his mother's love, the love of his family and his friends, and the enemy's intention of killing him seemed impossible. (228)

A Frenchman is running toward him with lowered bayonet. Rostov snatches up his pistol, and instead of firing with it, flings it at the Frenchman and runs to the bushes with all his might: "happy life took possession of his whole being":

he flew over the field, now and then turning his pale, good-natured, youthful face, and a chill of horror ran down his spine. (Ibid.)

The Frenchman fires at him, he ducks, and with a last effort runs into the bushes, where there are Russian sharpshooters.

This experience of fire, however, Rostov later turns into a splendid story, as when Boris asks him how and where he had been wounded.

He described to them his battle at Schöngraben exactly as men who have taken part in battles always do describe them, that is, as they would have liked them to be, as they have heard them described by others, and as sounds well, but not in the least as it really had been. (294)

He doesn't consciously lie, but puts a certain heroic gloss on it:

Rostov was a truthful young man: he would not have unintentionally told a lie. He began with the intention of telling everything precisely as it had happened, but imperceptibly, unconsciously, and inevitably he passed into falsehood. If he had told the truth to his listeners, who, like himself, had heard numerous descriptions of cavalry charges, and had formed a definite idea of what a charge was like and were expecting a similar description, either they would not have believed him, or worse still, would have assumed that Rostov was himself to blame for not having performed the exploits usually performed by those who describe cavalry charges. (295)

According to Tolstoy, such a soldier cannot tell the truth.

He could not tell them simply that they had all been charging full gallop, that he had fallen off his horse, sprained his arm, and run with all his might away from the French into the copse. And besides, to tell everything exactly as it happened, he would have had to exercise considerably self-control in order to tell nothing beyond what happened. To tell the truth is a very different thing; and young people are rarely capable of it. (Ibid.)

So, Rostov adds his own spice to his story, declaring that "you can't fancy what a strange frenzy takes possession of one at the moment of the charge." Andrey Bolkonsky, who comes in at that moment, finds it hard to endure such swaggering accounts, and treats Rostov with disdain—so much so that they quarrel: they almost challenge one another to a duel over it. Rostov is in a state of what Tolstoy calls "childish, uncontrollable embarrassment."

No doubt there is something of the same swaggering untruth in the letter Nikolay Rostov writes to his family, which is gone over and over by his mother and father, Natasha, Sonya, Petya, and others: to them he is a wounded hero.

> Nikolushka's letter was read over hundreds of times, and those who were considered worthy of hearing it had to come in to the countess, who did not let it go out of her hands. . . .

The countess, in reading it over, dotes on her son.

> How strange, extraordinary and joyful it was to her to think that her son—her little son, whose tiny limbs had faintly stirred within her twenty years ago, for whose sake she had often quarrelled with the count, who would spoil him, the little son, who had first learnt to say *grusha,* and then had learnt to say *baba*—that that son was now in a foreign land, in strange surroundings, a manly warrior, alone without help or guidance, doing there his proper manly work. . . . (287)

This is indeed, ironic, when the "manly work" consisted in falling off his horse, throwing his pistol at the enemy, and running away into the bushes where there were Russian troops. And in the course of this thinking of his mother's love, and the love of his family, and dwelling on these as a reason why the enemy should not kill him.

> Just as, twenty years before, she could not believe that the little creature that was lying somewhere under her heart, would one day cry and suck her breast and learn to talk, now she could not believe that the same little creature could be that strong, brave man, that paragon of sons and of men that, judging by this letter, he was now. (288)

This is at the heart of *War and Peace*—the distance between the woman-created new human being, the fantasy of prowess, and the horrible reality of the battlefield, in which tens of thousands of men are killed, who were once "little creatures" under their mother's hearts. With Petya Rostov, of course, the story is repeated: the myths of the loyal brave soldier are enhanced for him by his elder brother's prowess: he yearns to be in a military adventure and gets his saber sharpened specially—only to be shot dead at point-blank range in his first action.

* * *

A sensitive individual like Tolstoy, who suffers the terrible experience of losing his mother in infancy, remains deeply disturbed about the reality of the flesh. To be in the flesh is perpetually to suffer the vulnerability of the flesh: this is of course true of all of us, but to one whose very grasp on the reality of the world has suffered that primary unsettlement, it must be a perpetual torment. We can understand that torment if we read the biographical details of Tolstoy's life.

It must have been to encounter that torment, and to try to work through it, that Tolstoy chose to write about war. His most graphic war episodes present us with the reality of the flesh, as it is revealed by military action. One of the most painful episodes is the wounding of Prince Andrey for the second time, at the battle of Borodino: and this, of course, is followed by his long treatment and nursing, part of it by Natasha, which is virtually his slow death. The spiritual problem of whether there is any meaning to life, which is a concomitant of Tolstoy's perplexity that dates from his infant loss, is of course explored through Andrey's long sickness, and through his rediscovery of his love for Natasha. The coincidence of her appearance, through encountering his wagon train, may thus be seen as belonging to the arranged drama of the novel. Here there are two themes which emerge from Tolstoy's unconscious problems: here the dangerous woman is brought into the sphere of being a *nurse*, devoted to enabling the man to belong to life, rather than betraying him to death with a rival; and secondly, both he and she are involved in a love situation in which there can be no sex—and so the most menacing element between man and woman is removed.

The other coincidence is the presence of his rival, Anatole Kuragin, in the same hospital tent operating theater as Prince Andrey. In terms of the novel's realism this is extremely improbable. In terms of the theme of the insecurity of the flesh it is understandable. Prince Andrey remembered Natasha and how he understood her: later he is made to remember how much he loved her, after he has witnessed the terrible operation on Anatole. At the moment of the most terrible mutilation and violation of the human body by death, of fatal wounding, we find the presence of the idealized mother figure, the idealized woman image. The amputated leg of Anatole, held up for him to see, is his reward for his attempt to seduce this woman, by treating her as a part object, in contempt for her being. Prince Andrey's fatal wound is his reward for cruelly removing his love from her when she betrayed him: he is to find her love again, beyond the possibility of staying alive to be her fulfillment.

The presence of vulnerable flesh is terribly impressed upon us, throughout this episode. It begins by emphasizing the mass nature of the slaughter: "There was directed the concentrated fire of hundreds of the enemy's cannons." There come "flying hissing cannon-balls and slowly whizzing grenades":

> Several men out of the regiment would be swept off, and they were busy the whole time dragging away the dead and carrying off the wounded. (1020)

"With every fresh stroke the chances of life grew less and less for those who were not killed." In this dire situation, which is the reality of the machinations of Napoleon and Kutusov of which we have read in the previous chapters, the men fall into a strange mood, clinging, as it were, to cherishing being alive, by small gestures:

> One taking off his shako, carefully loosened and then drew up the folds of it; another, crumbling the dry clay in his hands, rubbed up his bayonet with it; another shifted and fastened the buckle of his shoulder straps; while another carefully undid, and did up again, his leg bandages, and changed his boots. Some built little houses of clods of the ploughed field, or plaited straws of stubble (Ibid.)

They "found a rest in the commonplace incidents of everyday life." One typical incident is recounted, when a dog runs on to the battlefield:

> The attention of all was attracted by a little brown dog, with its tail in the air, who had come no one knew from where, and was running about fussily in front of the ranks. All at once a cannon-ball fell near it, and it squealed and dashed away with its tail between its legs! Roars and shrieks of laughter rang out from the whole regiment. (1021)

The terror of death is never relaxed for an instant, and the men's pale and haggard faces grow paler and more haggard.

Prince Andrey walks about, all his energies "directed to restraining himself from contemplating the horror of his position." He, too, concentrates on futile acts which reassure him he is still alive:

> dragging one leg after another, making the grass rustle, and watching the dust, which covered his boots . . . or cut off the flowers of wormwood growing in the rut, and crushing them in his hands, sniffed at the bitter-sweet, pungent odour. (Ibid.)

The grenade which gives him his fatal wound seems almost insignificant when it arrives:

> like a bird, with swift whirring wings alighting on the earth, a grenade dropped with a dull thud a couple of paces from Prince Andrey. . . . The shell was smoking and rotating like a top between him and the recumbent adjutant. . . . (1022)

We experience a strange slowing or even stopping of the progress of time, in which Prince Andrey looking at the thread of smoke coiling from the rotating top, has time to ask himself, "Can this be death?" and to think "I can't die, I don't want to die, I love life, I love this grass and earth and air. . . ."

Then comes the explosion:

> there was a tearing, crashing sound, like the smash of broken crockery, a puff of stifling fumes, and Prince Andrey was sent spinning over, and flinging up one arm, fell on his face. . . . (1023)

Prince Andrey is still breathing in hard, hoarse gasps, and when they lay him on a stretcher one says, "What is it? . . . The stomach! It's all over then! Ah, my God."

They carry him to an ambulance station where there are three tents where for five acres around are wounded men sitting around waiting attention. Prince Andrey reflects, "There was something in this life that I didn't understand and don't understand. . . ."

There is a vivid picture of one of the doctors:

> with a blood-stained apron, and small, blood-stained hands, in one of which he had a cigar, carefully held between his thumb and little finger, that it might not be stained too. (1025)

Andrey is laid on a table that has just been rinsed over by an attendant.

> Everything he saw around melted for him into a single general impression of naked, blood-stained human flesh which seemed to fill up the whole low-pitched tent, as, a few weeks before, on that hot August day, the bare human flesh had filled up the dirty pond along the Smolensk road. Yes, it was the same flesh, the same *chair à canon*, the sight of which had aroused in him then a horror, that seemed prophetic of what he felt now. . . . (Ibid.)

Our imaginations, too, as we read, are filled like that tent, with suffering flesh, and these foreground perspectives illuminate the gruesome statistics, of the battles, the tens of thousands of men, slaughtered in these vast historical events.

Prince Andrey is the involuntary witness of a Tatar having a piece of shrapnel cut out of his back, while being held down by four soldiers:

> all of a sudden, throwing up his broad, swarthy, sun-burned face, and showing his white teeth, he began wriggling, twitching, and shrieking a piercingly shrill, prolonged scream. (1026)

This is the horrifying reality of war, a war, of course, without anaesthetics. (In the Normandy invasion each of us was given a little toothpaste-type tube fitted with a needle, to inject ourselves with morphia, if we were severely injured. The worst thing I ever saw in battle was the equipment of a field hospital laid out before a battle began.)

On the next table is Anatole Kuragin, having a leg amputated.

> Several assistants were holding him, and weighing on his chest. One white, plump leg was incessantly moving with a rapid, spasmodic twitching. This man was sobbing and choking convulsively. Two doctors—one was pale and trembling—were mutely engaged in doing something with the other red, gory leg. . . .
> "Show it to me . . . ooo! o! ooo!" he could hear his frightened, abjectly suffering moans, broken by sobs. Hearing his moans, Prince Andrey wanted to cry. Either because he was dying thus without glory, or because he was sorry to part with life, or from these memories of a childhood that could never return. . . . (1027)

Unconsciously, I believe, Tolstoy, in his imaginative exploration of this suffering, has arrived at his childhood and is experiencing his childhood fantasies. Remember that Andrey has gone into the fighting regiment in order to enact revenge on his rival Anatole, who, in that he has bemused Natasha, is his rival, and so stands, in terms of psychological myth, for the father who has taken possession of the mother, and who has threatened her with death: here he witnesses a terrible revenge, even as he too is dying from a fatal wound, acquired in the same battle. Prince Andrey asks the questions that perplex Tolstoy, even as he writes this scene:

> In the miserable, sobbing, abject creature whose leg had just been cut off, he recognised Anatole Kuragin. It was Anatole they were holding up in their arms and offering a glass of water, the edge of which he could not catch with his trembling, swollen lips. Anatole drew a sob-

bing, convulsive breath. "Yes, it is he; yes, that man is somehow closely and painfully bound up with me," thought Prince Andrey, with no clear understanding yet of what was before him. "What is the connection between that man and my childhood, my life?" he asked himself, unable to find the clue. (Ibid.)

Tolstoy does not recognize what he himself is doing, in bringing about this coincidence. It is an Oedipal phantasy, around his own Cimmerian fantasies about his mother's death, that he has turned into this drama of his alter ego being confronted with his rival, turned into a painful and realistic scene in his novel. This is the ultimate consequence of that risky behavior by which men seek parity with woman, by going to war. Anatole is presumably so traumatized that he dies of shock (incidentally, one of the realistic perceptions we draw from the scene is the effect such work must have had on the doctors and their attendants, who are pale and haggard, having to witness such suffering and to hear such cries.)

Andrey is brought to reminisce again about Natasha, whose idealization as I have said is a product of the original idealization by Tolstoy of his mother:

a new, unexpected memory from that childlike world of purity and love rose up before Prince Andrey. He remembered Natasha, as he had seen her for the first time at the ball in 1810, with her slender neck and slender arms, and her frightened, happy face, ready for ecstatic enjoyment, and a love and tenderness awoke in his heart for her stronger and more loving than ever. (Ibid.)

This prompts in him a "passionate pity and love for that suffering man" and "tears of love and tenderness over his fellow-men, over himself, and over their errors and his own."

"Sympathy, love for our brother, for those who love us, love for those who hate us, love for our enemies; yes, the love that God preached upon earth. . . . But now it is too late. I know that!" (Ibid.)

In the next chapter we return to Napoleon and to his egocentric musings: "he wrote to Paris that 'le champ de bataille a été superbe', because there were fifty thousand corpses on it." But in the flesh-overwhelmed picture Tolstoy has painted, and in the vivid detail of terrible suffering Tolstoy achieves the kind of effect achieved by few artists, of the horror of human war (Goya perhaps is a fair parallel), and in his portrayal of what human hate is capable of, he invokes something like the power of the Crucifixion of Christ as a symbol of the triumph of evil, to remind us of that spiritual awareness that is, by contrast, capable of good, as in Prince Andrey's final meditations. This leads him toward the ultimate reconciliation with Natasha, which is totally without sentimentality, and a realistic confrontation with the advance and triumph of death, and the finding of love, even as it is extinguished as earthly love is overwhelmed.

*   *   *

Some of the most striking passages in *War and Peace* are those which render the hopelessness that can overcome men, in the sphere of what I have called false male doing. In war, men can become elated—they shout "Vive l'Empereur!" and tell the czar that they are willing to die for him. Then they do die, in their tens of thousands, so that the field of battle looks as if it is covered with ridges of dung—the heaps of bodies. There are the wounded, shrieking or moaning, crawling away from the battles. But it is in the field medical stations that we experience the real hopelessness of war: as when Prince Andrey is carried to the field hospital.

The horror of hopelessness in war is brought home to us in another section in which Nikolay Rostov goes to seek Denisov at a hospital in a little Prussian town:

> As soon as Rostov went in at the door, he was conscious of the stench of hospital and putrefying flesh all around him. (497)

A cynical Russian army doctor warns him: "Couldn't you meet with a bullet that you want to pick up typhus? This is a pest-house, my good sir." Five doctors had already died of it. The doctor has four hundred patients.

Rostov goes to look in the soldiers' ward. The stench is stronger: the greater number of patients are unconscious:

> He had never expected to see anything like this. . . .

There is a wounded Cossack begging for water, and an old man with his leg amputated wants to ask him something.

> There lay with head thrown back the motionless figure of a young soldier with a waxen pallor on his snub-nosed and still freckled face, and eyes sunken under the lids. Rostov looked at the snub-nosed soldier and a shiver ran down his back.
> "Why, that one seems to be. . . ." he said to the assistant.

"We've begged and begged, your honour," said the old soldier with a quiver in his lower jaw. "He died early in the morning. We're men, too, not dogs. . . ." (500)

In the officers' ward Rostov meets Tuskin with one arm missing: there is the sound of several men laughing. "How can they live in this place, much less laugh?" thinks Rostov. When he gets to Rostov, he senses with grief that beneath his habitual swagger there is a "new, sinister, smothered feeling." His wound has not healed, even though it was somewhat superficial.

Denisov has been threatened with court-martial for seizing some rations for his men, which were destined for the infantry. He is quite obsessed with this problem and is persuaded to petition the emperor. But our concern is that he should survive the ghastly hospital where he is placed.

This hospital scene is only one of the most searing chapters in this novel which delineates with graphic realism the horrors of war.

* * *

The ordeals endured by Prince Andrey Bolkonsky and Pierre Bezuhov in *War and Peace* represent a kind of spiritual purgation. No doubt Tolstoy was drawing on his own experience, as during the Siege of Sevastopol, and embodying in these two alter ego figures his sense of how his own attitudes to human experience were modified by the experience of war, in a man who had a spiritual impulse, to ask "What for?" and to inquire into the meaning of life.

War is the most puzzling manifestation of human behavior, and Tolstoy examines it with a firm opinion that it is so bizarre as to escape explanation.

How and with what object were the battles of Shevardino and Borodino fought? Why was the battle of Borodino fought? There was not the slightest sense in it, either for the French or the Russians. The immediate result of it was, and was bound to be, for the Russians, that we were brought nearer to the destruction of Moscow (the very thing we dreaded above everything in the world); and for the French, that they were brought nearer to the destruction of their army (which they, too, dreaded above everything in the world). . . . In giving and accepting battle at Borodino, Kutuzov and Napoleon acted without design or rational plan. . . . (951–52)

Both Pierre and Andrey wander about the battlefields in which they are involved in a state of bewilderment and confusion. Of course Andrey is a military officer, and takes part in operations, as when he seizes the flag and stops a rout at Austerlitz. Pierre is on his battlefield merely as a curious observer, and is arrested as an incendiary in the occupation of Moscow. In a sense the use of both men is a literary ploy, so that the author can employ both wandering consciousnesses to perceive the events from a roaming perspective, not confined to any one corner of the field or any practical perspective. On the other hand we may take their sensitive awareness as a focus of what hundreds of thousands of men are enduring on each occasion, thus underpinning Tolstoy's overall purpose, which is to unravel the rational rearrangements of the development and conduct of war by historians and other commentators, who had tidied it up, to suit their theories of history and individual will, to make war seem sensible and an acceptable part of human development. Tolstoy is able to bear the horror and disorder of war and to show its destructive and miserable effect, on the ordinary human beings who become caught up in it.

War is depicted as a male activity, an inclination that is "irrational, masculine and perverse"—as embodied eminently in the tragic story of young Petya Rostov. Andrey and Pierre link it with the feminine world, of love and feeling, because they are both in love with Natasha, whose fate runs through the book from child to mature motherly woman: Natasha, who is all life and promise, has her life devastated by the war, through nursing until death the suitor whom she has betrayed, and by comforting her mother and family, over their loss of Petya. She is the focus of all the force of the suffering war imposes on the domestic realm of peaceful civilian living.

Andrey's experience of war is more straightforward: the things that happen to him happen in the course of duty, and in the face of death. Pierre's experiences are stranger, because his presence in danger is quite voluntary and he has no function to justify his participation.

The soldiers shook their heads disapprovingly as they looked at Pierre. But as the conviction gained ground among them that the man in the white hat was doing no harm, and either sat quietly on the slope of the earthwork, or, making way with a shy and courteous smile for the soldiers to pass, walked about the battery under fire as calmly as though he were strolling on a boulevard, their feelings of suspicious ill-will began to give way to a playful and kindly cordiality akin to the feelings soldiers always have for the dogs, cocks, goats, and other animals who share the fortunes of the regiment. The soldiers soon accepted Pierre in their own minds as one of their little circle, made him one of themselves, and gave him a name: "our gentleman" they called him, and laughed good-humouredly about him among themselves.

A cannon-ball tore up the earth a couple of paces from Pierre. Brushing the earth off his clothes, he looked about him with a smile.

"And how is it you're not afraid, sir, upon my word?" said a broad, red-faced soldier, showing his strong white teeth in a grin.

"Why, are you afraid, then?" asked Pierre.

"Why, to be sure!" answered the soldier. "Why, she has no mercy on you. She smashed onto you, and your guts are sent flying. Nobody could help being afraid," he said laughing. (1001)

Pierre's experiences at this soldier's battery are truly horrifying: this soldier and his boy-faced officer are killed:

he found no one left of that little fraternal group that had accepted him as one of themselves. There were many dead there, whom he had not seen before. But several he recognised. The boy-officer was still sitting huddled up in a pool of blood at the edge of the earth wall. The red-faced, merry soldier was still twitching convulsively; but they did not carry him away.

Pierre ran down the slope. "Oh, now they will stop it, now they will be horrified at what they have done!" thought Pierre. (1007)

More horrible than the smashing force of the cannonballs, the sharpshooting, and the bayoneting, however, are the manifestations of the breakdown of order when Moscow is occupied by the French.

The accounts of incidents in this part of the novel are humiliating in their savagery: one does not want to admit to oneself that human beings are capable of such cruelty and injustice—although in our century such atrocities have become more prevalent, more cruel, and more terrible. There is, for example, the fury of Count Rastoptokin, who is mortified by not being called to the council of war, and of whom Kutuzov has taken no notice of his offer to take part in the defense of Moscow. He is horrified at the possibilities of popular disturbance and terrorism. He becomes angry and excited, feeling "This is what they have done with Russia! This is what they have done with me!" feeling "a rush of irrepressible rage against the undefined some one to whose fault what was happening could be set down."

He is brought as prisoner a young man, Vereshtchagin, whom he accuses of deserting to Bonaparte: "he alone of all the Russians has disgraced the name of Russia, and through him Moscow is lost." He hands the victim over to the crowd, telling them to deal with him as they think fit. To the reader's horror, it is the cry of pain of this youth as he is struck on the head with the flat of a soldier's sword that turns the crowd into a murderous mob.

> Only when the victim ceased to struggle, and his shrieks had passed into a long-drawn, rhythmic death-rattle, the mob began hurriedly to change places about the bleeding corpse on the ground. Every one went up to it, gazed at what had been done, and pressed back horror-stricken, surprised and reproachful. (1124)

Rastoptchin turns white, but quickly assures himself that this death was necessary for *le bien publique*. But the image of the lynched man, he knows, will be forever deeply imprinted on his heart.

Pierre dresses as a peasant, arms himself with a knife, and sets out to assassinate Napoleon. However, he becomes involved in rescuing a child from a fire and is arrested as an incendiary: he is condemned to death. The executions are conducted in a kitchen garden.

> Several drums suddenly began beating on both sides of them, and Pierre felt as though a part of his soul was being torn away from him by that sound. He lost all power of thought and reflection. He could only see and hear. . . . (1213)

The French soldiers were discomforted by their task:

> it was evident that every one was in haste and not making haste, as people do when they are getting through some job every one can understand, but as men hasten to get something done that is inevitable, but is disagreeable and incomprehensible. (1214)

The French soldiers have "trembling hands and pale faces": the victims are "plainly unable to understand or believe in what was coming":

> They could not believe in it, because they only knew what their life was to them, and so could not understand, and could not believe, that it could be taken from them. (Ibid.)

When Pierre's turn comes (he is sixth on the list) one man steps forward: but Pierre cannot understand that he was saved. He watches the fifth victim intently. The man darts away in terror and clutches at Pierre. He cannot walk and is dragged to the stake screaming. The man is shot, though Pierre does not hear the volley:

> He only saw the factory lad suddenly fall back from the cords, saw blood oozing in two places, and saw the cords themselves work loose from the weight of the hanging body, and the factory lad sit down, his head falling unnaturally, and one leg bent under him. Pierre ran up to the post. No one hindered him. Men with pale and frightened faces were doing something round the factory lad. There was one old whiskered Frenchman, whose lower jaw twitched all the while as he untied the cords. The body sank down. The soldiers, with clumsy haste, dragged it from the post and shoved it into the pit.
>
> All of them clearly knew, beyond all doubt, that they were criminals, who must make haste to hide the traces of their crime.
>
> Pierre glanced into the pit and saw that the factory lad was lying there with his knees up close to his head, and one shoulder higher than the other. And that shoulder was convulsively, rhythmically rising and falling. But spadefuls of earth were already falling all over the body. (1216)

It is the cold-bloodedness of the deed that conveys its impact, in such close mordant description, of the bodily gestures of the victim, and of the fearful response of the soldiers to their own deed, that makes it such an appalling passage. For the most horrible aspect of the incident is that even the perpetrators reveal their humanness, even though they are serving the machine of war and repression. One of the firing party is badly affected:

> A young soldier, with a face of deathly pallor, still stood facing the pit on the spot upon which he had shot, his shako falling backwards off his head, and his fuse dropping on to the ground. He staggered like a drunken man, taking a few steps forward, and then a few back, to keep himself from falling. An old under-officer ran out of the ranks, and, seizing the young soldier by the shoulder, dragged him to his company. (1216–17)

To Pierre, to witness the fearful murder committed by men who did not want to do it,

> it seemed as though the spring in his soul, by which everything was held together and given the semblance of life, had been wrenched out, and all seemed to have collapsed into a heap of meaningless refuse. Though he had no clear apprehension of it, it had annihilated in his soul all faith in the beneficent ordering of the universe, and in the soul of men, and in his own soul and in God . . . the world was

collapsing before his eyes, and. . . . Nothing was left but meaningless
ruin. . . . (1217–18)

Immediately after this Pierre meets a soldier who is to prove important to him: Platon Karataev.

"And have you seen a lot of trouble, sir? Eh?" . . . There was a tone
of such friendliness and simplicity in the sing-song voice that Pierre
wanted to answer, but his jaw quivered and he felt the tears rising.
(1219)

Platon speaks in "that tender carressing singsong in which old
Russian peasant-women talk":

"Ay, darling, don't grieve . . . trouble lasts an hour, but life lasts for
ever. . . ." (Ibid.)

Pierre has met the feminine element in the folk tradition—the
element developed from the experience of great suffering.

"Our happiness, my dear, is like water in a drag-net; you drag, and it
is all puffed up, but pull it out and there's nothing. . . ."

Every evening Platon prays "Let me lie down, Lord, like a stone;
let me rise up like new bread." His peasant faith, his simple figu-
rative way of speaking, his dog, his kindliness make Pierre feel

that the world that had been shattered was rising up now in his soul, in
new beauty, and on new foundations that could not be shaken. (1222)

He becomes for Pierre "an unfathomable, rounded-off, and ever-
lasting personification of the spirit of simplicity and truth—so he
remained to him for ever."
   The structure of the novel is so cunningly worked that at this
point we turn to the last stages of Natasha's experience of nursing
Prince Andrey, to his death. And then we return to Pierre, four
weeks after he had been taken prisoner.

For long years of his life he had been seeking in various directions
for that peace, that harmony with himself, which had struck him so
much in the soldiers at Borodino. He had sought for it in philan-
thropy, in freemasonry, in the dissipations of society, in wine, in heroic
feats of self-sacrifice, in his romantic love for Natasha; he had sought
it by the path of thought; and all his researches and all his efforts
had failed him. And now without any thought of his own, he had

gained that peace and that harmony with himself simply through the horror of death, through hardships, through what he had seen in Karataev. (1274)

He feels a new feeling of joy and vigor in life such as he had never experienced before.

But before he is rescued, Pierre becomes aware that Karataev is sick, and is shot by the French escorts.

> There was the sound of a shot behind, at the spot where Karataev was sitting. Pierre heard that shot distinctly. . . . Two French soldiers ran by Pierre, one holding a still smoking gun. They were both pale, and in the expression of their faces—one of them glanced timidly at Pierre—there was something like what he had seen in the young soldier at the execution in Moscow. . . . (1341)

Pierre, who seems to be in a somewhat hallucinating state, through exhaustion and hunger, dreams in his deep sleep: an old man is showing Pierre a globe:

> This globe was a living, quivering ball, with no definite limits. Its whole surface consisted of drops, closely cohering together. And those drops were all in motion, and changing, several passing into one, and then one splitting up again into many. Every drop seemed to spread, to take up more space, but the others, pressing upon it, sometimes absorbed it, sometimes melted into it.
> "This is life. . . ."
> "God is in the midst, and each drop strives to expand, to reflect Him on the largest scale possible. And it grows, and is absorbed and crowded out, and on the surface it disappears, goes back to the depths, and falls not to the surface again. That is how it is with him, with Karataev: he is absorbed and has disappeared." (1342)

Platon Karataev thus seems to have a deep spiritual importance for Pierre, and for Tolstoy—perhaps parallel to the influence the peasants have for Levin when he works in the fields with them. He remembers a summer evening in Kiev:

> the picture of the summer night in the country mingled with the thought of bathing and of that fluid, quivering globe, and he seemed to sink deep down into water, so that the waters closed over his head. (1343)

So, Pierre ends his long passage of suffering with a kind of fantasy of rebirth, not least under the influence of Platon, who has died with his eyes bright with tears, and under the influence of the "ecstatic gladness that beamed in Karataev's face" as he told a mysterious story of sin and repentance, so that "the mysterious significance of that gladness vaguely filled and rejoiced Pierre's soul. . . ." Here Gustafson is correct in saying that "Karataev is the emblem of love, of universal love that flows from the soul untouched by passion and suffering" (Gustafson, 79)

But on the next page Dolohov is walking behind the Cossacks who are bearing to a hole freshly dug in the garden the body of Petya Rostov.

*   *   *

One question explored in *War and Peace* is the degree to which the individual is supported by the group to which he belongs—his regiment, the army, the czardom, the nation. There is obviously at times a conflict between what the group requires soldiers to do, and the individual conscience. But more importantly, there is the wider question of morale, a concept with which W. R. D. Fairbairn, the psychoanalyst who has made a special study of war neuroses, is especially concerned. (See Fairbairn, *Psychoanalytical Studies of the Personality* [1952].)

When individuals with a strong motive for military operations are functioning alone, with considerable experience, and are hardened by service, they work according to an equilibrium and determination that sustains them, as Denisov does in his guerrilla operations toward the end of the novel. Prince Andrey's response to battle is more complex: he moves between heroism, as when he seizes the flag when soldiers are fleeing, and giving up army service altogether—through in the end, disappointed by Natasha, he returns it, partly from a self-destructive impulse. But he can be said to be sustained by noble ideals at the highest level. Pierre, however, has no regiment to sustain him, and no military function. He endures all the horrors but has no function or even purpose, except curiosity and the pursuit of risk. He is often perplexed, by the way those soldiers who are sustained by morale exposed themselves to injury or death, by the way this morale can collapse so that the soldiers become an anarchic, fleeing mob, and by the way the French army operates by regulations that oblige men to perform acts that frighten them and which they loathe.

Pierre is thus a vehicle for examining human exposure to the horrors of war without the dependence on a group that sustains morale. This is perhaps why his progress and his experience is so terrifying, and so soul-purging. Pierre is reduced to a solitary survivor, and in delineating his ordeals Tolstoy is exploring his own exposure to the loss of all confidence in being dependent, and searching for the capacity to survive in a situation in which no support whatever is given to the individual faced with the most terrible onslaughts and exposure to human cruelty—to the rejection of all compassion, concern, and care.

In considering Tolstoy's account of war it is worth taking into account Fairbairn's findings further. This Scottish psychoanalyst at one stage became consultant neuropsychiatrist to the Ministry of Pensions, and thus was deeply concerned with war neuroses and with the psychology of the soldier. Fairbairn, of course, was very much a solitary and independent figure in his profession, and developed his own dynamic model of the psyche, which is discussed in detail in his two books by Harry Guntrip, who was himself much influenced by Fairbairn, with whom he underwent analysis.*

Fairbairn seems to believe that it is unlikely that a war experience actually causes a neurotic problem: the problem is there and is triggered off by a traumatic experience. All psychopathological developments in the adult, he declares, are ultimately based upon a persistence into later life of an exaggerated degree of that emotional dependence which is characteristic of childhood, and more particularly of infancy.

Fairbairn says "Separation-anxiety is so universal a feature of the war neuroses that it is difficult to believe that its prevalence can have escaped observation hitherto." The capacity to endure danger, he believes, varies with the extent to which the individual has outgrown the stage of infantile dependence. In military circles he points out that soldiers have been classified into three groups: (1) those who like it, (2) those who don't like it but stick to it, and (3) those who don't like it and don't stick to it. Those who don't like it and don't stick to it represent the neurotic individual who has, relatively speaking, failed to take the momentous step of outgrowing the stage of infantile dependence. Those who "like it" include a considerable proportion of psychopaths who have

> developed a denial of infantile dependence into such a fine art that callousness and indifference to ordinary human relationships have become embodied in the very structure of their personalities. (Fairbairn 1952; 267)

---

*Guntrip, *Personality Structure and Human Interaction* and Guntrip, *Schizoid Phenomena, Object-relations and the Self.* Fairbairn's book is *Psychoanalytical Studies of the Personality.*

Many of the least bearable scenes in *War and Peace* show individuals acting with "callousness and indifference to ordinary human relationships."

Separation-anxiety is a characteristic product of the tendency of individuals who have remained in a state of infantile dependence to make identification the basis of their emotional relationships with those upon whom they depend. It would seem clear from the biographies (and especially from the biography of Tolstoy's wife Sonya) that he himself suffered from this capacity to identify with those upon whom he depended: the way Tolstoy and his wife both kept diaries alone indicates that. And we may also see in his confusion over how he should treat Sonya, in pregnancy and as a nursing mother, a link with the intense anxiety he suffered, as an infant, over his mother's pregnancy and loss in childbirth. Of course, this capacity for identifying is the very basis of his art, too—especially his capacity to identify with women. Says Fairbairn,

> The figure with whom the dependent individual is originally identified is, of course, his mother, and, whilst it is not long before he begins to identify himself with other figures, particularly his father, the original identification persists underneath all others subsequently made. (Ibid., 276)

Fairbairn here makes an important point by referring to the fact that wounded soldiers often, in their agony, cry out for their mothers—a fact that I can verify from experience. Fairbairn goes on,

> In the case of the individual who fails to outgrow the stage of infantile dependence . . . the relationships which he is best able to sustain are such as conform most to the pattern of his early relationship with his mother; and the only relationships which he is able to sustain are such as conform most to the pattern of his early relationship with his mother; and the only relationships which he is able to establish with any measure of stability are relationships calculated to assume for him, by a process of transference, all or much of the significance of the original relationship. . . . (His home and loved ones) still tend to constitute for him, as was the case in his childhood, not only his emotional world, but even, in a sense, himself. He tends to feel that he is part of them, and equally that they are part of him. . . . (Ibid., 277)

This paragraph explains in some measure the creation of *War and Peace*, the novel. The presentation of Natasha conforms to the significance of Tolstoy's relationship with his mother, while Prince Andrey and Pierre are both himself in relationship with the mother-woman. With all of his characters, Tolstoy tends to feel that "he is part of them, and equally that they are part of him." The same is true even of Napoleon, Czar Alexander, and Kutuzov: these are drawn into the author's emotional world and so into himself. In order to find and place his being Tolstoy had to throw himself into this delineation of his emotional life, as a panorama of world history.

This explains his fascination with chaos and especially with the breakdown of morale. Fairbairn here refers to Freud's *Group Psychology and the Analysis of the Ego* (1921). Freud saw that the state of panic notoriously associated with the collapse of an army in the field is essentially a breakdown of the emotional bonds which unite members of the military group to one another under common leaders. According to the ordinary view, it is when the situation of "every man for himself" arises that the group spirit (esprit de corps) disintegrates. According to Freud, on the contrary, it is when the group spirit becomes weakened that the situation of "every man for himself" arises, and that panic invades the individual heart, as it does in *War and Peace* (229ff):

> The essential feature of the situation is that each *quondam* member of the military group becomes deprived of the support both of his former fellow-soldiers and of the military group as a whole, and is relegated to the status of an isolated individual facing the combined strength of a hostile force without any support. (Fairbairn, 280)

We also see in *War and Peace* the consequences of the neurotic element in the soldier which reduces him to the emotional state of the child who has not yet reached the stage of accepting his parents as authoritative conscience-figures:

> At this stage the child is not so much concerned whether his own behaviour is good or bad (morally) in the eyes of his parents or whether his parents appear to love him or not, i.e., whether, from his point of view, they present themselves as good (in the sense of "nice") or bad (in the sense of "nasty") figures. What happens, therefore, when a soldier develops a war neurosis is that, regressing to an infantile emotional level, he ceases to regard his superiors in rank and military organisation in general as representing authoritative parental figures to whom he is bound by a deep sense of moral obligation, and begins to regard them as "bad" parental figures who have no love or consideration for him. (Ibid., 286)

He thus may be consumed by an overwhelming desire to escape from the insecurity which he experiences at the hands of the "bad" figures, into whose clutches he feels that military obligations have delivered him, to the security which the "good" figures at home seem, by contrast, to offer him. Many of the characters engaged in operations in *War and Peace* hover around this ambiguity. And this also explains the intensely explored connections in the novel between "home" and "battlefield." Fairbairn also indicates the common feeling of traumatized soldiers: that they "can't stand being stared at," and that they "can't eat Army food": every word of command has become the shout of an angry father, and every army meal the indifference of a heartless mother. Tolstoy's preoccupation with the horrors and deprivations of war may thus seem to be linked with his separation-anxiety feelings about his parents.

Finally, the neurotic soldier feels himself, says Fairbairn, to be in the power of evil figures: they have a sense of being watched, and experience nightmares of being chased, or shouted at, crushed, strangled, or visited by ghosts. Fairbairn refers to a remark he made himself, confronting the predicament of war-neurotic servicemen: "What these people really need is not a psychotherapist, but an evangelist." And in the spiritual quests and yearnings in Tolstoy's novel they have it: it was in that spirit that he chose to confront the Napoleonic war in Russia. Tolstoy needed to confront this greatest of disasters in order to confront the problem of what men live by, and it is this question to which he tried to find an answer, in desperate need.

* * *

How true to reality are Tolstoy's portraits of Napoleon, Kutuzov, and other historical figures it is impossible for me to say, as I am no historian. It is sufficient to say that they are adequate for the purposes of the novel.

Perhaps the most striking portrait of Napoleon is that of him being flesh-brushed by his valet:

With snorts and grunts of satisfaction, he was turning first his stout back and then his plump, hirsute chest towards the flesh-brush with which a valet was rubbing him down. Another valet, holding a bottle with one finger on it, was sprinkling eau de cologne on the Emperor's pampered person with an expression which seemed to say that he alone knew where and how much eau de cologne must be sprinkled. Napoleon's short hair was wet and matted on his brow. But his face, though puffy and yellow, expressed physical satisfaction. (*War and Peace*, 981)

This is just before the battle of Borodino, in which, according to Tolstoy, Napoleon performed "the cruel, gloomy, irksome, and inhuman part destined for him."

Not on that day only he wrote to Paris that "*le champ de bataille a été superbe*", because there were fifty thousand corpses on it. (1029)

It is more difficult to accept Tolstoy's version of Kutuzov as a great military leader, because of his persistent inaction. Yet Prince Andrey, again just before the Battle of Borodino, feels complete approval for Kutuzov:

he went back to his regiment feeling reassured as to the future course of the war, and as to the man to whom its guidance was intrusted. The more clearly he perceived the absence of everything personal in the old leader, who seemed to have nothing left of his own but habits of passions, and instead of an intellect grasping events and making plans, had only the capacity for the calm contemplation of the course of events, the more confident he felt that all would be as it should be. "He will put in nothing of himself. He will contrive nothing, will undertake nothing," thought Prince Andrey; "but he will hear everything, will think of everything, will put everything in its place, will not hinder anything that could be of use, and will not allow anything that could do harm. He knows that there is something stronger and more important than his will—that is the inevitable march of events, and he can see them, can grasp their significance, and, seeing their significance, can abstain from meddling, from following his own will, and aiming at something else." (940–41)

This is, decides Prince Andrey, because he is Russian: and this feeling, says Tolstoy, was shared by all, and this determined the unanimous approval given to the appointment of Kutusov, in opposition to the intrigues at court. It is difficult to believe, though perhaps acceptable from a Russian point of view as inaction and passivity are heroic qualities in Russian culture.

Prince Andrey is the focus of the most sensitive portrayal in Tolstoy's novel of a man's consciousness in the experience of war, in the context of his life. Pierre's is a parallel spiritual progress, but his experience is wider and more concerned with human anarchy and man's cruelty. At one point for Prince Andrey life seems to be "a series of senseless phenomena following one another without any connection" (793). Before Borodino he is made to reflect on his betrothal to Natasha.

> "Love! . . . That little girl, who seemed to me brimming over with mysterious forces. How I loved her! I made romantic plans of love, of happiness with her! O simple-hearted youth!" he said aloud bitterly. "Why, I believed in some ideal love which was to keep her faithful to me for the whole year of her absence! Like the faithful dove in the fable, she was to pine away in my absence from me! And it was all so much simpler. . . . It is all so horrible and loathsome!" (971)

He is expecting to die in tomorrow's battle, and reflects in this disillusioned way on his betrayed affection. He tries to contemplate the way the world will go on in his absence, and then suddenly encounters Pierre, who tells him he is on the battlefield because it is "interesting."

Together they discuss the nature of war, and then part: Andrey urges Pierre to get to sleep: "before a battle one needs to get a good sleep." As Andrey tries to sleep, again he remembers Natasha, joyfully recalling her eager excited face as she told him about looking for mushrooms and getting lost in a great forest:

> every minute she broke off in her story, saying, "No, I can't. I'm not describing it properly; no, you won't understand me. . . ." Natasha was dissatisfied with her own words; she felt that they did not convey the passionately poetical feeling she had known that day. . . . (980)

Prince Andrey realizes how much he had been in sympathy with her (as Anatole Kuragin had not):

> "I understood her," thought Prince Andrey, "and more than understood her: that spiritual force, that sincerity, that openness of soul, the very soul of her, which seemed bound up with her body, the very soul it was I loved in her . . . loved so intensely, so passionately. . . ." And all at once he thought how his love had ended. "*He* cared nothing for all that. *He* say nothing of it, had no notion of it. He saw in her a pretty and *fresh* young girl with whom he did not deign to unite his life permanently. And I? . . . And he is still alive and happy." Prince Andrey jumped up as though suddenly scalded, and began to walk to and fro before the barn again. . . . (Ibid.)

It is extraordinary how Natasha's being is a lodestone that unites the experiences of these predominant male characters in the novel—Pierre, Andrey and to a lesser extent Anatole Kuragin. We may, I think, surmise that this may be taken as an index to Tolstoy's whole undertaking in this immense and extraordinary novel. That is, he is trying to bring together the exposure of men to the most terrifying and destructive dynamics of hate in the universe, so that they are pressed to question the nature, purpose, and meaning of their existence, and their extremes of adoration and being adored, in love, with women. At the end, married to Pierre, Natasha becomes much less of an inspiration: but throughout the battles, she remains an image in their consciousness by which they measure their life-situations, at the level of being. This is the connection that informs the novel, between war and peace.

* * *

Pierre Bezuhov idolizes Natasha. At one point she forms the focus of the solution to all his spiritual problems:

> he thought of her as he had seen her last, and all his doubts vanished; not because she had answered the questions that haunted him, but because her image lifted him instantly into another bright realm of spiritual activity, in which there could be neither right nor wrong, into a region of beauty and love, which was worth living for. (835)

The problem for Tolstoy, as we have seen, was to bring together the idealization, developed out of his infant experience of having to re-create the dead mother, with the real woman, the real object. It is perhaps significant that for most of this novel, Natasha, the intense love-object both of Andrey and Pierre, and in a way even of the philandering Anatole, is yearned for from a distance, and is as remote as the 1812 comet.

When he finds Natasha again, after her long misery following the death of Andrey, Pierre is seized by a "joyful, unexpected frenzy":

> The whole meaning of life, not for him only, but for all the world, seemed to him centred in his love and the possibility of her loving him. Sometimes all men seemed to him to be absorbed in nothing else than his future happiness. It seemed to him sometimes that they were all rejoicing as he was himself, and were only trying to conceal that joy, by pretending to be occupied with other interests. In every word and gesture he saw an allusion to his happiness. . . . (1419)

Such rapture is understandable, after so much suffering, and after so long a separation from the woman he has loved since she was a child. But at the same time it indicates an exaggerated extension of the pathetic fallacy, that "all men" were preoccupied with Pierre's happiness.

On Natasha's part, Pierre seems to have gone through a spiritual purgation that has made a new man of him:

> "He has become so clean and smooth and fresh: as though he had just come out of a bath; do you understand? Out of a moral bath. Isn't it so?" (1412)

Perhaps we may take this to refer to the author's own experience, of creating Pierre as an alter ego, and undergoing all the experiences with him—in the quest to be in touch with reality, and to press the existential problem to its ultimate limits. And one of the problems was to find in the woman-object a focus for the meaning of life.

Natasha's suffering parallels that of Pierre, through the huge misery of the French occupation of Moscow and the ensuing chaos. Natasha watches Andrey die and experiences, after a period of profound penitence ("I know that now I am good, and before I was wicked! But now I am good . . . but yet the best years, the best of my life, are all being wasted, and no good to anyone; . . ." [831]) a deep rediscovery of her love for him—a love that transcends because it is beyond any sexual fulfillment, and develops in the face of imminent death: it thus has a powerful existential dimension. Pierre, on his part, goes through the refining fire of exposure to death—he is nearly executed, witnesses the most terrible scenes of conflict, cruel punishment, and execution, and finds a kind of love that transcends by his acquaintance with the resigned and suffering humanity of Platon Karataev:

> Only now Pierre grasped all the force of vitality in man. . . . The harder his lot became, the more terrible his future, the more independent of his present plight were the glad and soothing thoughts, memories and images that occurred to him. (1336)

The scene in which Pierre meets Natasha again is deeply moving, because she has become virtually unrecognizable because of her suffering, while he has little hope of finding joy and love again. But what binds them is Natasha's capacity to hear and understand him:

> He experienced now in telling it all to Natasha that rare happiness given to men by women when they listen to them—not by *clever* women, who, as they listen, are either trying to remember what they

are told to enrich their intellect and on occasion to repeat it, or to adapt what is told them to their own ideas and to bring out in haste the clever comments elaborated in their little mental factory. . . . (1411)

For a moment Tolstoy reveals his prejudices and his Schopenhauerian proclivity for despising women—by contrast with this exception mother-woman whom he has created in Natasha. He goes on:

This rare happiness is given only by those real women, gifted with a faculty for picking out and assimilating all that is best in what a man shows them. Natasha, though herself unconscious of it, was all rapt attention; she did not lose one word, one quaver of the voice, one glance, one twitching in the facial muscles, one gesture of Pierre's. She caught the word before it was uttered and bore it straight to her open heart, *divining the secret import of all Pierre's spiritual travail.* (Ibid.; my italics)

What Pierre demands—what Tolstoy demands—in a woman are those maternal capacities to attend, hear, and understand what her son is giving her—because, as an infant, he lost that "creative reflection" and needs it desperately, in his quest for meaning in life. So his best women, his heroines, must have that life-giving gravity such as the mother has, and which he idealized.

But what happens when Natasha becomes his wife, and, in sexual union, the ideal has to be merged with the libidinal?

I believe that in these final pages we move from a realization of a real woman into the realm of Tolstoyean propaganda: propaganda for how he liked a woman to be, or shall we say how alone he was able to tolerate a woman, once she became a sexual partner.

Natasha, he tells us, was married in the early spring of 1813, and by 1820 has three daughters and a son.

She had grown stouter and broader, so that it was hard to recognise in the robust-looking young mother the slim, mobile Natasha of old days. (1456)

She is stripped of all those aspects that have made her so inspiring:

Her face had no longer that ever-glowing fire of eagerness that had once constituted her chief charm. Now, often her face and body were all that was to be seen, and the soul was not visible at all . . . only on rare occasions now the old fire glowed in her again. (Ibid.)

She is allowed to have "rare moments," when "the old fire glowed again" and then she becomes "more attractive, with her handsome, fully-developed figure, than she had ever been in the past."

But the portrait of Natasha as a wife suffers from Tolstoy's preoccupation, to put a woman under strict control, once she is a sexual partner, of "duty" and "the family." It is surely a sad disappointment to the reader that this exceptional woman, who has been such an inspiration to so many people, and to the two central male characters of the novel, such an embodiment of life and spirit, should be acclaimed for giving up all her achievements of a cultural kind, neglecting herself and tyrannizing over her husband?

This is not to deride Tolstoy's recognition of the fulfillment and satisfaction a couple may achieve, through creating a family, and fostering their children. But Tolstoy adds such a devastating re-duction of Natasha to a plain, dutiful wife that one suspects that he is here introducing into the novel propaganda for his own psychopathological patterns, that he indulged to such a tyrannical and brutal effect on the devoted Sonya. Of course, such an accep-tance of the woman's role was predominant in Russia at the time, though Tolstoy shows himself aware of the change in her image.

For he blames "society" for noticing the changes in Natasha and concerning them:

> those who had seen her there (i.e., "in society") were not greatly pleased with her. . . . She was neither charming nor amiable. . . . (1457)

Apparently she "could not meet all these demands on her except by renouncing society."

> Everyone who had known Natasha before her marriage marvelled at the change that had taken place in her, as though it were something extraordinary. (Ibid.)

Her mother declares that Natasha always wanted a husband and children, and that this was always at the root of her wild outbursts of feeling—but even she feels that Natasha carries her devotion to a foolish extent.

One would not, of course, expect a wife to continue to pursue the more frivolous preoccupations of an unattached girl. But Na-tasha gives up more than that, and seems to want to become positively uncultivated:

Natasha did not follow the golden rule preached by so many prudent persons, especially by the French, that recommends that a girl on marrying should not neglect herself, should not give up her accomplishments, should think even more of her appearance than when a young girl, and should try to fascinate her husband as she had fascinated him before he was her husband. Natasha, on the contrary, had at once abandoned all her accomplishments, of which the greatest was her singing. . . . (Ibid.)

Yet earlier this singing, when she returned to it, had been the mark of life and hope returning to her, and belonged to that natural capacity she exhibits, in the hunting lodge, when she begins to dance, to belong to Russian culture and consciousness.

She gave that up just because it was such a great attraction. . . .

Why? Why should Natasha want to detract from her own self-esteem, as by no longer being charming and attractive? For instance, Denisov, when he arrives, looks on Natasha "with melancholy wonder, as at a bad likeness of a person once loved": "A bored, dejected glance, random replies, and incessant talk of the nursery was all he saw and heard of his enchantress of old days" (1462). One has to say "Because Tolstoy liked it that way"—and then add, because he was afraid of women and so needed to suppress women's creativity.

Natasha troubled herself little about manners or delicacy of speech; nor did she think of showing herself to her husband in the most becoming attitudes and costumes, nor strive to avoid worrying him by being over-exacting. . . . (1457)

How extraordinary, for this writer, who throughout his enormous novel, has written so ecstatically about Natasha's beauty, grace, and charm, to tell us that she gives it up and becomes a dreary, broad mother-figure, of Russian proportions, simply because she is married!* And because her husband is assumed to be, like Tolstoy, afraid of the fully sexual woman.

Natasha does not need "romantic feelings" any longer: her feeling of being bound to her husband

rested on something else undefined, but as strong as the tie that bound her soul to her body.

---

*Denisov, for example, sees Natasha at this stage "with wonder": she seems to be "a bad likeness of a person once loved" (1462).

There follow paragraphs of theoretical rationalization, about "the faculty of entire absorption in one subject," which make one feel that Tolstoy is not now working from "life" but from propaganda.

> The subject in which Natasha was completely absorbed was her family, that is, her husband, whom she kept such a hold on that he should belong entirely to her, to his home and her children, whom she had to carry, to bear, to nurse and bring up. . . . (1458)

Well, yes, that is indeed a prodigious task. But why does Natasha have to exercise such a "hold" on Pierre, since he has in a sense "belonged" to her all his life? And the Rostov family has shown itself throughout the book as a close-knit family, with a powerful sense of honor and values, and intensely mutually supportive—so it ought to come naturally to Natasha, who has been adored by Petya and Nikolay: and, indeed, a family which has recognized its duties to the rest of the community and to its cultural links with "society." Why should Natasha, in order to bring up three children, have "no time" to think of "the careful choice of words" and cease to "adorn herself"? What might be the effect on the children themselves, to see their mother neglect herself, her art, her speech, her charm—for some theoretical concept of "the family"?

From Tolstoy's satisfaction with his own biased propaganda we proceed to an attack on "women's rights":

> There were in those days, just as now, arguments and discussions on the rights of women, on the relation of husband and wife, and on freedom and rights in marriage, though they were not, as now, called *questions*. But those questions had no interest for Natasha, in fact she had no comprehension of them.
>
> Those questions, then as now, existed only for those persons who see in marriage only the satisfaction the married receive from one another, that is, only the first beginnings of marriage and not at all its significance, which lies in the family. (1458–59)

And what, may one ask, happens once "the family" has grown up? Are the couple to go on finding meaning and satisfaction in love, as at "the first beginnings of marriage"? To ask such a question reveals that what lies behind Tolstoy's tendentiousness here is guilt and fear: he must try to surround the dangerous and threatening element of sexual love by some theoretical object of concern, that is, the welfare of the family. (Later as we know he ceased to believe that "the family" did provide this control over dangerous women and dangerous sex.)

He extends his tendentious argument by comparing marriage with dinner:

> Such discussions and the questions of today, like the question how to get the utmost possible gratification out of one's dinner, then, as now, did not exist for persons for whom the object of dinner is nourishment, and the object of wedlock is the family.
>
> The end of dinner is the nourishment of the body, the man who eats his dinners obtains possibly a greater amount of pleasure, but he does not attain the object of it, since his dinners cannot be digested by the stomach. (1459)

The argument has become a sermon which sounds convincing, but is based on false analogies. Marriage is not to be compared to dinners: sexual relationships are not like eating. The "family" is not like "nourishment." Of course, for marriage to develop, requires attention to the family, in the sense of the upbringing of children: but even here it is important for the children to be forced to recognize that a secret and exciting bond exists between father and mother, to whom it is of the first importance to preserve their sexual attraction and satisfaction, for the benefit of the family. And then, taking into account the needs of family upbringing, must one member of the partnership have all her interest sacrificed to this task?

Tolstoy goes on to say that the person who prefers to have several wives and several husbands "will not in any case have a family." But having more than one man is not like indigestion: "eating more than the stomach can digest." The objections to adultery, infidelity, divorce, and promiscuity cannot be based on the parallel with the dangers of overeating: behind such a view lies Tolstoy's guilt, over his own lustfulness, and a feeling that *sex is like eating* (and probably killed his mother). The real objections, surely, must be based on the kind of truth patients under psychotherapy tell their therapists: that what they yearn for is the sense of value and meaning that can be gained from a relationship that feels like the commitment of one unique being to another, as the expression of the authenticity of each. In this, loyalty and integrity (like that felt between Levin and Kitty) is at one with the sense of uniqueness that yields the sense of meaning. Of course, the uniqueness of each family bond enhances this.

But as Tolstoy goes on, we get a sense that he is rationalizing on the one hand, and justifying his own attitude to marriage, about which he was uncertain:

Natasha needed a husband. A husband was given her; and her husband gave her a family. And she saw no need of another better husband, and indeed, as all her spiritual energies were devoted to serving that husband and his children, she could not picture, and found no interest in trying to picture, what would have happened had things been different. (Ibid.)

Of course, a woman who is happy in her married life and with her family does not think about "another husband"—but Dolly does in the other novel, and Tolstoy here is surely seeking to persuade himself that a woman can gain exclusive satisfaction in the home alone.

Natasha . . . cared for the society of those persons to whom she could rush in from the nursery in a dressing-gown with her hair down; to whom she could, with a joyful face, show a baby's napkin stained yellow instead of green, and to receive their comforting assurances that that proved that baby was now really better. (Ibid.)

—but we know from his depiction of Dolly that there can be women who feel that they have sacrificed their good looks, their years of toil, their happiness, for "the family," and even feel that, despite all their efforts, ugly and vicious dynamics have taken over their children at times. What about the later stages of marriages, as when adolescents come into conflict with parental values? Or the crisis when they leave home, and the concentration on "the family" seems to have evaporated—at a time when a woman could exercise her faculties, but may have failed to sustain them?

In return for her complete devotion, Natasha exerts a formidable possessiveness on Pierre: Natasha neglects her appearance, but yet is intensely jealous.

The general opinion was that Pierre was tied to his wife's apron strings, and it really was so . . . Pierre . . . was surprised at his wife's demands, but he was flattered by them, and he acquiesed in them. Pierre was so far under petticoat government that he did not dare to be attentive, or even to speak with a smile, to any other woman: he did not dare to go to dine at the club . . . did not dare to spend money on idle whims . . . did not dare to be away from home for any long time together. . . . (1460)

This is surely a recipe for domination by one partner, and a relationship based on tyranny and fear.

To make up for all this, Pierre had complete power in his own house . . . Natasha made herself a slave to her husband. . . . He had but to express a wish and Natasha jumped up at once and ran for what he wanted. . . . (Ibid.)

So the chapter goes on, and since this is one of Tolstoy's deline-ations of what Leavis called a "normative" relationship in mar-riage, we have to say that it is a recipe for disaster—the kind of disaster Tolstoy endured, and Sonya endured, in their tormented domestic life, until, at the end, everyone more or less went mad.

Tolstoy is aware of the particular sympathetic entente between husband and wife, as he shows a little later:

> Natasha, as soon as she was alone with her husband, had begun talking too, as only husband and wife can talk, that is, understanding and communicating their thoughts to each other, with extraordinary clear-ness and rapidity, by a quite peculiar method opposed to all the rules of logic, without the aid of premises, deductions, and conclusions. Natasha was so used to talking to her husband in this fashion that a logical sequence of thought on Pierre's part was to her an infallible symptom of something being out of tune between them . . . she knew it would invariably lead to a quarrel. . . . (1483)

In the next paragraph she creeps up to him and presses his head to her bosom, crying "Now you're all mine, mine! You shan't es-cape!" It would seem that Tolstoy is protesting too much, and, by his insistence on their mutual slavery, rationalizing a pattern of false solutions in marriage. The sympathetic sense of union in consciousness is exploited, to make the implicit threat that when the man takes resort to male, abstract, logical thinking, this must lead to a "quarrel": sharing "female" thinking means acquies-cence in overpossessiveness. Again, it is a recipe for disastrous collusion in the solutions of overdependence, arising out of fear.

It is just after this that Natasha reflects, "Is it possible that a man of such value, of such importance to society, is at the same time my husband? . . ." And they fall into a conversation that seems organized to vindicate Tolstoy's attitude to marriage (un-troubled by any sense that he was making Sonya's life hell):

> "I like you awfully!" said Natasha all at once. "Awfully! awfully!"

> "you talk about separation. But you would not believe what a special feeling I have for you after separation. . . ."
> "And, besides. . . ." Natasha was beginning.
> "No, not so. I never leave off loving you. And one couldn't love more; but it's something special. . . ."

He did not finish, because their eyes meeting said the rest.

"What nonsense," said Natasha sudenly, "it all is about the honeymoon and that the greatest happiness is at first. On the contrary, now is much the best. If only you wouldn't go away. . . ." (1485–86)

(There follows the mysterious reference to another woman, discussed below, pp. 164–5.)

In Tolstoy's overdependent relationships there is always great trouble when the man "goes away": Vronsky bridles about his "freedom" to go to political meetings, while Anna makes absurd plots to get him back. Levin is always anxious, even during his shooting expeditions, about leaving Kitty. And here Pierre and Natasha discuss it as if "going away" placed an almost intolerable strain on their relationship.

It is as if the presence of their baby, to Pierre and Natasha, reassures them of their security: it is as if the man leaves the woman, she may be exposed to terrible danger, and die (as Levin thinks Kitty may have done, in the storm). To be reunited with the woman together with her baby is blissfully reassuring—and again we are taken back to the anguish of the infant whose mother died in childbirth.

Much of Tolstoy's own deeply disturbed behavior as a husband can be traced to that traumatic loss: but so, too, can much of his portrayal of marriage. I believe it could also be shown that his portrayal of disturbed jealousies, even when the woman is in late pregnancy, as with Kitty and Vasenka, are from autobiographical experience, and demonstrate a failure in the Oedipal process in Tolstoy himself: the "rival" being in the father's place undislodged in the collapse of the son's challenge. According to Troyat, Natasha was made up of a mixture of his daughter Tanya, and Sonya. She is also a mixture of his impulses to idealize women, and to reduce them to strict and fearful control.

And what are the implications of the last few pages of *War and Peace*, before the final long essay on history and war? As at the end of *Anna Karenina*, the man is still full of ultimate philosophical investigation:

> It seemed to him at that moment that he was destined to give a new direction to the progress of the whole of Russian society and of the whole world. . . . (1486)

He has an idea which he wants to communicate to his wife: she has something to say to him but says "it wasn't anything, only nonsense." He comes out with it:

"All my idea really is that if vicious people are united and form a power, honest men must do the same. It's so simple, you see."

"Yes."

"But what were you going to say?"

"Oh, nothing, nonsense."

"No, say it though."

"I was only going to tell you about Petya. Nurse came up to take him from me today, he laughed and puckered up his face and squeezed up to me—I suppose he thought he was hiding. He's awfully sweet. . . . There he is crying. Well, goodbye!" and she ran out of the room. (1486–87)

As in *Anna Karenina,* the heroic leading couple find an ultimate solace in the antics of their baby, and this somehow silences the great philosophical-poetic ambitions of the man. Is Tolstoy making the point that the larger philosophical gestures have their origins in the failure of the primary infantile processes (which were for him tragically interrupted)? Significantly perhaps this incident in *War and Peace* is followed by a tormented passage in which Nikolinka is endeavoring to re-create his dead father and trying to live up to an idealized image of self and father, to sustain him through his growth to manhood.

But how are we to take the final implication about Natasha and her inspirational role throughout the novel? Is the woman only a spur to the search for the meaning of life when her beautiful image and her lively spirit promotes love in the man—but turns inevitably to a down-to-earth preoccupation with babies in the event, making the man's continued uplift seem rather ridiculous, a male obsession with insoluble problems? Or is the implication that the men had better give up their metaphysical yearnings, now that their quest for a mate has been satisfied, and the business of creating and sustaining a family has been entered into?

* * *

In a sense, the war provides the kind of background Tolstoy needed, to press the question of human emotional needs to the limit. Of course war is terrible, and no novel conveys this grim truth more forcibly: but it is also exciting, and enhances the problems of dependency.

These emotional needs are focused in Natasha. At one point it is clear that the Rostovs can be gay, even though the war has touched them badly:

Natasha was gay, because she had too long been sad, and now nothing reminded her of the cause of her sadness, and she was quite strong again. She was gay too, because she needed someone to adore her (the adoration of others was like the grease on the wheels, without which her mechanism never worked quite smoothly), and Petya did adore her. And above all, they were both gay, because there would be fighting at the barriers, because arms were being given out, and everybody was rushing about, and altogether something extraordinary was happening, which is always inspiring, especially for the young. (1075)

At the same time, war brings loss by death, and exposes the nature of love and deprivation. There is a solemn episode, for example, just before news of the death of Petya reaches the Rostov household. Tolstoy is describing the aftermath of the death of Prince Andrey:

When a man sees an animal dying, a horror comes over him. What he is himself—his essence, visibly before his eyes, perishes—ceases to exist. But when the dying creature is a man, and a man dearly loved, then, besides the horror at the extinction of life, what is felt is a rending of the soul, a spiritual wound, which, like a physical wound, is sometimes mortal, sometimes healed, but always aches and shrinks from contact with the outer world, that sets it smarting. (1355)

After Andrey's death, Natasha and Princess Marya felt like this. All the everyday processes of life seem to be an insult to the wound. They cling to the "needful silence" in which they were trying to listen to the "stern, terrible litany" and to gaze into the "mysterious, endless vistas" that seemed to have been unveiled before them.

To admit the possibility of a future seems to be an insult to Andrey's memory.

Princess Marya has to return to everyday life, however, since she is forced to deal with its details—one Nikolushka, Andrey's son, and problems of her estate. Natasha, however, refuses to go with Marya to Moscow and she spends most of her time

alone in her room, huddled up in a corner of her sofa. While her slender, nervous fingers were busy twisting or tearing something, she kept her eyes fixed in a set stare on the first object that met them. (1357)

She feels she is close to understanding some great mystery associated with his death. She has a vision of the dying man, his eyes shining, bearing intolerable pain, and she goes over the words she might have said to him, might have put better:

in her imagination she said to him other words of tenderness and love, which she might have said then, which she only said now. . . ." I love thee! . . . thee . . . I love, love thee. . . ." she said, wringing her hands convulsively, and setting her teeth with bitter violence. . . . (1358)

"But to whom was she saying that? where is he, and what is he now?" She tries to gaze into the world where he was, and again believes she is just penetrating the mystery.

But at this moment a maid brings news of Petya's death, and she has to come out of her spell of despair and comfort her parents, her mother above all.

An electric shock seemed to run all through Natasha. Some fearful pain seemed to stab her to the heart. She felt a poignant anguish; it seemed to her that something was being rent within her, and she was dying. But with the pain she felt an instant release from the seal that shut her out of life. . . . (1359–60)

But the wound that half killed the countess, that fresh wound brought Natasha back to life. (1362)

Her love for her mother shows her that the essence of her life—love—was still alive within her. "Love was awakened, and life worked with it."

* * *

It is impossible to pursue one's exploration of *War and Peace* further without raising the question of what must seem to be a serious fault in its construction. There are so many coincidences in it that it strains one's credibility: Andrey, for instance, reaching the hospital tent at the moment when Anatole Kuragin was having his leg off: Natasha finding him in the convoy of wounded prisoners who call at their house.

The novel tries to paint a picture of real life as it is—both of the peacetime strengths and weaknesses of human beings, and of the disasters that they bring on themselves in war, as well as their courage. It is essentially a realistic novel, so much so that certain events which are portrayed in gruesome realism are almost unbearable—the death of the little princess, for example, or Prince Andrey's own woundings and death, Anatole Kuragin's amputation, the executions witnessed by Pierre Bezuhov, the attempted seduction of Natasha, and the death of Petya.

Yet the coincidences seem to belong to a manipulation of the mythology and symbolism that places a strain on the realism. I find that today students of literature are much troubled by Dickens's coincidences: they find them too much to stomach, and feel that the novelist is shown to be manipulating his material to a fraudulent extent. Perhaps Tolstoy took a clue from Dickens?

In *War and Peace* there are coincidences all the time and they are bound up with the structure of the novel. There are, of course, the meetings with the czar and Napoleon: by Nikolay Rostov, by Prince Bolkonsky. Some of these could have been possible, though they could not have occurred so plentifully. The most difficult coincidences to swallow are the meetings between characters that fit an artistic pattern: Natasha, for example, seeing Pierre at the moment he sets off disguised as a peasant, to seek out Napoleon and to assassinate him. The meeting between the convoy of wounded officers and soldiers and the Rostovs is also just credible, but it seems to be too much of a manipulated maneuver to bring Natasha and her rejected and humiliated suitor together in this, so that she can nurse him until his death. It is also unbelievable that, just as the moment Bolkonsky is brought to the awful field hospital on the battlefield, that he should see his rival Anatole Kuragin having his leg amputated at that very hour. And it is also unbelievable that Pierre Bezuhov should be liberated by a gang of guerrilla fighters which includes not only Dolohov and Denisov, but also Petya Rostov, who dies at the moment of delivery.

There is a puzzling aspect of Tolstoy's point of view, about historical events, such as the progress of war. At one point he makes Prince Andrey reflect on Kutusov:

> "He knows that there is something stronger and more important than his will—that is the inevitable march of events, and he can see them, can grasp their significance, and, seeing their significance, can abstain from meddling, from following his own will, and aiming at something else. . . ." (941)

Of course, we can agree with Tolstoy that historians tend to tidy up events, and that military men rewrite their deeds, to counter their dread at the chaos of the battlefield. But did Tolstoy believe that human volition, choice, and action were ineffectual, and that there were and are "historical processes" that march on by themselves, regardless of generals, czars, and emperors?

Or did Tolstoy have a feeling that God actually intervened in human affairs and guided events, so that these characters made their entrances and suffered their faults by some divine plan? Of course one may be falling into the trap of judging Tolstoy by the standards of Western realism: and it is true that there are mysterious coincidences—we may remember Karl Jung and sychronicity. Of course, a Christian critic like Gustafson sees these coincidences in the light of what he calls "emblematic realism." But all the same, one cannot but feel that Tolstoy fell into the trap of authorial omnipotence allowing his creative authenticity to be overruled by a wilfull desire to make connections where the odds were too long against them, by his own realistic mode.

It was necessary for Tolstoy to punish Anatole Kuragin in the sight of Prince Andrey, in order to prepare him for his transformation, through forgiveness, into a man who can love Natasha again, when there is no hope of survival. It was necessary for him to persist in establishing a mystical union between Pierre and Natasha, so that Pierre must appear to her at certain significant moments (there is a parallel between her sighting of him, as he goes off in disguise and the way Kitty glimpses Levin from her carriage on the way to Dolly's in *Anna Karenina*).

Of course, such chance but coincidental encounters do take place, especially in war, in which normal patterns of movement are radically altered, and it does not strike us as strange, for example, that Petya should find himself in the adventure with Denisov. In that episode culminates all that "false male doing" in which Pierre Bezuhov is caught up: indeed, in which the whole world is caught up, in *War and Peace*. The female element behind the novel is aware of this, and the death of Petya embodies the whole clash between true and false, male and female, in modes of behavior. The countess, Petya's mother, is aware of this:

> The countess looked in timid horror at her son's eager, excited face, as he told them this. She knew that if she said a word to try and dissuade Petya from going to this battle (she knew how he was enjoying the prospect of it), he would say something about the duty of a man, about honour, and the fatherland—*something irrational, masculine and perverse*—which it would be useless to oppose, and all hope of preventing him would be gone. . . . (1078; my italics)

She tries, with "the instinctive, feminine duplicity of love," to get the family away—but fails in the end to curb Petya's desire to be a bold soldier. The moment in the episode of his death, where he gets his saber specially sharpened is highly symbolic, and adds to the poignancy of his waste, that even makes the hardened Denisov make a "sound like the howl of a dog" as he clutches at a fence, after he has looked at the dead face of the Rostov boy.

Of course, if we approach the coincidences from the point of view of the artistic purpose, they feel much more acceptable than they really are. On the other hand they are impelled by a powerful will that insists on there being a meaning to events despite the more truthful perception that there are none. Perhaps one could say that one or two such coincidences might have been acceptable, but that half a dozen, in such a hugely realistic work, somewhat strains one's credulity, and reveals a certain intrusive pressure in Tolstoy that seems to come from some intense personal need, though one can understand his struggle to bind this massive novel together.

*   *   *

There is one strange reference in *War and Peace,* which makes one suppose that there was an incident in the original novel that came to be cut in later versions. It seems possible that this incident ran parallel to incidents concerning characters in *Anna Karenina*— for instance Anna's jealousy over Vronsky's attending a display in which a famous beauty was performing underwater. Was there an incident in *War and Peace* concerning some old flame of Pierre's?

The incident comes when Pierre and Natasha are discussing love: Natasha exclaims, as we have seen,

"I like you awfully!" said Natasha all at once. "Awfully! awfully!"

and Pierre says he has a special feeling for her after separation.

"I never leave off loving you. . . ."

But in his interest in making their married love something special, Tolstoy makes Natasha say,

"What nonsense," said Natasha suddenly, "it all is about the honey-moon and that the greatest happiness is at first. On the contrary, now is much the best. If only you wouldn't go away. Do you remember how we used to quarrel? And I was always in the wrong. It was always my doing. And what we quarrelled about—I don't remember even."
"Always the same thing," said Pierre smiling. "Jea. . . ."
"Don't say it, I can't bear it," cried Natasha, and a cold, vindictive light gleamed in her eyes. "Did you see her?" she added after a pause.
"No; and if I had, I shouldn't have known her."
They were silent. (1486)

A cloud has come between them: but who is it that Pierre might have seen? *And who is it that Natasha has been jealous of?* Pierre has not paid attention to any other woman since his wife died, and there has been no occasion on which Natasha and Pierre have quarreled about another woman. The reference thus remains mystifying.

* * *

I have attended more or less exclusively to the personal dramas in *War and Peace,* to illustrate my investigation of Tolstoy's preoccupation with men and women, and especially man's vision of woman. In the sphere of war and of the historical forces that lead to war he takes the view that mass movements happen under their own impetus, and that individuals do not have, leaders do not have, the impact they suppose they have, on events. Yet he shows us a Napoleon who is a massive egotist, who sees everything in terms of his own glory, while Kutusov is a monument to the ideal of Russian inactivity and stoicism: these elements of personality surely must have had some effect on the historical processes. Certainly, with Andrey and Pierre, their very different attempts to find meaning, influenced by their devotion to the ideal inspired by Natasha, has an influence on events, and at times the action of individuals definitely alters circumstances and their outcome—as when Nikolai Rostov rescues Princess Marya from the truculent and drunken peasants. We can surely take Tolstoy's theories here with a pinch of salt, as we can take the long historical essay with which he ends his novel. It is the human dramas which he devises, in his pondering of the truth of human nature, as an artist, that make this immense novel such a European masterpiece.

4

Anna Karenina

Anna Karenina is a fully mature and feminine woman: as Tolstoy says at one point, when she is first seen traveling by train, she steps out

> carrying her rather full figure with extraordinary lightness (*Anna Karenina*; 77)*

When he falls in love with her Vronsky becomes submissive: he looks at her in a subdued way, as if overwhelmed by the power of her femininity. She is far from being a bad or degenerate woman. Anna Karenina is full of benign impulses. She has a strong conscience, and she wants to be good. *She wants to live.*

On the one hand she is full of feeling for others, as when she displays her compassion for Dolly and her affection for her son Seriozha. But there is another side to her character: Vronsky has encountered this side, which displays a "superficiality and lightness of judgment," when he raises serious questions:

> she, the real Anna, retreated somewhere inside herself and another woman appeared, a stranger to him, who he did not love and whom he feared, and who was in opposition to him. (207)

It is this "other" woman who betrays Kitty, regards her husband with revulsion, takes morphine, screws her eyes up so as not to see certain aspects of reality, and, in the end, succumbs to insane fits of jealousy and uncertainty and ultimately kills herself. She is an enigma—the enigma of woman.

Judith Armstrong makes the valid point that what Tolstoy loves in Anna is "his own sexuality," and because she is his own sexuality,

---

*Page numbers in my discussion of this novel refer to the Penguin edition, translated by Rosemary Edmonds, published in 1954.

of which he was deeply afraid, he kills her. But that will not serve, either, as a definitive comment on Anna, for she comes to life in a powerful way, and acts from her own center—carrying us with her, joyously and painfully. She gets out of hand and, as Tolstoy himself implied, did things that he did not intend.

* * *

The novel opens with her trying to effect a reconciliation between Dolly and Oblonsky ("Stiva") who has been unfaithful to his wife: or, rather, he has been found out for the first time: Dolly proclaims,

> "with *maman's* upbringing, I was not merely innocent, I was stupid. I knew nothing. People say, I know, that husbands tell their wives about their past lives, but Stiva . . . Steven Arkadyevich . . . told me nothing. You will hardly believe it, but until this happened I suppose she was the only woman he had ever loved. . . ." (82)

Anna declares that she understands.

> "And do you imagine he realises all the horror of my position?" exclaimed Dolly. "Not a bit! He is happy and contented."

Now we learn something of Anna's capacity to understand her brother to the extent of making allowances for him, and also her capacity to make the best of a difficulty.

> "Oh no!" Anna interrupted quickly. "He's in a pitiful state, weighed down by remorse. . . . "
> "Is he capable of remorse?" broke in Dolly.
> "He's good-hearted, but he is proud, too, and now he feels so humiliated. What moved me most of all. . . . " (and here Anna guessed what would touch Dolly most) "he is tormented by two things: that he's ashamed for the children's sake and that, loving you—yes, yes, loving you more than anything in the world. . . . " (83)

We also get a clue here to Anna's capacity for self-delusion. It must strike the reader as comic, to think of Oblonsky ever being "weighed down by remorse" or even "tormented." And at the end, Anna tells Dolly she would forgive: "I should forgive, and forgive as utterly as if it never happened, had never happened at all."

Anna has a romantic idea of love, and in her womanly consideration for Dolly, an excessive expectation of the possibility of forgiveness, in such a situation. Her goodwill and benign inten-

tions are by no means presented ironically at this point, nor is
there any suspicion that her intervention is futile, or absurd, or
lacking in sincerity. Indeed, what we glimpse here is her capacity
for a kind of deception and self-deception that is based on a good-
natured concern for women friends—though (as we shall see) this
consideration does not extend to Kitty, whom she treats cruelly—
under the impulse of the passion that overwhelms her, at the ball.
Even at the end, she feels Kitty is somewhat alien to her: and by
then she has a sense of alienation from herself.

Her romantic (deluded) view comes out in her conversation
with Kitty later:

> "I remember that blue haze, like the haze on the mountains in Switzer-
> land. That haze which envelops everything at the blissful time when
> childhood is just coming to an and and its huge merry circle narrows
> to a path which one treads gaily yet with dread into life's corridor,
> bright and splendid as it appears. . . . Who has not been through
> it?" (87)

Anna talks of Vronsky and of what his mother told her about
him: "He is a hero," she says. But it is also significant that she
does not tell Kitty about the money Vronsky gives to the stationmaster: "She felt that there had been something in the incident
to do with her personally, that should not have been." She has a
sense of a fatal premonition already, around Vronsky and his
reckless generosity: and so we see the selectiveness in Anna's consideration of experience. There are always aspects she will not
see, or will not mention.

She is duplicitous only because she is aware of the many dimen-
sions of her being, and aware that there are some beyond her
consciousness. In recognizing this, in creating Anna, Tolstoy became able to write this great tragic novel, allowing his characters
to live beyond the delineations of his strong views, about men,
women, sex, and marriage, that, if he had merely illustrated them
in his fiction, would have resulted in novels that would have failed
to come alive. He was artist enough to recognize that the life he
imagined must be allowed to live, according to its own truths,
under the mysterious impulses of an inner voice that speaks of
things as they are, not of how they ought to be.

It is an astonishing example of the *art* taking over, being generated as it were from a source outside or beyond the individual:
of a writer giving himself up to some power in his imagination
that a greater, more subtle, more generous, more aware of human

complexity and need, than he, in his opinionated and tormented life outside the great novels, ever was. This novel is by no means the moral fable enacting his point of view, such as Gustafson would have us believe, but a true work of art, conveying living truth.

*   *   *

One aspect of *Anna Karenina* that becomes apparent to the reader very quickly is the complex symmetry of the relationships between the characters. This must have a symbolic significance: Oblonsky, good-natured, sensual, and unfaithful, is the brother of Anna Karenina. Dolly, Oblonsky's faded wife, is the elder sister of Kitty Shcherbatsky, while Levin has been in love with the whole family and only recently has learned that the woman he has come really to fall in love with is Kitty.

A contrast is clearly implied between Oblonsky and Levin. They have lived together as young men but while they get on well together as friends they find the other's modes of behavior to be beyond understanding. Early on, they have a discussion of relationships with women (around the theme of "stealing rolls") and Levin simply cannot grasp Oblonsky's view—though Levin, it is clear, has sowed his own plot of wild oats. He has come, however, to believe in pure love, and in conversation he fills Oblonsky with "mental and moral strain," by being too serious on this whole issue. The problem of authenticity thus comes to the fore, and it is this question that is pursued over Vronsky and Anna. These are taken over, as if by a force of destiny greater than themselves, by an irresistible mutual attraction. However much they resist this force, they find themselves overruled by it, and inclined, in pursuit of it, to bring on their own doom, indifferent, too, to the fate of others. Kitty herself is abandoned by Vronsky, who has been paying court to her (without really thinking of marrying her), while Anna very quickly falls into contempt and hatred for her husband—so quickly that we feel she has never known real love from him, but has married him from conventional pressures and out of a misguided sense of duty: certainly, she is unawakened, and Vronsky awakens her. Yet this awakened passion, as it becomes the only way of "holding" Vronsky, eventually destroys her.

*   *   *

It becomes clear that, in one sense, *Anna Karenina* is a tragedy of a woman who has never known love, gets married to a respected but cold and mechanical man, and then finds herself in an impossible situation, because she cannot find any way to get out of her marriage, to start a new life with the man with whom she does fall in love. In Russia at the time only the injured party as in adultery could sue for divorce, and the children would not be left with the guilty party. So, there is no hope for Anna of keeping the son, Seriozha, whom she loves so much. Her husband Karenin is not willing to undergo the shame of producing evidence of his wife's adultery, which would have to be from witnesses. And if she commits herself totally to Vronsky, Anna comes to feel that he will only get tired of her, by finding her expression of her sexual needs, exerted to keep him, distasteful.

Yet in a sense Anna is a wronged woman, or, rather, a woman who has made a mistake—the mistake of marrying without love, or perhaps in supposing that her relationship with her partner was love, when it was not, and in her ignorance she did not know this. So, we have great sympathy for her. (Gustafson seems to be seriously unsympathetic and is indeed hostile to Anna.)

Musing on the "people" who believe Karenin to be "religious, so high-principled, so upright, so clever," she reflects that they have not seen what she has seen:

> They don't know how for eight years he has crushed my life, crushed everything that was living in me—he has never once thought that I'm a live woman in need of love. They don't know how at every step he's humiliated me and remained self-satisfied. Haven't I striven, striven with all my might, to find something to give meaning to my life? Haven't I struggled to love him, to love my son when I could no longer love my husband? But the time came when I realized I couldn't deceive myself any longer, that I was alive, that I was not to blame, that God made me so that I need to love and live. . . . (314)

So, Anna's taking a lover is to her a manifestation of authenticity—a claim of someone alive to find that which seems to her the truth of love, to fulfill herself as a "live woman."

To her "anything is better than lies and deceit": but she does not have the strength to tear down the fabric of her old situation, "however false and dishonourable it might be." The idea that she can now have her position cleared up and made definite is destroyed forever:

> She knew beforehand that everything would go on as it was—would in fact be far worse than before. She felt that the position she enjoyed in society, which had seemed of so little consequence that morning, was precious to her after all, and that she would not have the strength

to exchange it for the shameful one of a woman who has deserted husband and child to join her lover: that, however much she might struggle, she could not be stronger than herself. She would never know freedom in love, but would always be the guilty wife continually threatened with exposure, deceiving her husband for the sake of a disgraceful liaison with a man living apart and away from her, whose life she could never share. (315–16)

It is important to note that Anna is made to reflect that her position in society was "precious to her after all." D. H. Lawrence's view that Vronsky and Anna only had to thumb their noses at "society" and all would be well, simply won't do (Lawrence's "Reflections on the Death of a Porcupine," p. 2): the dissociation from her position among other people is deeply distressing to Anna, and we need to take account of the societal context in Russia at the time, when adultery was felt to be outrageous (even if a subject for salacious gossip) and divorce deplorable.

* * *

We know very little of Anna Karenina's early married life, or, indeed, why she married a man who is twenty years older than herself, without loving him, or, as Oblonsky declares "before she knew what love was."

We learn a little since. Karenin had grown up as an orphan. There were two brothers.

They did not remember their father, and their mother died when Alexei Alexandrovich was ten years old. Their means were small. Their uncle, Karenin, a distinguished Government official and at one time a favourite of the late Emperor, had brought them up. (*Anna Karenina*, p. 534)

Karenin did well in school and at university and devoted himself entirely to political ambition. But he made few friends and his brother had been his only intimate: he died shortly after Karenin's marriage.

Karenin had been governor of a province and Anna's aunt, who was a wealthy provincial lady, had thrown him into the society of her niece. He was not young in years, but was young to be a governor. She seems to have obviously been ambitious for her niece, and managed to place Karenin in such a position that he had to declare himself or leave the town. He hesitated for a long time, and one can imagine him debating what to do:

There were then as many arguments for the step as against it, and no overwhelming consideration to outweigh his invariable rule of abstaining when in doubt. Anna's aunt, however, managed to insinuate, through a common acquaintance, that he had already compromised the girl and was in honour bound to make her an offer. He made the offer, and bestowed on his betrothed and wife all the feelings of which he was capable. (535)

It was obviously a marriage planned and organized by a member of Anna's family—and, like Lady Russell's prohibition in Jane Austen's *Persuasion,* at odds with the true feelings of the participants: or, rather, the marriage did not arise from emotional commitment on both sides. It was not so much a shotgun wedding, but one in which an emotionally naive man was made to feel it was his duty to make a girl an honest woman, because of behavior which, he was led to suppose, made the world at large feel that it committed him to this path. In his own emotional deficiency Karenin bears some relationship to George Eliot's Casaubon: paradoxically, he becomes sympathetic and compassionate through the birth of Vronsky's baby, when Anna nearly dies.

* * *

It is a marvelous piece of perspective, for us to see Anna at the beginning of the novel through Kitty's eyes. Kitty is the first to get Anna in focus, when they meet in the Oblonsky's house: Anna is a "fashionable Petersburg lady" to her, and Kitty falls in love with her "as young girls do fall in love with married women older than themselves." Tolstoy's capacity to portray the intersubjectivity between women characters is superb:

> Anna was not like a society lady, nor the mother of an eight-year-old son. Her lithe movements, her freshness, and the persistent animation of her face, which broke out now in her smile, now in her glance, would have made her look like a girl of twenty, had it not been for the grave and at times mournful expression in her eyes, which struck and drew Kitty to her. Kitty felt Anna was completely natural and was not trying to conceal anything, but that she had another and higher world of complex and poetic interest beyond Kitty's reach. (86)

Why does Anna have that "grave and at times mournful expression in her eyes"? It can only be because she remains unawakened and is secretly aware that there are joys of sexual love she has never known.

So, Kitty suddenly sees a very different Anna at the ball:

now she suddenly saw her again in a different and unexpected light. She noticed that Anna was elated with success, a feeling Kitty herself knew so well. She saw that Anna was intoxicated with the admiration she had aroused. . . . She saw the quivering, flashing lights in her eyes, the smile of happiness and excitement that involuntarily curved her lips, and the graceful sureness and ease of her movements. (95)

Tolstoy is uncannily aware of the woman's capacity to be excited, by displaying an appearance to which a man will respond. Anna has dressed for the occasion (and we see her through Kitty's eyes):

Anna was not in lilac . . . but in a low-necked black velvet gown which displayed her full shoulders and bosom, that seemed carved out of old ivory, and her rounded arms with their delicate tiny wrists. Her dress was richly trimmed with Venetian lace. In her black hair, which was all her own, she wore a little wreath of pansies, and there were more pansies on the black ribbon winding through the white lace at her waist. Except for the wilful little curls that always escaped at her temples and on the nape of her neck, adding to her beauty, there was nothing remarkable about her coiffure. She wore a string of pearls round her finely-modelled neck. (93)

She is, in fact, a very beautiful woman, displaying all her cunning charm, because of her excitement that she was going to meet Vronsky. Kitty, seeing Anna in black, feels that she had never before realized all her charm.

She saw her now in a new and quite unexpected light and realized . . . that her charm lay precisely in the fact that she stood out from whatever she was wearing, that her dress was never conspicuous on her. And the black velvet, with its rich lace, was not at all conspicuous but served only as a frame. It was Anna alone, simple, natural, elegant, and at the same time animated, whom one saw. (Ibid.)

This portrayal of Anna through a young naive woman's eyes enables us also to share the shock, of the naive Kitty, who loves Anna, when she sees in her face the way she responds to someone's admiration ("Can it be *he*?"):

Every time he spoke to Anna, her eyes lit up joyously and a smile of happiness parted her red lips. (95)

And when she looks at Vronsky's face, she sees an expression she had never seen before. Gone was his usually quiet, firm manner and tranquil carefree expression. Instead, he bowed his head a little, as if wanting to fall at her feet in adoration, and his eyes held only submission and fear. "I would not offend you" his every look seemed to say. "I only want to save myself but I do not know how." (96)

Kitty has a crisis of despair and terror. She has looked in Vronsky's face and has given him a look that was full of love: but it meets with no response, and this pierces her heart with tormenting shame. She remembers that wounding moment forever.

Vronsky, to Kitty, has "an expression like that of an intelligent dog conscious of having done wrong." His animal instinctual life of being is being aroused by Anna's hunger for admiration—and for the sexual awakening she has never had.* It is as if she is possessed by this instinctual need, and it overpowers Vronsky. Vronsky has had many sensual escapades obviously: but, as we shall find, this *affaire* is very different. Later, when he is obliged to entertain a foreign prince, and leads him into a social life that mirrors the one Vronsky used to lead, he becomes aware of how he used to behave, and becomes aware, too, of how different his commitment to Anna has made him: he sees the prince only as a "beefy ass" and ultimately as "fat and spiteful." But Vronsky is the kind of responsive, living, sexually available man for whom Anna's soul is calling out: he is to her a manifestation of "life."

Much later we learn of Anna's feelings of dissatisfaction with her marriage, as we have seen in the paragraph beginning" for eight years he has crushed my life, crushed everything that was living in me—he has never once thought that I'm a live woman in need of love. . . ." (*Anna Karenina*, p. 314).

This is a very revealing paragraph, showing that Tolstoy recognizes that Anna has a claim to "love and live," and that Karenin was incapable of giving her this experience—which is bound up with her need for a *sense of meaning in her life*. Hers is an existential need, and the power with which her love of Vronsky takes her over comes from the deepest needs of being. Yet in her situation, it leads to circumstances that are intolerable, and inescapably destructive.

She cannot now adhere to the principles of religion "unless she were prepared to renounce that which made up for her the whole meaning of life." So, she begins to feel a sense of duality about

---

*I find it somewhat farfetched to find in this comparison of Vronsky to a dog an echo of the incarnation of Mephistopheles in the form of a dog in Goethe's *Faust*, as Mandelker argues (Mandelker 152).

everything, and because the two halves of her being are at odds, she begins to feel bitterness toward Vronsky himself, as the cause of her confusion and shame.

*   *   *

It is the existence of Seriozha that first begins to bring home to Vronsky and Anna the gravity of their situation, and the realities of relationship and time:

> This boy was more often than anyone else a check upon their freedom. When he was present, neither Vronsky nor Anna would allow themselves to speak of anything—or even refer by hints to anything— the boy would have understood.

They don't want to deceive the child. But Vronsky notices

> the child's attentive, bewildered gaze fixed upon him and a strange timidity and uncertainty in the boy's manner to him. . . . It was as if the child felt that between this man and his mother there was some important bond which he could not understand. (203)

Seriozha is puzzled, about Vronsky's identity, his relationship with his mother, and what ought his relationship to be with this man. As we know from reports by psychotherapists, the child is aware of the sexual relationship between his parents, even if he is not explicitly aware: and it is important to children that they should feel there is a special, even mysterious, relationship between their parents, in which they have no part. But if the mother, like Anna, takes on an illicit relationship, the child is naturally confused, by his unconscious awareness of this, at a very deep level—and so is Seriozha:

> "What does it mean? Who is he? How ought I to love him? If I don't know, it's my fault: it means I am a silly boy, or a bad boy," thought the child. And this was what caused his scrutinizing, inquiring, and to some extent hostile expression and the shyness and uncertainty which so embarrassed Vronsky. (Ibid.)

This childish reaction has an effect on Vronsky and Anna:

> The child's presence invariably called up in Vronsky that strange feeling of inexplicable revulsion which he had experienced of late. The child's presence called up both in Vronsky and Anna a feeling akin to that of a sailor who can see by the compass that the direction in

which he is swiftly sailing is wide of the proper course, but is powerless to stop. Every moment takes him farther and farther astray, and to admit to himself that he is off his course is the same as admitting final disaster.

This child, with his innocent outlook upon life, was the compass which showed them the degree to which they had departed from what they knew but did not want to know. (203–4)

Vronsky and Anna are caught in a love that it would be impossible for them to withdraw from: it has become the primary reality of their existence. Yet, as revealed by the child's innocent response, it is wrong, sub specie aeternitatis—so wrong that it threatens ultimate disaster.

Throughout the novel, the main protagonists are aware that they are on a disastrous course, and they cannot see a way out. At one point Vronsky, although he has gone away with Anna to live with her all the time as man and wife, and although she loves him "for himself and for his love for her," and feels unpardonably happy, finds that he is *not* happy.

He soon began to feel that the realization of his desires brought him no more than a grain of sand out of the mountain of bliss he had expected. (490)

From this Tolstoy establishes a universal principle:

It showed him the eternal error men make in imagining that happiness consists in the realization of their desires.

For a time he has experienced the charm of freedom in general, and of the freedom to love, and he was content, "*but not for long*,"

Soon he felt a desire spring up in his heart for desires—*ennui*. (491)

Anna cries, "Oh, why did I not die? It would have been better!"—and she now resolutely refuses a divorce. Vronsky has declared, "Our love, if it could grow stronger, would do so because of there being something terrible in it. . . ." But Anna, even in her "unpardonable happiness" begins to fear she will lose Vronsky's love—a suspicion that eventually destroys them.

Karenin, either, cannot see a way out—though he vacillates between being persuaded by Oblonsky to seek a divorce, and being persuaded by the countess Lydia Ivanovna not to. At one point he has a gush of forgiveness toward his wife, when she seems to be dying. But after Oblonsky has sought to persuade him into divorce, Karenin realizes that this is impossible:

> An action for divorce, with the details of which he was now acquainted, appeared to him out of the question, because of his feelings of self-respect and his regard for religion forbade his pleading guilty to a fictitious act of adultery, and still less could he allow his wife, forgiven and beloved by him, to be exposed and put to shame. (456)

Divorce also seems to him impossible on other still more weighty grounds:

> In the event of a divorce, what would become of his son? To leave him with his mother was out of the question. The divorced mother would have her own illegitimate family, in which the position and upbringing of a stepson would in all probability be wretched. Should he keep the child himself? He knew that would be an act of vengeance on his part, and he did not want that. But apart from this, what ruled out divorce more than anything in his eyes was that by consenting to a divorce he would be handing Anna over to destruction. (456–57)

To give her a divorce, he feels, since he had forgiven her and had grown fond of her children, would be to take from her the last prop that supported her on the path of virtue, "to thrust her to perdition."

He believes at this point that, while Anna could not marry Vronsky, Vronsky would get tired of her, and she would take on another illicit union—and he become the cause of her ruin. Listening to Oblonsky he feels that his words

> were the expression of that mighty brutal force which controlled his life and to which he would have to surrender in the end. (457)

Oblonsky, of course, regards the calamity as "an act of fate . . . an accomplished fact"—that must be accepted.

But what does Tolstoy mean by the "mighty brutal force" that Karenin believes "controls his life" and "to which he would have to surrender in the end?" A month later Anna goes off with Vronsky, and Karenin is left in his house with Seriozha. Is the brutal force fate? Is this force symbolized by the malevolent little peasant who mutters that the iron must be beaten? It seems to be a strange remark, and suggests a hint of Tolstoy having his thumb in the scales, a question to which we shall return—yet, at the same time, a bias which he manages to resolve into tragedy.

* * *

Tolstoy is able to write so poignantly about Seriozha because the boy's situation echoes his own, when he lost his mother.

> When the candle was taken away, Seriozha heard and felt his mother. She stood over him and caressed him with a loving look. But then windmills appeared, and a penknife, and everything began to be mixed up, and he fell asleep. (555)

Tolstoy conveys with vivid precision the phenomenology of Seriozha's mind: the way, for instance, he cannot believe in death, and the way he can only think of Enoch, among the characters in the Old Testament which he is instructed to study. Enoch was taken up alive to heaven.

> Enoch had not died, so not everybody died.
> "And why shouldn't anyone else deserve the same in God's sight and be taken up to heaven alive?" thought Seriozha. (554)

Above all, he does not believe his mother is dead, though he is told she is. As soon as Lydia Ivanovna tells him his mother is dead, Seriozha begins looking for her when he was having his walk:

> Every comely, graceful woman with dark hair was his mother. At the sight of every such woman his heart would swell with tenderness until his breath failed him and the tears came into his eyes. And he was on tiptoe with expectation that she would come up to him, would lift her veil. All her face would be visible, she would smile, she would take him in her arms, he would sniff her fragrance, feel the tender clasp of her hand, and cry with happiness, just as he had done one evening when he had rolled at her feet and she had tickled him, while he shook with laughter and bit her white hand with the rings on her fingers. (552)

There are several such passages of ecstatic imagining of the bodily presence of the mother to Seriozha and of play with her. And they are close in spirit to passages I have analyzed elsewhere in the writing of George MacDonald, who lost his mother as a child, a loss which evoked for him painful memories of her sudden weaning of him: he spent his life fantasying the refinding of his mother's breast. I find a parallel phenomenon in the writings of C. S. Lewis who also lost his mother as a child, and whose world seemed blighted by his lost mother. What we find with such writers is the deep disturbance of their capacity to relate to reality, their profound need to exercise fantasy in the attempt to put this right, and their poignant need to recover the mother who has been lost.

We recall Tolstoy's portrait of Nikolay's mother in *Childhood*:

> So many memories arise when one tries to recall the features of a beloved being, that one sees those features dimly through the memories as if through tears. They are the tears of imagination. When I try to recall my mother as she was at the time I can only picture her brown eyes, always expressing the same kindness and love, the mole on her neck, just below the place where the short hairs curled, her embroidered white collar, and the delicate dry hand which so often caressed me and which I so often kissed, but her general expression escapes me. (Quoted in Benson, 5)

Seriozha learns from his old nurse that his mother is not dead, while his father and Lydia tell him she is dead because she was a wicked woman (which he cannot believe): he goes on looking for her in the same way.

> That day in the public gardens there had been a lady in a lilac veil, whom he had watched with a throbbing heart, believing it to be her as she came towards them along the path. The lady had not come up to them, but had disappeared somewhere. Today, Seriozha felt a wish of love for her, stronger than ever, and now as he sat waiting for his father he forgot everything, and notched all round the edge of the table with his knife, staring before him with shining eyes and dreaming of her. (*Anna Karenina*, (552)

Karenin cannot understand this devotion to a phantom and he and the tutor suppose Seriozha's behavior is mere naughtiness. The desire for the mother is inexpressible, and is satisfied at a less than conscious level, of being and body. The mother feels the same need, to be with her firstborn, and much of Anna's final disintegration happens because she loses this contact.

When she makes her bold and unsanctioned visit to Seriozha he has changed from the four-year-old baby, which was the age at which she loved him most: but it is the same child, albeit taller and thinner:

> "Seriozha!" she repeated almost in the child's ear. He raised himself again on his elbow, turned his tousled head from side to side as if seeking something and opened his eyes. Slowly and inquiringly he gazed for several seconds at his mother standing motionless before him. . . . (562)

Seriozha has, so to speak, to "make" or "re-make" his mother, bringing her reality into focus with his imaginings of her:

> then all at once he smiled blissfully and closing his sleepy eyelids toppled not backwards but forward into her arms.
> "Seriozha, my darling boy!" she murmured, catching her breath and putting her arms round his chubby little body.
> "Mama!" he whispered, wriggling about in her arms so as to touch them with different parts of him. (Ibid.)

This marvelously realized moment heightens our awareness of Anna's feelings, and of her poignant situation: for there is no solution to the problem of her loss of Seriozha—for even if she gets a divorce, she won't be able to keep him (Russian law as I have pointed out would not allow the guilty party to have custody). It also deepens our awareness of Karenin's cruelty, because he does not understand Anna's feelings as a bereft mother, while Vronsky is not able to understand (and Anna is aware of his limitations over the matter).

> Smiling sleepily, with his eyes shut, he moved his plump little hands from behind him, enveloping her with that sweet fragrance of warmth and sleepiness peculiar to children, and began rubbing his face against her neck and shoulders. (Ibid.)

The intensity of the moment has its roots in Tolstoy's own poignant experience of trying to remember his own lost mother:

> "My precious little Kootik!" she murmured, calling him by the pet name she had used when he was a baby, "you won't forget me? You. . . ." But she could say no more. (565).

A look of dread has come over her face: Karenin comes in and sees her, and she hurriedly departs feeling loathing and hatred for her husband, and jealousy over her son. She is so preoccupied that she carries with her the toys she had chosen "so sadly and with so much love" away with her, a harrowing touch which brings home to us the misery of her loss.

Anna tries to console herself with Ani, but the latter does not grip the heart as Seriozha does: for

> Seriozha was now almost a personality, and a beloved one, already struggling with thoughts and feelings of his own; he understood her, he loved her, he judged her, she thought, recalling his words and his

eyes. And she was for ever separated from him, not physically only but spiritually, and there was no help for it. (567)

All the passages around this theme of the intersubjectivity between mother and child in Tolstoy's novel have their origins in his own experience in infancy, of the need to use the imagination, with intense application, to re-create the lost mother and to reestablish the formative links with her, to discover his own and the world's reality.

* * *

In one sense, *Anna Karenina* is a dissertation on femininity. Oblonsky, we need to remember, is Anna's brother. His view of women is at the opposite pole from Levin's, but perplexed all the same:

"You know the Ossian type of woman . . . such as one only sees in dreams? . . . Well, such women do exist . . . and they are terrible. Woman, don't you know, is the sort of subject that study it as much as you will it is always new." (179)

Thus Oblonsky. Levin, to whom he is speaking, cannot "even begin to enter into the feelings of his friend and understand his sentiments and the charm of studying women of that kind." These two characters represent opposing attitudes to women, love, and sex, at a level below that of the main protagonists, Vronsky and Anna. Anna, of course, is Oblonsky's sister, and she is closer to his views: but Levin represents the approach of total authenticity—even though, as a young man, he has been guilty of coarse and promiscuous relationships with women. In the light of what we know about Levin, it is clear that Oblonsky, despite this aphorism, knows nothing at all about women, despite his prowess as a philanderer. Oblonsky is a marvelous comic character—utterly immoral in his self-indulgent way, and yet so full of good nature that few of the other characters can condemn him. Yet Levin and Oblonsky can be friends, because they have shared childhood experiences, though each is baffled by the attitudes to personal relationships of the other.

Oblonsky has assumed that his wife knew of his unfaithfulness and had turned a blind eye to it. She has faded, largely through bearing his children, and he no longer loves her. She has become a "no longer young, a simple, uninteresting woman." So, it seemed to him "she really ought to be indulgent." In all this there is a

certain "straightforwardness," but Oblonsky really "lives from day
to day" and regards upsets as his wife's unforgiving rage at her
discovery of his infidelity as things that happen "to spite him."

His is one kind of egoism: he regards it, merely, as "something
banal and vulgar" about making love to one's own governess ("But
what a governess!")—though he didn't actually permit himself any
liberties while she was actually under his roof. When his wife
bursts out at him "let them (the children) all know what a scoundrel you are! I am going away this very day, and you can live with
your mistress!" Oblonsky regards all this shouting as "so vulgar"—
"terribly vulgar, terribly!"—"the maids may have heard"—"recalling her screams and the words *scoundrel* and *mistress.*"

The price he pays, of course, is to be limited to the sphere of
l'homme moyen sensuel: his *affaire* with the governess is trivial, and
it is not long before he has another favorite, a young ballet dancer
to whom he is giving dinner and gifts. Yet Oblonsky is so full of
goodwill that he seeks to deal with all kinds of difficult situations,
such as Levin's alienation from Kitty and Karenin's from Anna,
sometimes successfully, but often falling short of a real understanding of the problems involved.

Levin's earnestness, his authenticity, and the depth of his love
for Kitty are beyond Oblonsky, and he finds that he causes him
"too great a mental and moral strain." He lapses with relief into
a conversation with an aide-de-camp about an actress and her
protector, to refresh himself after a conversation with Levin,
about women. Levin finds Oblonsky's account of how he loves his
wife but is attracted by other women quite incomprehensible.
Levin says he separates women into two categories—women and
fallen women:

> I have a horror of fallen women. You are afraid of spiders, and I am
> afraid of these women. . . . (55)

Oblonsky dismisses Levin's view with "Oh, you moralist!" and yet
Levin is reduced to some confusion:

> "If you want my opinion, I can only tell you that I do not believe there
> is any conflict about it. For this reason: to my mind, love—both kinds
> of love (Plato defines them in his *Symposium*) serve as a criterion. Some
> men only understand one sort, and some only the other. And those
> who only understand the non-Platonic love have no need to talk of
> conflict. In such love there can be no conflict. 'Much obliged for the
> gratification, my humble respects'—and that is all there is to it. And

in Platonic love there can be no conflict because in that love all is clear
and pure, because. . . . "

At that instant, Levin recollected all his own sins and the inner
conflict he had lived through. And he added unexpectedly:

"However, perhaps you are right. You may very likely be. . . . But I
don't know, I really don't know. . . ." (Ibid.)

This is more or less the spirit in which Tolstoy (whose Levin
has much in him that is autobiographical) wrote *Anna Karenina*:
"I don't know"—and so, as his characters take life and develop,
they show him how these beliefs affect life, and how life is lived,
despite adherences, assumptions, and moral beliefs.

Anna has some of the characteristics of her brother, though
she is not capable of the same capacity for the trivial or for the
complacently comfortable. In relating to Dolly how she was responsible for spoiling Kitty's evening at the ball, and, indeed, spoiling Kitty's life, Anna comes to realize her own capacity for self-
deception.

> "I have spoiled. . . . It was because of me that the ball was a torture
> instead of a joy to her. But truly, truly, I am not to blame, or only a
> little bit," she said in a high-pitched voice, drawling the words "a
> little bit."
>
> "Oh, how exactly like Stiva you said that!" laughed Dolly.
>
> Anna was offended.
>
> "Oh no, oh no! I am not Stiva," she said, with a frown. "The reason
> I'm telling you in that I could never let myself doubt myself for an
> instant." (113)

But then Anna Karenina recognizes that she has in fact the same
capacity for self-deception that Stiva has:

> But as she was uttering the words she knew they were not true: she
> not only distrusted herself, but the thought of Vronsky disturbed her,
> and she was leaving sooner than she had intended solely in order not
> to meet him again. (Ibid.)

Indeed, this womanly capacity to deceive herself is what makes
for tragedy, as she is always supposing that she can cope with
the violent love that intrudes upon her life, and deal with its
consequences, when the reverse is true—so much so that death
increasingly presents itself as the only alternative answer. Anna,
however, is "not Stiva" in that, out of her own perverse authenticity, compromise is not possible for her: she does not share his
superficial attitudes. Yet in her increasing shrinking from the real-

ity of her predicament—as by her recourse to morphine and by the way she screws up her eyes—she seeks to avoid looking reality in the face. Moreover, there is something witchlike about Anna Karenina, because she is a woman: in her charm, as it is first expressed to Vronsky at the ball, Kitty perceives "something terrible and cruel." It is cruel both to Kitty, and to Vronsky—because what excites Anna most is Vronsky's submissive stance toward her, as he becomes ensnared.

> "Yes, there is something strange, diabolical, and enchanting about her," thought Kitty. (97)

*   *   *

Tolstoy is anxious to distinguish between the different views of women that men hold. To Oblonsky, women are rather like the little decanters in his dream in the opening pages:

> "the tables were singing *Il mio tesoro*. No, not *Il mio tesoro*, something better: and there were some little decanters who were women," he remembered. (14)

Levin, of course, is gravely respectful of the mystery that is woman, and cannot conceive any other approach but that of total fidelity to the woman he loves.

Vronsky, contemplating Levin and the pain he suffers when rejected by Kitty, says:

> "Yes, that is a painful position. That's why most of us prefer our Claras, the women of the *demi-monde*. If you don't succeed with them it only means you've not got enough cash; but with the others it's our merits that are weighed in the balance." (74)

This is insightful, but it also reveals the limitations of the sophisticated view. Lower down on the same page, the origin of Vronsky's limitations are indicated:

> In the depths of his heart he had no great respect for his mother and, though not confessing as much to himself, he did not love her; but, in accordance to the ideas of his set and with his upbringing, he could not imagine treating her otherwise than dutifully and with the greatest respect, and the more outwardly dutiful and respectful he was, the less he respected and loved her in his heart. (Ibid.)

This aspect of Vronsky is rendered in his last quarrel with Anna, and the last phrase is true, in a different way, of his final clash with her.

Vronsky as a lover is more plainly driven on by egoism and vanity, though this is not all there is about him. He is for one thing as much a product of his milieu as the Crawfords in Jane Austen's *Mansfield Park* are of theirs. He belongs to the entourage of Betsy, Princess Betsy Tverskoy, Anna's cousin's wife. These people make fun of the other entourage, that surrounding the very Christian Lydia Ivanova. Vronsky, from the point of view of Betsy's set, is

> well aware that he ran no risk of appearing ridiculous in Betsy's eyes or in the eyes of fashionable people generally. He was well aware that in their eyes the role of disappointed lover of a young girl or of any single woman might be ridiculous; but the role of a man pursuing a married woman, who has made it the purpose of his life at all costs to draw her into adultery—that role had something fine and grand about it and could never be ridiculous. . . . (144)

Listening to the gay prattle of Baroness Shilton, a friend of Petritsky's, Vronsky reflects that

> In his Petersburg world people were divided into two quite distinct classes. One—the lower class—commonplace, stupid, and, above all, ridiculous people, who believed that a husband should live with the one woman to whom he was married, that young girls should be virtuous, women chaste, and men virile, self-controlled, and strong; that children should be brought up to earn their bread and pay their debts, and other such nonsense. These were the old-fashioned, ridiculous people. But there was another class: the real people, the kind to which his set belonged, in which the important thing was to be elegant, handsome, broad-minded, gay, and *ready to surrender unblushingly to every passion* and to laugh at everything else. (129; my italics)

Some of Vronsky's colleagues are described as is Gashvin: "a man not merely without moral principles but of immoral principles." Vronsky's own code of principles is clear, though it demonstrates the wilfull confusion of those of his class: gambling debts must be paid, but the tailor need not be; one must not lie to a man but one might to a woman; one must never cheat anyone but may a husband; one must never pardon an insult but may insult others oneself, and so on.

> These principles might be irrational and not good, but they were absolute and in complying with them Vronsky felt at ease and could hold his head high. (327)

His tragedy, however, is that his love for Anna takes him beyond the realm in which life can be operated by such principles, and he falls into such grave and committed love that he is presented with "doubts and difficulties for which he could find no guiding thread."

*   *   *

Dolly, of course, Kitty's sister and Oblonsky's wife, represents yet another perspective in the merry-go-round of differing modes of relationship in Tolstoy's novel. Indeed, the novel opens with her responding bitterly to her discovery of her husband's infidelity. Dolly remembers the early days of her marriage at Kitty's wedding, but reflects elsewhere on the common lot of women, who lose their attractiveness as they have child after child.

Ought Dolly to have been tolerant, as Stiva believes, since she must know he is no longer in love with her, and prefers ballet girls and other temporary indulgences? She indulges herself in fantasies of infidelity, as she travels to stay with Anna, where, in the well-appointed house of Count Vronsky, she feels humiliated by her patched and worn-out clothes. Yet when Anna reveals that she has prevented herself from having children, in order to preserve her figure for Vronsky, in order to keep him, Dolly is shocked. So, must she simply accept the common lot of married women? She is, in fact, a sad victim of the circumstances of bourgeois marriage and by no means a heroine of the novel.

Her most bitter reflections on these problems are made when she is traveling from Levin's house to Anna and Vronsky's mansion, where they are living as man and wife:

> At home, looking after the children, left her no leisure for reflection. So, now, during this four-hour drive, all the thoughts she had suppressed before rushed swarming into her brain, and she reviewed her whole life, from every aspect, as she had never done before. (636)

After some anxious reflections on the care of the children and the costs she contemplates the possibility of having another baby. ("Stiva, of course, there's no counting on.") Tolstoy says, "It occurred to her how untrue was the saying that woman's curse was to bring forth children in travail"—but as we follow Dolly's reflections it would seem rather that she is finding this true indeed:

> "The birth itself, that's nothing—it is the period of pregnancy that is torture," she thought, recalling her last pregnancy and the death of the baby. (637)

She recalls her shock at hearing a young peasant woman speaking of the death of her own baby as "freeing" her: she was shocked, but although she found it "cynical," "there was some truth in what the girl had said."

> "Yes, it comes to this," she thought, looking back over her fifteen years of married life, "nothing but pregnancy, sickness, mind dulled and indifferent to everything and, most of all—the disfigurement. Even Kitty, young and pretty as she is, has lost her looks, and when I'm with child I become hideous, I know. The birth, the agony, the hideous agonies, that last moment . . . then nursing the baby, the sleepless nights, the fearful pains. . . . " (Ibid.)

And Dolly recalls her sore nipples which she had in feeding every child. She remembers the children's illnesses, and the death of her last baby.

> "And what is it all for? . . . what agonies, just for that—my whole life ruined!"

She then turns to Anna and asks herself in what way is she better than her? "As least I have a husband I love—not as I should like to love him, but still I do love him, while Anna never loved hers." How is she to blame?

She wants to live: "*We were born with that need in our hearts.*" (639, my italics). It is in entering into that reflection himself that Tolstoy is able to present the tragedy of Anna Karenina.

Dolly reflects that she should have left Oblonsky when she found out his infidelity. Instead, she listened to Anna. She might instead have loved and been loved the right way. Is what she is doing now any better? She doesn't respect her husband, but he is necessary to her, and she puts up with him.

All kinds of passionate, impossible romances present themselves to Dolly's fantasy. She invents a romance identical with Anna's with an imaginary composite figure, "the ideal man who was in love with her."

> She saw herself, like Anna, making a clean breast of it to her husband, and Oblonsky's amazement and perplexity at this avowal made her smile. (Ibid.)

But neither Dolly's mischievous sense of humor nor her fancy can really alleviate her distress, and while he is sympathetic Tolstoy can offer no answers to her plight, anymore than he could supply answers for Anna.

Not that it is the task of the artist-writer to offer solutions: yet the novel *Anna Karenina* has an "upshot," even if it is not that of the moralist Tolstoy. It is that when a woman follows her impulse to "live" and not submit to the pains and indignities that Dolly suffers, she will inevitably come to be destroyed by the damage caused to her sense of her place in society, as it erodes her capacity to uphold her sense of identity and her authentic being. And while we admire and endorse Anna Karenina's courageous gesture, much as we admire Shakespeare's Cleopatra's, we cannot but feel that her self-destruction is inevitable, as real existence cannot contain such impulses to love on a higher plane, in defiance of the limitations of reality.

That Anna Karenina's passion is on a higher plane deepens her predicament. Society obviously had double standards here. For Stiva, Vronsky, and Betsy Tverskaya it was all right for them to have *affaires*—so long as they were not serious. Anna's *affaire* is a deeply serious one, and it was this that was unacceptable.

* * *

What is perhaps missing, if we approach the novel with insights derived from psychotherapy, is any indication of a *reason* for Anna's destructiveness. She has, after all, only been awakened from a marriage that has destroyed life in her, and it is life that she chooses: she is such a charming, beautiful, intelligent, and benign woman that it seems difficult to believe in her cruelty and ultimate madness, despite all the strains to which her social position puts her, despite her guilt and her anguish over Seriozha. We cannot deny that life does entrap individuals in such circumstances, and they do die or kill themselves: only, if one knows Tolstoy's theories about the dangers and destructiveness of sexual intercourse, one cannot help finding his presentation of Anna's final madness somewhat contrived, out of a theory of the inevitable consequences of sexuality. That is, it has something in it of propaganda, sustained by Schopenhauerian distortions and prejudice: as one critic (Dorothy Armstrong) says, he is in Anna also killing an aspect of himself—his own sexuality. He does not give us adequate grounds—an adequate etiology—for Anna to be that kind of person. It is as much a surprise to us as to her when she comes to feel that "side by side with the love that bound them there had grown up some evil spirit of discord, which she could not exorcise from his heart, and still less from her own" (739).

There are a number of recurrent links which are noticeable, if we know the book well:

> some strange spirit of evil held her back, as if the rules of warfare would not permit her to surrender. (738)

Psychologically penetrating is the novelist's rendering of the tendency in a loving couple when they quarrel, to be unwilling to retreat: but at the same time there is an evocation here of the "strange spirit of evil" that plagues Anna throughout the book—a dynamic that comes from Tolstoy's unconscious mind and from his strange paranoia.

There is a sense that while Anna is undoubtedly divided against herself the "evil" that haunts her is imposed by fate, as if she were being pursued by an evil spirit.

The presentation of Vronsky is more convincing:

> the realization of his desires brought him no more than a grain of sand out of the mountain of bliss he had expected. . . . (490)

He has made the "eternal error" that men make in imagining that "happiness consists in the realization of their desires" (pp. 490–91). He begins to feel a desire spring up in his heart for desires—ennui (491). This we may set, for its truth, alongside those views that have developed in psychotherapy, in its rejection of Freudian instinct theory. Our satisfaction is not to be found in the realization of our desires, but in finding our authenticity and whatever sense of meaning in existence we can achieve. The mere satisfaction of desires leads to ennui, indeed, Vronsky has a (sensual) hunger for satisfactions:

> As a hungry animal seizes upon everything it can get hold of in the hope that it may be food, so Vronsky quite unconsciously clutched first at politics, then at new books, then pictures. (Ibid.)

So, Vronsky finds his love for Anna, in the end, "burdensome" (697). He cannot turn round from his possession of her in all her beauty, and all their passion, to devote himself, secure in her love, to tasks that serve the rest of the world and contribute to it what each has gained from their love. Later, whenever he looks at Anna, he is aware of her beauty but divides himself from it:

> "Well, I'm very glad," he said, coldly surveying her, her hair and the dress which he knew she had put on for him. He liked and admired

it all, but he had admired her so often! And the stern, stony expression which she so dreaded settled on his face. (699)

Even as he declares to Anna, that "there is nothing I wish for
more than never to be parted from you"

the look that flashed in his eyes as he spoke the tender words was not
merely cold—it was the vindictive look of a man persecuted and
lashed to fury. (701)

Vronsky might be seen as a man who "loves women":

In her eyes Vronsky, with all his habits, ideas, desires—his whole spiritual and physical temperament—could be summed up in one thing—
love for women, and this love, which she felt ought to be wholly concentrated on her, was diminishing. . . . (772)

Yet despite his "love of women" Vronsky has only contempt for
Anna's attempt to educate her protégée Hannah, and for the education of women in general. The exchange over this provokes a
sharp and bitter passage between them (773).

Vronsky's love for women extends only to them as agents of
sensual satisfaction. Yet, of course, when he falls in love with Anna
he finds himself more deeply involved than he had ever found
himself, and becomes committed beyond all the conventional
views of his milieu. Even so, he falls short of rising sufficiently to
a level of noble being to be worthy of her.

* * *

The death of Anna is precipitated by the collapse of trust between her and Vronsky. In the process of this we perceive their
limitations. It is not only a matter of mutual narcissism, but of a
mutual incapacity to really meet as beings—a far more important
matter than mere sexual fulfillment, and a question that takes
one into the realm of authenticity. They cannot escape out of their
huis clos of love, into giving themselves to the world in a wider
sense. She becomes suspicious of his commitment to her, begins
to believe that he is succumbing to his mother's interest in
marrying him to the princess Sorokin. Much of this springs from
her frantic imaginings, but for whatever the reason the couple
begin to quarrel, and both notice the coldness in the eyes or the
face of the other, and are brought to reflect that their love is
turning to hate. And as their burning passion turns to hate, it
generates an inauthenticity. An example is the moment when

Vronsky conceals a telegram from Oblonsky. Oblonsky is doing his best to persuade Karenin to seek a divorce, though he has run into difficulties. He tends to fire off telegrams on occasions, and this is one of them: it arrives at a delicate moment between Anna and Vronsky

> "Who was your telegram from?" she asked, taking no notice of what he said.
> "From Stiva," he replied reluctantly.
> "Why didn't you show it to me? What secrets can Stiva have from me?"
> Vronsky called the valet back and told him to bring the telegram.
> "I didn't want to show it to you because Stiva has a passion for wiring. Why telegraph when nothing is settled?"
> "About the divorce?"
> "Yes, but he wires 'Could get nothing out of him. Promises definite answer soon.' But read it for yourself."
> Anna took the telegram with shaking fingers and saw exactly what Vronsky had said. But at the end were added the words: "little hope but will do everything possible and impossible".
> "I said yesterday that it is all the same to me when I get the divorce or whether I never get it," she said, flushing crimson. "There was not the slightest necessity to hide it from me."
> "If he conceals this, he can also conceal his correspondence with women, and probably does," she thought. (pp. 779–80)

Vronsky now talks to her with a tone of "cool composure" and this irritates her. We are shocked to perceive that this is now a couple who no longer trust one another. Anna is likely to fly into insane fits of jealousy and fear, with which Vronsky can only cope by cold indifference.

> "It's love, not the outward form that counts," she said. . . . "Oh, Lord, love again?" he thought, with a grimace. (780)

And when she asks why he should want "things to be definite," she asks:

> "Why should you want it?"
> He replies: "You know very well why—for your sake and that of the children we may have," he said.
> "We shan't have any."
> "That's a great pity," he said.
> "You want it for the sake of the children but you don't think of me, do you?" she pursued, quite forgetting or not having heard that he had said, "for *your* sake and that of the children."

The question of having children had long been a thorny subject of dispute. His desire to have children she interpreted as a proof of his indifference to her beauty.

"Oh, I said *for your sake*! Most of all for your sake," he repeated, his face contorted as though in pain, "because I am sure that a great deal of your irritability is due to the uncertainty of your position." (Ibid.)

This is a quite dreadful quarrel—virtually their last, and it is marked by hate and distrust, arising, characteristically, from problems arising from the possibility of children, pregnancy being a threat to her beauty and so to her hold on Vronsky: and from other complexities of their relationship to others and "society." Vronsky says that

"The indefiniteness consists in your imagining that I am free."

"As far as that goes, you can set your mind at rest," she said. . . . (781)

But the expression on his face shows her that he finds "her hand, her gesture, and the sound of her lips (as she sips her coffee) *repulsive*" (my italics).

On her part, she makes scathing references to Vronsky's mother (who, we know, despises Anna):

"A woman whose heart does not tell her where her son's happiness and honour lie has no heart." (Ibid.)

And Vronsky coldly tells her that she should not speak disrespectfully of his mother. (Elsewhere it is made plain that he has no great attachment to his mother: but it is a conventional point of tension, that a woman should not insult a man's mother.) She remembers, looking at him, every detail of his caresses, during their reconciliation the night before:

"Just such caresses he has lavished, and longs to lavish on other women," she thought.

"You don't love your mother! That's all talk, talk, talk!" she said, looking at him with hate in her eyes. (Ibid.)

At the end of the scene Vronsky shrinks from a reconciliation, and this time the breach is final: or, at least, there is one final brief exchange in which the last thing she says is:

"You . . . you will be sorry for this. . . ."

Tolstoy is perceptively aware of the way love can give way to hate—can turn itself into hate, the more even it is imbued with passion. And he is aware of the many levels of response between lovers, of which they are only partially aware, and cannot sometimes control. Anna is in terror of herself, in terror of her obsession with the thought that death is the only solution to an impossible situation. And predominant in that situation is the impossibility of holding onto any security in this relationship, when the questions of children, their name and paternity, cannot be solved. Anna's powers over Vronsky are in any case losing their effectiveness: for a long time her beauty has ceased to exact a compelling force on him. At the time when she was being insulted in the theater by Mme. Kartasov, Tolstoy writes:

> The poise of her head on her lovely, broad shoulders and the restrained excitement and brilliance of her eyes and her whole face reminded him of her just as he had seen her at the ball in Moscow. But he felt utterly different towards her beauty now. In his feeling for her now there was no element of mystery, and so her beauty, though it attracted him even more than before, gave him now a sense of injury. (pp. 575–76)

By degrees, the mystery goes, and the sense of injury grows, so that their love comes to turn to pain and hate. They have tried to live abroad; Vronsky has tried to become an artist, by taking up painting; he has built a hospital on his estate. But none of these impulses succeed, and these lovers cannot go out from their self-consuming love, to find a modus vivendi by going out to the rest of humanity. They are haunted by the sense that other people are suspicious and hostile, and that their alienation cannot be overcome. Because of their inability to relate to society, they are unable to find any sphere in which they can be reconciled and content, while Anna gradually becomes cut off from aspects of her reality she cannot bear to witness.

* * *

Heinz Kohut makes a crude distinction where Tolstoy is concerned, between tragic man and guilty man.* Tolstoy was at one stage of his life a moralizer, religious moralist, and philosopher: at others, when he was a novelist, he was "deeply in tune with the drama of human existence."

---

*Heinz Kohut, *The Search for the Self, Selected Writings,* ed. Paul Ornstein, 761ff.

The suggestion is that his moral concern inspired Tolstoy's art. But this does not solve the problem, because such a novel as *Anna Karenina* was only made possible by a deep underlying moral concern—a concern to pursue the truth about men and women, wherever the quest led. Take, for example, the moment at which Anna reveals to Vronsky that she is pregnant with their child. The portrayal of the inwardness of each character is one with great subtlety, and here we see that the problem is not only their failure with "society" but a failure to understand or "find" one another.

Vronsky has asked Anna what she is thinking of. Her hands are cold and her lips are quivering. Vronsky's mind is filled with his races, and Anna doubts whether she should tell him as he will find it difficult in such a mood to feel the gravity of her new situation.

> She did not answer and, bending her head a little, looked inquiringly at him from under her brows, her eyes shining beneath their long lashes. Her hand, toying with a leaf she had pulled off, shook. He noticed this and the look of humble, slavish devotion which so captivated her come over his face.

> "Yes, I should never forgive him if he did not realise all the gravity of it. Better not say anything. Why put him to the test?" she thought, still staring at him in the same way and feeling the hand which held the leaf trembling more and more.
> "For God's sake!" he repeated, taking her hand.
> "Shall I?"
> "Yes, yes, yes. . . ."
> "I am with child," she whispered slowly. (205)

Tolstoy is aware throughout of the paradox in these two of intimacy, of mutual attraction, and yet division—the fact that they belong to different worlds and have to struggle to understand one another. Anna, being a woman, wants this man to understand her predicament and to be grave about it: yet she doubts his capacity to rise to the occasion. He is aware that she is cold and trembling, and that he is in his mood of slavish devotion that captivates her. But their response remains divided.

> The leaf in her hand shook more violently but she did not remove her eyes from his face, watching to see how he would take her news. He turned pale, tried to say something but stopped, dropped her hand and sank his head on his breast. "Yes, he realizes the gravity of it," she thought, and gratefully pressed his hand.

But she was mistaken in thinking he realized the gravity of the fact as she, a woman, understood it. *Her words gave him that strange feeling of revulsion for someone with tenfold force.* But at the same time he realized that the turning-point for which he had been longing for was now near. . . . (pp. 205–6; my italics)

It is a bitter perception, that Vronsky's reaction would be "revulsion." (I am not clear of the meaning of the phrase "for someone with tenfold force," though I pick up the strength of that word "tenfold.")

The lovers argue over whether it is possible to unite their lives: but the reality of the fact that she is married to Karenin presses into the exchange:

"Oh, he does not even know," she said, and suddenly her face flushed a vivid red. Her cheeks, her forehead, her neck crimsoned, and tears of shame welled into her eyes. "But we won't talk of him." (206.)

Anna is evidently feeling a conflict of emotions (including shame at her own adultery) that are womanly, and beyond Vronsky's capacity to share or understand them. And in this division we have the seeds of their tragedy.

But the writer is open to what is happening on both sides, as he allows his drama to happen—without leaning on his text, to point a moral. Yet in his penetration to the truth of what is going on inside these characters, he is pursuing a deeper moral purpose, which is to find the truth of human nature, male and female, and to seek to find modes by which life may be lived between them.

* * *

The torment that Anna goes through is not merely a consequence of her awkward problem of her relationship to "society." It is a consequence of her division within herself. Soon after her seduction by Vronsky we learn that

She dreamed that she was the wife of both of them and that both lavished caresses on her. Alexei Alexandrovich was weeping, kissing her hands, and saying, "How happy we are now!" And Alexei Vronsky was there too, and he, too, was her husband. And she was marvelling that this had once seemed impossible to her, and she would explain to them, laughing, that it was ever so much simpler this way and that now both of them were contented and happy. But this dream weighed on her like a nightmare and she awoke from it in terror. (166)

When she is suffering from puerperal fever and near death she greets her husband with "her eyes gazing at him with such tender and ecstatic affection as he had never seen in them," and she cries:

> "Don't be surprised at me, I am still the same. But there is another woman in me, I'm afraid of her: it was she who fell in love with that man, and I tried to hate you, and I could not forget the self that had once been. I'm not that woman. Now I'm my real self, all myself. I'm dying now, I know I am; you ask him. . . ." (438)

She asks forgiveness, and Karenin gives it, but he is really deceived and later withdraws his forgiveness.

Oblonsky tries to persuade Anna at one point that "Nothing is so very terrible"—a characteristic Oblonsky attitude. He smiles at this point and, as Tolstoy says, "No one else in Oblonsky's place, having to do with such despair, would have ventured to smile . . . but in his smile there was so much kindness and almost feminine tenderness that it did not wound but soothed and calmed her" (Anna). Anna, however, replies:

> "No, Stiva," she said, "I'm lost, lost! Worse than lost! I'm not lost yet— I can't say that all is over: on the contrary, I feel that it's not ended. I'm like an overstrained violin string that must snap. But it's not ended yet . . . And the end will be terrible."

Oblonsky then tries a reasonable interpretation of her predicament:

> "you married a man twenty years older than yourself. You married him without love, or without knowing what love was. That was a mistake, let's admit it."
> "A fearful mistake!" said Anna.
> "But I repeat—it's an accomplished fact. Then you had, let us say, the misfortune to fall in love with a man not your husband. That was a misfortune, but that, too, is an accomplished fact. And your husband accepted it and forgave it. . . . That is how matters stand. . . ." (pp. 452–53)

Strangely, the consequence of this *terre-à-terre* account, putting an Oblonsky pragmatic account on the matter, is for Anna to become confused. When Oblonsky asks her whether she now wishes to live with her husband she says,

> "I don't know, I don't know at all."

And later adds that

> "I feel I'm flying headlong over some precipice, but ought not to save myself. And I can't."

and later still

> "There's nothing, nothing I wish . . . except for it to be all over." (453)

This death wish comes early to Anna, and deepens as her predicament seems to become increasingly insoluble, but also as her inner division against herself becomes more strained.

Oblonsky says at this point that "a divorce would solve everything." But Anna makes no reply to this assertion, and shakes her cropped head in dissent: Oblonsky sees in her face that she sees this as "unattainable happiness." And "unattainable happiness" makes a good motif for Anna's condition. Oblonsky's mission to Karenin, to urge a divorce, comes, of course, to nothing. He (Oblonsky) prides himself on his function as a "fixer."

> "What is the difference between me and a chemist? A chemist makes solutions and no-one is any the better—but *I* arranged a solution which makes three people happier. . . ." (458)

But it cannot be so easy as this, because of the deep divisions within Anna herself.

* * *

Vronsky's attitude to women, his particular posture, and his experience of a very different situation from any he has known before, are eventually made more clear.

This is largely taken up with a conversation with Serpuhovskoy, a prince who had been a playmate of Vronsky's childhood, and who was a man of the same set, the same coteries. Prince Serpuhovskoy had been Vronsky's comrade in the Corps of Pages, and has just returned from Central Asia, where he has been twice promoted and has won a distinction seldom awarded to so young a general.

He is regarded as a newly risen star of the first magnitude, even as Vronsky, as merely a cavalry captain, was allowed to remain as independent as he pleased—albeit beloved by a charming woman. "With her love," Vronsky reflects, "I cannot feel envious of Serpuhovskoy."

Serpuhovskoy has all the confident air of a successful man. He declares that he is glad he is ambitious: "that's my weakness and I confess to it." He tells Vronsky that men like him are needed by Russia: "what's wanted is a powerful party of independent men like you and me . . . Men who are difficult to buy. . . . " Vronsky, however, declares that he has lost his desire for power, "now." But "that *now* will not last for ever" declares Serpuhovskoy—meaning Vronsky's state of being in love with Anna Karenina. Vronsky hedges, saying only "maybe."

Serpuhovskoy challenges him: he does not believe Vronsky was right to allow himself to be passed over. He urges Vronsky to retire from the regiment and he will advance him.

> "But don't you see, I want nothing," said Vronsky, "except that things should remain as they are." (334)

Serpuhovskoy admits that Vronsky may have known more women than him.

> "But I am married and, believe me, in getting to know your wife, if one loves her, as someone has said, a man gets to know all women better than if he knew thousands of them." (Ibid.)

Women, declares Serpuhovskoy, are the chief stumbling block in a man's career. "It's difficult to love a woman and do anything. There's only one way of having love conveniently without it being a hindrance—and that is to marry."

Serpuhovskoy talks about tying the burden to oneself, in order to leave one's hands free: but Vronsky declares, "you have never loved."

Riding away, Vronsky is possessed by a feeling of a "joyous impression of life." He has put his affairs in order, he has a vague sense of Serpuhovsky's friendship and his flattery in considering a man that was needed, and most of all he is in anticipation of his rendezvous with Anna. We get here a glimpse of a level of egoistic sensuality in Vronsky, that goes with the limitations of his love—those limitations that lead to his downfall.

> This impression was so strong that he could not help smiling. He dropped his legs, crossed one leg over the other knee and, taking it in his hand, felt the springy muscle of his calf, where he had bruised it in his fall the day before, and then, leaning back, he drew several deep breaths.
> "Good, splendid," he said to himself. (336)

There is a certain sensual complacency about Vronsky, that brings him to be increasingly separated from Anna, because it stands in the way of a genuine understanding of her. (Serpuhovsky has warned him that "women are all more materialistic than men. We make something immense out of love, but they are always *terre-à-terre*. . . . " So, there are aspects of Anna's existence which Vronsky can never fathom, such as her love for Seriozha, and her sense of shame vis-à-vis her husband.)

Vronsky's love, although it goes far beyond what he expects, keeps something of complacent egoism in it:

> he had often had this sense of physical joy but he had never felt so fond of himself, of his own body, as at that moment. . . . The bright, cold August day which had made Anna feel so hopeless seemed exhilarating to him and refreshed his face and neck that still tingled after the drenching he had given them under the tap. The scent of brilliantine on his moustache struck him as peculiarly pleasant in the fresh air. Everything he saw through the carriage window, everything in that cold pure air, in the pale light of the sunset, was as fresh and jolly and vigorous as he was himself. . . . (Ibid.)

"I want nothing, nothing but this happiness," he thinks, as his imagination pictures Anna as he had seen her last time. When he sees her he drinks in with glad eyes "the special manner of walking, peculiar to her alone, the slope of her shoulders, the poise of her head; and at once a thrill ran through his body like an electric current:"

> with new intensity he felt *conscious of himself* from the elastic spring of his legs to the rise and fall of his lungs as he breathed, and *something set his lips twitching*. (337, my italics)

Anna's appearance has the purpose, to Vronsky, of making him pleased with himself. And even though Anna tells him what is for her momentous news—that she has told her husband—he does not understand it as she does:

> she was reading his thoughts from his face. She could not guess that the expression arose from the first idea that presented itself to him— that a duel was now inevitable. The possibility of a duel had never crossed her mind, and so she put a different interpretation on this fleeting look of severity . . . the news had not produced the effect she had expected in him: he only looked as though he were resenting some affront. . . . (pp. 337–38)

So, there develops a sense between Anna and Vronsky that they do not know one another. When Vronsky is alarmed that someone is coming who might know them, Anna cries, "Oh, I don't care."

and he fancied that her eyes looked with *strange malevolence at him from under her veil.* (338, my italics)

He is contemplating the duel he feels sure he will have to fight, and remembering Serpuhovskoy's warnings about tying himself down, while also being aware that he could not tell Anna this thought.

She knew that whatever he might say to her, he would not say all he thought. And she knew that her last hope had failed her. This was not what she had been reckoning on. (339)

She protests that there is one thing, and one thing only—his love, and she tries to say she is proud of this, but "tears of shame and despair" choke her and she stands still and sobs. Vronsky is conscious of a smarting in his nose and something swelling in his throat and for the first time in his life feels on the point of weeping. He even feels he is to *blame* for her wretchedness; *"that he had done wrong."* And they part with Anna with her foreboding that everything would remain as it was had not deceived her. There is an ominous note to this chapter, not least because Vronsky's self-absorption, despite his being drawn to understand Anna and to feel blame for what he has done to her, makes it impossible for him to understand her—as Levin understands Kitty. There are barriers even in their preoccupation with "happiness" and in their inability to come to terms with the reality of their situation. In many respects, though he is thought of as a manly man, and although he brings "life" to Anna as Karenin cannot, Vronsky is a limited man, and his self-preserving egoism emerges more and more as a barrier to their future: though it has to be said it is difficult to conceive what their future might have been, to guarantee the survival of their relationship.

* * *

A most significant piece of symbolism in *Anna Karenina* is that of Vronsky's accident with his horse. There is a link in terms of unconscious symbols between Vronsky's accident in the point-to-point race, and his relationship to Anna. He goes to see Anna unannounced just before the race. This is a crucial moment in the story, because many things come together: Anna reveals to Vronsky that she is with child: she tells her husband that Vronsky is her lover and that she hates him, Karenin: Vronsky is told he should keep calm before the race, but he does everything that might be supposed to disturb him. And so, just as he reaches the last fence in this race that is so important to him and makes him the cynosure of all eyes, he fails to keep in sympathy with the bodily movements of the mare, and in essence, kills her. In this is symbolized the particular failure of both Vronsky and Anna to be in touch with reality—including the reality of one another—and its fatal consequences.

When Anna tells him she is with child, she is mistaken over his response:

> She was mistaken in thinking he realized the gravity of the fact as she, a woman, understood it. *Her words gave him that strange feeling of revulsion for someone with tenfold force.* . . . (206; my italics)

He realizes that they must now face the reality of their situation in a new way: but the impact of the revelation has a deeper impact. And so, he is bitterly resentful, when he realizes how he has destroyed his own horse, by an inadequate response to her.

> His face distorted with passion, pale, and with lower jaw trembling, Vronsky kicked her in the belly with his heel and again fell to tugging at the rein. (218)

She gazes at her master with eloquent eyes: and Vronsky cries: "What have I done? . . . And it was my own shameful unforgiveable fault!"

The mare's response to Vronsky makes the parallel with his woman even more clear.

> Vronsky cast another look at the exquisite lines of his favourite mare, who was quivering all over, and tearing himself with an effort from the sight of her, he went out of the stable. . . . (210)

Only a few pages back, Vronsky has paid his unarranged visit to Anna:

> He was thinking of one thing only—that he would see her directly, not merely in his imagination but living, all of her, as she was in reality. . . . (203)

And this moment follows chapter 21 in which he visits Frou-Frou, the mare, against the wishes of his English trainer.

> Her whole appearance, and in particular her head, was spirited yet gentle. She was one of those creatures who seem as if they would certainly speak if only the mechanism of their mouths allowed them to.
>
> To Vronsky, at any rate, it seemed that she understood all he was feeling while he looked at her.
>
> "Oh, you beauty, you!" said Vronsky, moving up to the mare and trying to soothe her.
> But the nearer he came the more excited she grew. (pp. 199–200)

He strokes the horse, and the horse gives a start.

> "Quiet, sweet, quiet!" he said, stroking her flank again; and in the happy knowledge that his mare was in the best possible condition he left the horse-box.
> The mare's excitement had infected Vronsky. He felt the blood rushing to his heart and that, like the horse, he, too, wanted to move about and attack. *It was a sensation both disgraceful and delicious.* (200; my italics)

Vronsky is a sensualist and appreciates beautiful, well-groomed, and elegant creatures, like Frou-Frou and Anna. There is an element of narcissism in this: his delight in the horse is a delight in a possession that extends to his ego. It is another facet of the same appreciation of his own body that Vronsky enjoys. At the same time, Vronsky is now beyond the customary bounds of an ordinary love affair. Storming inwardly about the attitudes of his brother and his mother, he thinks:

> "If it were an ordinary, vulgar, society intrigue, they would have let me alone. They feel that this is something different, that it is not a mere pastime, that this woman is dearer than life to me. That is incomprehensible, and therefore it annoys them. . . . They haven't the remotest idea of what happiness is; they don't know that without our love, for us there is neither happiness nor unhappiness—there would be no life at all. . . ." (201)

At the same time, in his heart, he felt that they were all of them right. The love which bound him to Anna was not a momentary infatuation that would pass. It was a tormented situation in which they had to conceal their love, lie, and deceive, "when the passion which united them was so intense that they were both oblivious of everything but their love."

He remembers both the *shame* he has detected in Anna, and the necessity for deceit and lies.

> And he experienced the strange feeling which had sometimes come upon him since his liaison with Anna. *It was a feeling of revulsion against something*; against Karenin, against himself, or the whole world—he hardly knew which. But he always drove away this strange feeling. (202; my italics)

It is this "strange feeling" at which he is protesting when, in passion, he kicks his broken horse in the belly: it is in one sense a protest against the unknown forces of being—as with Anna's pregnancy—but also a protest against the reality of the world and of his vulnerability, and the ominous nature of the mysterious love that consumes himself and Anna, which is going to lead to her death and his extinction, by its all-consuming sensual fire.

On the other hand, their love is also *life*. Anna declares:

> "I unhappy?" she said, drawing near him and gazing at him with a rapturous smile of love. "I feel like a starving man who has been given food. He may be cold, his clothes may be in rags, and he may feel ashamed, but he is not unhappy. I unhappy? No, this is my happiness. . . ." (208)

We do not learn much about the original circumstances of Anna's marriage to Karenin, which has lasted seven years. While Anna seems at one point content to return to her everyday marriage, it is clear that she is unawakened by it. Karenin finds that his wife's capacity to fall in love with someone else is "life."

> he felt face to face with something illogical and irrational, and he did not know what to do. Karenin was face to face with life—with the possibility of his wife's loving somebody else—and this seemed to him very irrational and incomprehensible because it was life itself. All his life he had lived and worked in official spheres, having to do with the reflection of life. And every time he had come up against life itself he had stepped aside. . . . (158)

In fact, in this novel, we perceive Karenin almost saved by being claimed for life, when he experiences the agony of Anna's near-death in childbirth. There is a moment when Anna's dream of being loved by both her husband and lover comes true: but it is afterward spoiled by Karenin's taking refuge in the spurious affection of Lydia Ivanovna—spurious because she had such a vainglorious view of herself as an agent of Christian virtue.

Karenin, on his part, we know to be a man who fears the emotional life—indeed, fears life. He is characteristically totally thrown by any indication of distress, as when a woman begins to cry in his presence—a feature of which Tolstoy makes good use, as when Vronsky begins to weep as Anna lies dying in her puerperal fever, and at other moments.

We learn this aspect of Karenin's personality early, as he begins to ponder the fact that his wife is taking an unusual interest in another man: "As he thought it over, he grudged having to expend his time and intellect on such domestic matters" (160). He is that kind of man, who in his capacity to distract himself from questions of being, loses himself in male activity and intellectual abstraction, to avoid being confronted by "life." He talks a lot about duties and responsibilities, but never accepts his own responsibility, to try to understand his wife—or, indeed, to understand himself. He is also making abstractions about his own experiences: of his conclusion about Anna's conscience Tolstoy says, he was "feeling relieved at having found the category of regulating principles to which the newly arisen situation rightly belonged" (161).

Anna's tragedy is that, having become bound to a husband of this kind, she falls into a passionate relationship with a man who does not understand her much better. At the moment of her first seduction Vronsky declares, "I can never forget what is life itself to me. For one moment of happiness like this. . . ." (166)—and although he becomes as serious as he is capable of being, we feel a certain shallowness in Vronsky's view of "life," and that (as Theodore Redpath avers) he is not worthy of Anna.

*   *   *

One aspect of human nature about which Tolstoy is superb, is the way people can avoid thinking about the more disturbing aspects of their lives. As Anna and Vronsky enter upon the first stages of their adulterous liaison, of course, they have to become deceitful, and this becomes mingled with their capacity to deceive themselves about their situation.

As well as this, they are reminded from time to time by feelings described as "inexplicable" of areas of feeling over which they have no control. And the accident with Frou-Frou the mare reminds

Vronsky, too, of areas of his own existence and character over which he has no control: when he drops back into the saddle in a clumsy movement the dreadful blunder is said to happen "for some inexplicable reason."

And of course he and Anna are continually having dreams whose symbolism relates to their predicament—the sources of which are also inexplicable (and, indeed, would seem at times, so to speak, to come from Tolstoy's unconscious mind).

From time to time Vronsky is troubled by an "inexplicable revulsion"—not least by the presence of Seriozha who is puzzled by his presence and who has a scrutinizing, inquiry "and to some extent hostile expression" when he looks at him.

Seriozha is the embodiment of the fatal flaw in their love, since it is impossible for it to be reconciled with circumstances, fate, and society. Anna loves her firstborn boy and yearns to keep him with her: yet her attachment to Vronsky will divide her from him forever.

> The child, with his innocent outlook on life, was the compass which showed them the degree to which they had departed *from what they knew but did not want to know.* (204; my italics)

The problem becomes even more complicated when Anna confesses that she is with child by Vronsky and her words give him "a strange feeling of revulsion . . . with tenfold force."

He hopes now to put an end to their continual need to exercise deceit. But this is easier said than done, and Anna mocks him: "Am I not the wife of my husband?" And though she dismisses her husband ("I never think of him. He doesn't exist.") and declares, "Oh, he does not even know," she is still full of shame:

> Suddenly her face flushed a vivid red. Her cheeks, her forehead, her neck crimsoned, and tears of shame welled into her eyes. . . . (206)

Maliciously, she admits that one alternative is to become Vronsky's mistress, but that this would be intolerable:

> "Yes," she went on, "become your mistress and complete the ruin of. . . . "
> Again she was going to say "my son", but could not utter the word. (208)

And she speaks of the "degradation" and the "horror" of her position. She says she feels sorry that she has "ruined your whole life on my account," and he replies that he "cannot forgive myself that you are unhappy." But the ambiguity of their situation is brought out by her reply, which has just been quoted, about her feeling like a starving man who has been given food.

And she makes an assignation, to receive him at 1:00 in the morning, to make love.

This tryst hangs over the race, in Vronsky's mind: as he gallops about to his appointments he thinks of "the blissful meeting awaiting him that night." Yet, his ghastly error with the mare, even as he feels completely self-possessed and confident, is ominous. At the beginning of the race Tolstoy writes, "From the first instant Vronsky was master neither of himself nor the mare" (215) and in the end he commits a "shameful" and "unforgiveable" offense against this creature, whose form and beautiful eloquent eyes are described as if she were a woman. Yet in the end Vronsky is kicking her in the belly and cannot understand why she does not rise to her feet: her back is broken.

We may detect behind this powerful sequence the same element we find behind D. H. Lawrence's scene with Gerald on his horse in *Women in Love,* struggling to control it as a goods train passes: the primal scene. Tolstoy believed that sex was dangerous, even murderous, and Vronsky's error with the mare at the culminating moment of their race is an act of murder: when he kicks the dying horse in the belly we may suspect an unconscious impulse attributed to Vronsky by Tolstoy of hatred and hostility toward the pregnant Anna, and a recognition that her pregnancy deepens the disastrous predicament in which they find themselves.

Yet, even as Vronsky is reported to be safe after the accident, the focus of the distress felt by Anna becomes whether or not Vronsky will come to her that night!

> "Is he killed or not? Is it true what they said? Will he come or not? Shall I see him tonight?" she was thinking. (230)

Her despair when Vronsky fell is felt by her husband to have been "unbecoming," and he on his part is unable to grasp the true reality of his situation: when he sees her smile "with a pretence of irony" he supposes that she is going to tell him that his suspicions are ridiculous.

Instead, out of despair, she tells him the truth:

> "You were not mistaken. I was, and I could not help being in despair. I listen to you, but I am thinking of him. I love him, I am his mistress;

I cannot endure you, I am afraid of you, and I hate you . . . you can do what you like with me." (231)

She bursts into tears, and, since Karenin cannot face tears in anyone, his "whole face suddenly assumed the solemn immobility of the dead." When they reach their villa she looks at her watch.

> She had three hours to wait, and the memories of their last meeting fired her blood.
> "Heavens, how light it is! It's dreadful but I do love to see his face and I do love this fantastic light. . . ." (232)

Anna, clearly, is two women: and at this moment, when she has made this desperate declaration to her husband, she is also yearning for her sexual tryst with Vronsky. But he, too, has had experience of this kind of duplicity: he has tried to get her to consider her position,

> and each time he had encountered the same superficiality and lightness of judgement. . . . It was as though there were something in it which she could not or would not face, as though directly she began to speak of it she, the real Anna, retreated to somewhere inside herself and another woman appeared, a stranger to him, whom he did not love and whom he feared, and who was in opposition to him. . . . (206–7)

Anna's duplicity, of course, plays all kinds of tricks with her husband, before her declaration which was just quoted. There is a moment before the race, and after her promise to Vronsky to receive him at 1:00 A.M., when suddenly she hears Karenin's carriage arriving. "How unfortunate!" she exclaims to herself. "Can he be going to stay the night?"

> and the consequences that might result therefrom struck her as so awful and terrible that, without a moment's hesitation, she went to meet him with a gay and smiling face; and *conscious of the presence within her of the already familiar spirit of falsehood and deceit*, she immediately abandoned herself to it, and began talking, hardly knowing what she was saying. (223; my italics)

To Karenin she says, "How nice! . . . You are staying the night I hope. . . ." These, say Tolstoy, "were the first words the devil of deceit prompted her to utter." She talks too much, however, at this interview: talking "lightly, rapidly, and with a peculiar brilliance in her eyes." Karenin does not notice, but "never afterwards could

Anna recall this brief scene without an agonising pang of shame" (p. 224)

At the end of the scene Karenin kisses her hand, and she becomes "conscious of the spot on her hand that his lips have touched and gave a shudder of revulsion." Sexual relations between Anna and Karenin must have ceased some time ago, and this is a critical moment in all three lives: but the internal forces in all three must be tearing them apart. Here, Anna is shown as the deceitful, sensual, and evil woman whom Tolstoy regarded as so destructive, determined to enjoy her sexual pleasure, no matter who was destroyed in the process. And every move she makes focuses on the one end—her ecstasy in the night with Vronsky.

*   *   *

The courtship and marriage of Constantine Levin and Kitty is, of course, set against the story of the passionate relationship between Vronsky and Anna, in order to try to define marriage. The story of Levin is close to Tolstoy's own marriage, and much of the material is autobiographical, as we know. The use of these two couples, in the diagram of the novel, is not unlike the contrast between Birkin and Ursula on the one hand and Gerald and Gudrun on the other, in D. H. Lawrence's *Women in Love*: maybe, indeed, the pattern of that book may have been inspired by Tolstoy's. Birkin "is," in the same way, his author, and this lends a certain touch of realism, as in the chapter in which Ursula throws his ring at him: but also makes possible some serious misrepresentation, as indeed in that very chapter, in which Birkin becomes a "son of God" and exerts a triumphant mastery over the woman. With Levin, however, the autobiographical element does not lead to distortion so much as to several passages in which we become involved in incidents and reflections in which Tolstoy was intensely interested—but which we may find tedious: for instance, the passages about going snipe-shooting, the passages about farming and farm organizing (though the episode in which Levin enjoys mowing with his peasants is magnificent), and the passages in which Levin contemplates the meaning of his life, in a rather heavy and desperate philosophical fashion. But, again, one has to say that in portraying his love and his need for love in relation to the problem of the meaning of existence is often marvelously done—as, for instance, when Levin is made to take confession before his wedding, or when he fears for his wife and infant in the storm at the end.

As in *War and Peace*, however, one senses that Tolstoy's view of women is that their role and duty is to serve the family—to have a number of children, to provide comfort and solace for their husbands, and to subdue their lives and interests to the home: Natasha in *War and Peace* becomes a characteristic Russian house-wife and mother to Pierre, while there is also a marked contrast between the vivacious Kitty in the skating episode at the beginning of *Anna Karenina* and the mother so deeply involved in family life at the end, so subservient to her husband's interests in running his estate. The one episode in which one gets the sense of Kitty asserting her equality and independence is when she insists on going with her husband to nurse his dying brother, knowing as she does that he will be helpless in that situation. But there is a sense at the end that while Levin goes on pondering the stars and the possibility of the meaning of life, Kitty is much simpler, more *terre-à-terre*, like Dolly, and absorbed in the minutiae of daily chores:

> The lighting showed her his face distinctly, and seeing that he was calm and happy she smiled at him.
>
> "She understands," he thought. "She knows what I am thinking about. Shall I tell her or not? Yes, I will. . . . " But just as he opened his mouth to speak she turned to him first.
>
> "Oh, Kostya, be nice and go and see if Sergei Ivanich will be comfortable in the corner room. I can't very well go myself. See if they're put the new washstand in."
>
> "Very well, I'll go directly," said Levin, straightening up and kissing her.
>
> "No, I'd better not speak of it," he thought, as she passed in before him. "It's a secret for me alone, of vital importance for me, and not to be put into words. . . ." (pp. 852–53)

Of course, we have no sense that Kitty will lose her looks, so that Levin loses his interest in her: he finds the possibility that he could ever have relationship with another woman incomprehensible: his and Kitty's love is sub specie aeternitatis, and as such it is in complete contrast to the egoistic love of Anna and Vronsky, in which the woman becomes desperately anxious that the only things that "hold" her man is her beauty and sensuality, and the fear is that he will tire of both. And it is in complete contrast to the comfortably compromised relationship of Kitty's sister Dolly, who has lost her attractiveness through childbearing, whose husband has ceased to love her, and who had to make do as best she can, with her children, whom she adores (but is anxious about their characters) and with her good-natured but hopelessly indulgent and unfaithful husband.

Levin has an all-or-nothing attitude to his love: Oblonsky recognizes this early on:

> He knew that feeling of Levin's so well—that, for Levin all the girls in the world were divided into two classes: one class included all the girls in the world except Kitty, and they had all the human weaknesses and were very ordinary girls: while Kitty was in a class by herself, without the least imperfection and above all the rest of humanity. (51)

To Levin, whether Kitty will have him is "a question of life or death" for him. He declares,

> "it's not love. I have been in love, but this is not the same thing. It's not my feeling, but a sort of force outside myself has taken possession of me. . . ." (52)

Levin is also obsessed with his own unworthiness:

> "it is awful when we—who are already getting on in years—we have a past . . . not of love but of sins . . . are suddenly close to a pure innocent creature! It is loathsome, and that is why one can't help feeling oneself unworthy." (Ibid.)

Oblonsky declares that Levin cannot have much on his conscience.

> "Alas, all the same," said Levin, "all the same, looking back on my life, 'I tremble, and bitterly I curse the day I was born. . . .' Yes."
> "What's to be done? The world is made that way," said Oblonsky. (Ibid.)

Oblonsky is a great placater of consciences: later in talking to Anna and Karenin he seeks to minimize trouble, and, of course, is most indulgent of his own misdemeanors. But Levin wants Kitty—long before she knows of his intentions—to forgive him, in the spirit of Christ: "Pardon me not according to my deserts but according to Thy loving kindness" (Ibid.)

* * *

Levin idealizes Kitty: he goes to meet her at the skating rink with a beating heart. Everything he sees around him seems in tune with his excited mood:

It was a bright, frosty day. At the gates there were rows of carriages, sleighs, drivers, and policemen. Well-dressed people, with their hats shining in the sunlight, crowded about the entrance and along the well-swept little paths between the little old-fashioned Russian chalets with their carved eaves. The old curly birch-trees in the gardens, their branches all laden with snow, looked as though they had been freshly decked in sacred vestments. (40)

The spot where Kitty stands "seemed to him unapproachable holy ground" and there is a moment when he nearly turns away, "so filled with awe was he."

He walked down, for a long while averting his eyes from her, as though she were the sun, but seeing her, as one sees the sun, without looking. (41)

Kitty is pleased to see him, but becomes increasingly puzzled by his state of agitation, and by the confused hints in the things he says to her. Levin has carried an image of her in his heart, but the real Kitty transports him:

When he thought about her, he could conjure up a vivid picture of her whole appearance and especially the charm of the little fair head, poised so lightly on the shapely girlish shoulders, and the expression of child-like serenity and goodness. That child-like innocence of expression, together with the slender beauty of her figure, made up her special charm, which he always remembered; but what struck him afresh every time was the look of her gentle, tranquil, honest eyes and, above all, her smile, which never failed to transport him into some enchanted world, where his heart softened and he felt full of peace— as he remembered feeling on rare occasions in his early childhood. (42)

It is interesting to note the repetition of the word little, both in the description of the scene, and of Kitty: it seems to have been a significant feature of the attitude of the nineteenth-century novelist (like Dickens and Tolstoy) to find attributes of women they admired described by the word little: it also seems to be an attractive aspect of a woman that she was childlike, and brought to man's soul the kind of peaceful feelings he knew in childhood (where his feelings about women were those of his response to his mother). Presumably the strange humiliation that Levin and Kitty experience in the first months of their marriage arises from the experience of behavior that is *not* childlike. The ideal woman seems to have been an "innocent" woman. One cannot, of course, idealize the woman with whom one has had sexual intercourse in the way Levin idealizes Kitty in these opening chapters.

I do not want to deny that a young lover may feel like Levin toward Kitty (whom we learn he has called "Tiny bear" when he was staying with the Schcherbatsky family). The Levins and the Schcherbatskys belonged to the old nobility of Moscow and have always been on intimate and friendly terms. Levin went to college with the young prince, brother to Dolly and Kitty: Levin has fallen in love with the family. He had been deprived of family life by the death of his own father and mother and so he enjoyed that of the Schcherbatskys, in which, especially the feminine half, "appeared to him as though wrapped in some mysterious, poetic veil. . . . " behind which are "the loftiest sentiments and every possible perfection" (34). He was "in love with the very mystery" of their household. Levin first fell in love with Dolly, before she married Oblonsky: then with Natalie, before she married a diplomat. At last, he realized which of the sisters he was really destined to love—the girl who had been a child when he went to college.

> Levin was in love and therefore Kitty seemed to him so perfect in every respect, a being above all earthly beings, while he himself was so earthly and insignificant a creature that there could be no hope of his seeming worthy of her, by others or by himself. (35)

So, after seeing Kitty every day, in society, which he began to frequent in order to meet her, Levin decided that the union was impossible, and went back to the country. He felt she could not love him—he was a fellow without talent, merely spending his time living and working on his estates.

> The mysterious, enchanting Kitty could not love such a dull fellow as he believed himself to be, a man so ordinary and undistinguished. Besides, his former attitude to Kitty—that of a grown-up person to a child . . . seemed to him an additional obstacle in love's path. (Ibid.)

He himself "could not have loved any but beautiful, mysterious, exceptional women." But in leaving Kitty for so long, he had made a serious mistake: and now he comes back to Moscow to make her an offer, by which time she is bewitched by Vronsky. Kitty is only eighteen. Vronsky has no intention of marrying her, but Kitty's mother is pleased by his attentions, and expects her to make a brilliant match. The old prince is disgusted by his wife's matchmaking, and for Levin the situation is disastrous.

*   *   *

So, how do we account for the creation of this enigmatic, out-standing novel? In the event, the novel does not convey the "message" or "upshot" that Tolstoy intended. He said, "In *Anna Karenina* I love the idea of the family." There are several drafts of the novel: in the earlier ones, as we have seen, the characters are quite different: in the final version they virtually reverse their original qualities and characteristics, and the "upshot" becomes complex and not at all straightforward. What power was it, that overturned the original moralizing impulse that made Tolstoy start out on this endeavor, and generated a great work of art?

The answer can perhaps be best found in the scene in which Dolly goes to visit Anna at Vozdvizhenskoe, and reflects on her plight and on Anna's love affair and discusses her situation with her. It is true that at the end Dolly thinks "her own home and children rose in her imagination with a new and peculiar charm":

> So sweet and precious did her little world now seem that she would not on any account spend another day away from it. . . . (672)

It is also true that at the end of this section, the feelings she has aroused in Anna she knows to have "belonged to the better part of herself, which was fast becoming smothered by the life she was leading" (673)—so, Anna is falling into false solutions.

But the episode itself, and Dolly's reflections, do not at all bear out Tolstoy's insistence that in *Anna Karenina* he was "loving" the idea of the family. The family rather appears as a *faute de mieux*—as perhaps the best one can expect in this life, given the evil nature of man's sexual propensities. But we sense a different perception coming through—the eye of the artist who is capable of confronting the truth of circumstances on the one hand, while perceiving the deepest and primary human needs at the same time, notably the need for authenticity. This generates a completely different conclusion from what Tolstoy originally intended.

Dolly has a four-hour journey during which to reflect:

> all the thoughts she had suppressed before rushed swarming into her brain, and she reviewed her whole life, from every aspect, as she had never done before. Even to herself her thoughts seemed strange. (636)

First the worries about her children, and the forthcoming need to move into another flat in Moscow. Might she have another baby? A young peasant-woman has said to her that she was glad her child had died ("God set me free. . . ."). Rather curiously, Dolly is said to think:

how untrue was the saying that woman's curse was to bring forth
children in travail. (637)

Untrue? Here, obviously, we are at the heart of Tolstoy's anguish,
around the experience of pregnancy and childbirth that cut his
mother off from him, at the time of his greatest need, with all
the ambiguity that followed, in his soul.
Dolly reflects,

> "The birth itself, that's nothing—it's the period of pregnancy that is
> torture. . . ." (Ibid.)

Looking back over fifteen years of married life, she sees

> "nothing but pregnancy, sickness, mind dulled and indifferent to
> everything and, most of all, the disfigurement . . . when I'm with child
> I become hideous, I know. . . ." (Ibid)

She reflects on her pain from sore nipples, during feeding; the
children's illnesses, their "nasty tendencies," and the death of her
last baby.

> "And what is it all for? What will come of it all? Here am I . . . unbear-
> able to my husband.
> So I shall go on for the rest of my life, producing a lot of unfortu-
> nate, badly-brought up, penniless children . . . what agonies, what toil,
> just for that—my whole life ruined!" (638)

She feels that everyone else is enjoying life except her:

> "And they are all down on Anna! What for? Am I any better than
> she is? I at least have a husband I love—not as I should like to love
> him, but still I do love him, while Anna never loved hers. How is she
> to blame? *She wants to live. We were born with that need in our hearts.*"
> (639; my italics)

The last two sentences come from the vision of the great artist.
Despite all Tolstoy's complex hang-ups about making love to a
pregnant woman or to a nursing woman: despite his own tyranny
to his own wife, despite his explicit contempt and hostility for
women at large, his demon as artist accepts that *women need to
live*—they know, at the level of being, when their relationships in
life fall below their existential fulfillment: "we were born with that
need in our hearts."

Dolly reflects that she should not have accepted Anna's counseling when she found out about Oblonsky's infidelity: "I ought to have left my husband then, and started life afresh. Then I might have loved and been loved the real way."

> Is what I am doing any better? I don't respect him. *He's necessary to me.* (Ibid.; my italics)

She wants to look in a mirror to ponder the degree to which she is still attractive, but dare not, because of the possibility of being seen by the coachman or by her escort.

What Dolly reflects upon is the inauthenticity of her own position, in her reconciliation with Oblonsky, who goes on spending money (having sold her forest for much less than it was worth), pursuing his inclination to indulge himself as a bachelor as by his womanizing, and by merely maintaining his relationship to Dolly for his own comfort and peace of mind. She has massively compromised, while Oblonsky simply does not make the connections he ought to make, between his egoistic fantasies and his wife's wretchedness. Despite his perpetual geniality, Oblonsky is a total failure as a man and as a "family man": so in what sense can this novel be said to be a manifestation of devotion to the "family"?

Dolly comforts herself with romantic fantasies: she thinks of possible affairs—with Koznyshev, with Turovtsyn, with another younger man: "all sorts of passionate, impossible romances presented themselves to her fancy." She decides that "Anna did quite right," and ends up daydreaming of a love affair for herself on the lines of Anna's, with an "ideal man who was in love with her":

> She saw herself like Anna, making a clean breast of it to her husband, and Oblonsky's amazement and perplexity at this avowal made her smile. (Ibid.)

But the truth is that Dolly cannot extract herself from her predicament anymore than Anna: her personal life is at a pretty low level, sunk to a miserable compromise, for the sake of the "family": and she here reflects on the price to be paid.

So what can a woman do? There follow two serious conversations between Dolly and Anna. Dolly is impressed by the high life that Anna can lead—the luxurious rooms, the well-organized household, the new hospital, the lawn tennis, Anna's flirtation with Veskovky, and her handsome and courteous lover. At last, she is alone with Anna and can talk: of Anna's treatment of Kitty, by allowing Vronsky to fall in love with her, Anna says:

"I was not to blame. And who is to blame? What does being to blame mean? Could things have been otherwise?" (666)

The artist allows this point of view to exist, as the moralist could not. Indeed, the novel as tragedy emerges from this artist's sense that things could not have been otherwise. The deepest needs to fulfill oneself lie behind events and relationships as they develop, and so fate draws individuals into impossible situations. It is the true creative eye, that sees this enigma: the moralist (the kind of novelist who could write the moral tale that Leavis tries to turn *Anna Karenina* into) could not.

In her private conversation with Dolly, Anna reveals her more intimate self. She resents Vronsky's freedom and independence, and fears "living alone without him, alone. . . ." ("Everything goes to show that it will often happen. . . ."). "Of course. . . ." she declares, "I won't try to keep him by force. . . ."

This theme is another which arises from Tolstoy's eccentric attitudes to man-woman relationships: his couples suffer agonies over letting the other go—Levin continually debates his "freedom" with himself, is accused of being under "petticoat government," and both he and Vronsky are aware of a clash between their absence on civic duties and their need to be with their women. This problem eventually leads to that coldness in Vronsky, that prompts Anna's final derangement and suicide.

It is surely abnormal for men and women to be so disturbed by mere physical absence? Does it not suggest a profound overdependence in Tolstoy himself, that he sees it as a major problem? Of course, it enables him to dramatize Anna's anxieties about "keeping" Vronsky, when he is not married to her and so has no legal ties to her. But in normal relationships, surely, the partners feel they have taken the other sufficiently into themselves, to endure actual physical separation with less stress than Tolstoy's main protagonists (Oblonsky seems to cherish separation from Dolly, on the other hand). (A related idiosyncracy is the distress Levin feels over the flirtatiousness of Veskovsky with Kitty: but no doubt here Tolstoy is writing from his own personal experience, again.)

Dolly and Anna move on to discuss Vronsky's anxiety, that any children he has by Anna will not bear his name:

"What children?" asked Anna, half closing her eyes and not looking at Dolly.
  "Ani, and others that will come."
  "He can be easy on that score: I shall have no more children."
  "How can you say that—how can you tell that you won't?"
  "I shan't, because I don't wish it."

"The doctor told me after my illness. . . ." (668)

Tolstoy doesn't go into details, presumably to avoid disturbing readers at the time, but this must be a reference to the use of a sponge or some other contraceptive system. (Since Vronsky doesn't know about it it can't mean coitus interruptus.) Dolly, grasping the implication with surprise, reflects that she must "reflect a great, great deal upon it": but she does not appreciate the relational implications—that Anna has not discussed the problem with Vronsky (who is later shocked to find that Anna has decided not to have anymore children).

> This discovery . . . aroused so many ideas, reflections, and contradictory emotions, that she was unable to say anything, and could only stare at Anna wide-eyed with amazement. . . . (Ibid.)

She had been reflecting on the problem of continual childbearing, but now she learned it was a possibility, she is horrified: "*N'est-ce pas immoral?*" she says.

Anna declares she has two alternatives: "either to be with child, that is, an invalid, or to be the friend and companion of my husband—practically my husband." There may be reasons for others to hesitate

> "but for me . . . remember, I am not his wife: he loves me as long as he loves me. And how am I to keep his love? Like this?" She curved her white arms in front of her stomach. (669)

To most normal men, I suppose, their wife becomes more dear and attractive to them when pregnant, though they have to adjust to the woman becoming more of a breeding creature than a sexual object: but for Tolstoy, obviously, the period of pregnancy was full of anguish: and, of course, for the women of the time, it was far more dangerous, and an almost permanent state of her body (in Britain, the wives of authors like Dickens and George MacDonald were almost continually pregnant). But Dolly assumes that if a woman becomes unattractive because she is pregnant, her husband will find his pleasures elsewhere:

> "I . . . lost my attraction for Stiva; he left me for others, and the first woman for whom he betrayed me did not keep him by being always pretty and gay. He threw her over and took up a third. And can Anna attract and hold Vronsky in that way? If that is all he looks for, he will find dresses and manners more attractive and charming. And however white and shapely her bare arms, however beautiful her stately figure and her eager face under that black hair, he will find others still lovelier, just as my poor dear reprobate of a husband does." (Ibid.)

What perhaps interests us is that, apart from the word repro-
bate Dolly does not seem to consider that there is something seriously wrong with the *man* in her contemplation of the problem.
Levin, of course and also Pierre in *War and Peace*, would not want
to indulge themselves with other women, while their wives are
pregnant—though, of course, it is also true to say that in their
marriages both partners keep one another under tight scrutiny
and control. But over this problem, I believe, we have an indication
of Tolstoy's own difficulties: having been bereft of his idealized
mother by an early and abrupt weaning, he tends to fasten his
attention on the female face and body, often with extreme guilt,
because he himself was very susceptible to beauty and attractiveness (and, of course, he himself was unfaithful). His novels are
scattered with almost savage references to the "near-nudity" of
society women, at dinner or at the opera, while Levin (his autobiographical self) is at one point totally disoriented by the low-cut
dress of a girl in a household he visits. So, in generalizing about
sexual relationships, he seems to suppose that men whose wives
become unattractive in pregnancy will face temptations from
other women—just as deprived of his mother, he himself was left
in perpetual hunger, and cannot avoid (for instance) making love
to his own wife, even when she is pregnant, nursing, or has just
given birth, when at the rational level of belief he was strongly
opposed to such behavior.

What the psychotherapist discovers, surely, is that it is not the
availability of other attractive women that prompts men to infidelity, but a basic problem of finding fulfillment in a relationship:
where a man is insecure and unable to find satisfaction in his
basic relationship he may well be tempted to adventure elsewhere.

In the ensuing conversation, however, Tolstoy does raise a number of crucial issues. Anna asks,

"What was my reason given me for, if I am not to use it to avoid
bringing unhappy beings into the world?" (Ibid.)

And she is unable to reach the kind of argument people use
nowadays to justify abortion:

"I should always feel I had wronged these unhappy children. . . . If
they do not exist, at any rate they are not unhappy; while if they are
unhappy, I alone should be blamed for it." (Ibid.)

—But (we remind ourselves) Anna has made Seriozha himself
desperately unhappy, by entering into her love affair. Dolly is

shocked by this point of view: "How can one wrong creatures that don't exist?" she thinks, reflecting on her own children. And she now feels a great gulf between herself and Anna. The conversation drives home, in the most serious mode, the problem that sexual relationships cannot be discussed without taking into account the adults' responsibility for bringing children into the world, or for destroying the possibility of their birth: and the need to set their potential being against adult self-interest, or their destruction against their own "happiness." (Behind these considerations, of course, lurk the question of individual human worth.)

Dolly drives on, to ask Anna whether she will reconsider a divorce, and here emerges both the impossibility of Anna's situation, and her deep distress—the distress that, she admits, she can only escape by taking morphine.

> You say I look on the dark side . . . I try not to look at all . . . what can I do? Nothing. You tell me to marry Alexei, and say I don't think about it. I not think about that! . . . Not a day, not an hour passes without my thinking about it, and upbraiding myself for doing so . . . because thinking of it may drive me mad. . . . (671)

She declares that she loves two beings—Seriozha and Alexei: and yet the claims of these are irreconcilable: "I cannot have them both; yet that is my one need"—and so "nothing matters"—and she falls into such a nihilistic state that she believes that only death can end her perplexity: as, indeed, it ultimately does.

It is at this point that, left alone, Dolly sees her own domestic life as "sweet and precious." But this seems to offer no solution—and, we may say, his penetration to the problems explored here leaves Tolstoy with a sense of their being no easy solution—one might say no *moral* solution—and so he is able to create his tragic novel, rather than write a tract. Anna, clearly, is becoming, in her bafflement, locked in a hardening predicament, and so she and Vronsky, under the surface, begin to develop hostility, vindictiveness, and coldness, so that she feels "panic" and he is "lashed to fury": and their progress toward a dreadful end becomes inevitable. Anna's dynamics are beginning to take on a "false solution" quality, because she cannot find any way out of her "slavery" ("what wife could be more of a slave than I am in my position?"), and yet of course cannot relinquish what is always "life" to her, her reflection in Vronsky's regard—that is by now taking on an impulse to exert power over him, and to control him, in order to "keep" him.

"Marriage" and "family" are no answers to such a proclivity, and in this Tolstoy plumbs the human condition deeper than his own moralizing. He is wrong, of course: it won't do to look to *marriage* or *family* to provide control over the dangerous presence of the sexual urges in men and women, and to reconcile these with society. It is true that there are dangers in sex, but not in the way a man supposes who has been traumatized by a sudden weaning and by the loss of his mother. The meaning of the sexual dangers, whose force and power deludes people even as it deluded Freud, need to be seen from another perspective—that of the problem of seeking equal relationships between men and women, of the need for good relationships, and for that meeting between unique beings that can contribute to a sense of the meaning of life. Of course, in nineteenth-century Russia society did not give equality to men and women and we need to take this into account. On the other hand, all the greatest art explores this problem, from Chaucer and Shakespeare to Jane Austen and Henry James: there is a dimension in which we judge art by the degree to which it attends to authenticity. It is this deeper theme of authenticity that the artist Tolstoy serves, even as the moralist Tolstoy was impelled by his preoccupation with the sense of a "brutal force" that fatefully interfered with people's lives as, of course, it did in his own.*

* * *

Tolstoy's original and formative traumatic experience as an infant gave him a particular fascination with women—with women's *difference*: "*la différence*." Of course, he was a genius: of course he had especial powers of language: of course, he was a man of wide-ranging intelligence—his novels alone show him to be interested in matters of government, agriculture and farming, military adventures, hunting, philosophy, and religion. But there is also no doubt that his uncanny capacity to identify with women is outstanding, and that central to his creative concerns was with what one of his characters (Pestsov) calls "where woman, *dasewig Weibliche* (the eternal womanly), enters into conflict with fate," and with the special nature of women, as different from men.

Having spent all his life mourning for his mother, so to speak,

---

*Despite his exploration of the possibility of contraception in *Anna Karenina*, Tolstoy did not practice it and would no doubt have considered it "immoral" or sinful. Yet the problems between him and his wife would surely have benefited from family planning.

he is sensitively aware that women not only have a problem such as that discussed between Anna and Dolly, but a special role to play in the formation of the emerging human consciousness. We have looked at the marvelous way he is able to portray the anguish of Seriozha, as his mother takes a lover, leaves him for her lover, and is said by others to be dead or wicked—neither of which he can believe. The portrayal of Seriozha is as sensitive a portrait of a wronged child as anything in literature.

But so, too, is his portrayal of the parturition of Kitty when she has Levin's first child. Obviously, Tolstoy himself must have been acutely alert to his wife's first experience of giving birth, and so when he writes of Kitty's he is able to portray the experience in exact detail, to make his account grave and deeply moving, while at the same time making a comedy out of Levin's response, as a new husband.

The episode, like that of Anna's near-death from puerperal fever, underlies his dealings with sexual love—for we must never forget that sexual love has as its purpose and consequence the creation of new life—and so demands responsibility and gravity, even as it is bound up with the claim to "live," to be fulfilled in a rich sexual experience, that Tolstoy tacitly recognizes as men and women's needs. It is this connection with procreation that the modern world denies—and thus offends against life, as by taking recourse to abortion on trivial grounds, seeking to determine the sex of a baby, or arranging other manipulations in the processes of conception and birth by "technology": such mechanization tending to obliterate the truth that each fetus that is conceived is a *being* with a right to existence. This tendency, of course, is a culmination of the very biologic mechanism in science (as in Darwinism) that seemed to Tolstoy himself to threaten the meaning in life, and, indeed, it does threaten meaning by reducing human beings to machines whose existence has no point, and whose being has no value.

Here we may perhaps refer to the last chapter of that fascinating work by a Catholic psychotherapist, Karl Stern's *Flight from Woman*:

Wherever individuals become ciphers, the feminine is wounded. For on the purely natural level—apart from the question of grace, or even apart from all theological or philosophical reflection—the sense of the infinite importance of the single individual is rooted in the experience of pregnancy, birth and nursing . . . while somebody is reading this line, a woman gives birth, with that immediate certainty that the world has been created for this particular human being. (Stern 1966, 286)

This, one might say, is Tolstoy's theme in his depiction of Kitty's parturition.

Later, Levin is woken by Kitty, as her labor begins. The woman has obviously given herself to the new primeval experience as the man cannot:

> Though her quietness, as if she were holding her breath, and especially the peculiar tenderness and excitement with which . . . she had said, "It's nothing," seemed to him suspicious, he was so drowsy that he at once fell asleep again. (*Anna Karenina*, 739)

Afterward he remembered that bated breath and "realised what must have been taking place in her dear, sweet soul while she lay motionless by his side, awaiting the greatest event in a woman's life."

The state into which the woman passes is seen through the eyes of the man, who cannot understand it.

> He thought he loved her face, knew her every expression, but never had he seen it like this. (740)

Kitty has periods of painful contraction, and in Levin the problem arises "who is to blame?" and he seeks for a scapegoat to punish (as an infant, presumably, he felt his father was to blame for his mother's death). But for Kitty "something sublime was being accomplished in her soul, but what it was *he could not understand*" (my italics).

As is common among husbands, Levin is excited, but feels strangely "out of it": in his terror he begins to pray "Lord have mercy on us! Pardon us and help us!"

> To whom was he to turn, if not to Him who held in His hands himself, his soul, and his love? (741)

In this deeply religious frame of mind, and seized by a sense of the all-embracing importance of the moment, Levin goes to fetch the doctor and to get some laudanum from the chemist. These people, of course, are used to all this, and treat it as routine—which Levin cannot bear. The chemist's assistant slowly produces the drug, and is about to wrap it up, in spite of all Levin's entreaties to the contrary.

This was more than Levin could stand: he firmly snatched the phial from the man's hands and rushed out. . . . (742)

He implores the doctor to hurry, but to his astonishment hears a smile in his voice as the man calls "Coming, coming!" The doctor offers him a cup of coffee, and amusedly tells him how another patient of his "always takes refuge in the stables on such occasions." He starts on his coffee and makes a reference to yesterday's news:

> "It seems the Turks are decidedly getting the worst of it. Did you read yesterday's dispatch?"
> "No, I can't stand this!" said Levin, jumping up. "You'll be with us in a quarter of an hour, then?" (744)

Levin has steeled himself to endure and keep his heart under control, but he finds the waiting intolerable. After five hours he feels he has reached the "utmost limits of endurance and that his heart would burst with compassion and pain."

> All the ordinary conditions of life without which one can form no conception of anything had ceased to exist for Levin. He lost all sense of time (745)

He seems almost to be sleepwalking through this episode, whose time belongs to the primeval forces of natural processes. People tell him not to worry, but also look at him "gravely and with commiseration." The predicament of the husband faced with the first birth of his child (although he is not physically involved) is superbly done, and significantly, the experience is seen as being like that of *waiting for death*:

> He only knew and felt that what was happening was similar to what had happened a year ago at the deathbed in a provincial hotel of his brother Nikolai. Only that had been sorrow, and this was joy. But that sorrow and this joy were equally beyond the usual plane of existence: *they were like openings through which something sublime became visible.* (745; my italics)

In this experience "the soul soared to heights it had never attained before, while reason lagged behind, unable to keep up." It is not so for Kitty, of course, just as it is different for her, in dealing with Nikolai's death. Being a woman, she is equipped to endure. Kitty's cries give Levin a disturbed feeling that he is to blame, and he has to consciously reject this, and remember, that he is only anxious to protect and help her. He has to struggle to remain calm but he goes on praying. His response seems close to Tolstoy's, who must have associated childbirth with the threat of death: but is is also a picture with great universality, delineating the experience of any sensitive husband.

Kitty is giving "unearthly screams," yet while her face is distorted with pain she declares, "I'm not afraid!" Yet she also cries, "Oh, this is terrible! I am dying . . . I shall die!" Dolly declares, "It's nothing, it's nothing, everything is going all right." But Levin becomes convinced that "all was over": his wife becomes "what had once been Kitty"—"someone shrieking and moaning in a way he had never heard before." She has been quite taken over by the primeval processes of emerging new life. Instead of Kitty's face was

> something fearful—fearful in its strange distortion and the sounds that issued from it. . . . The terrible screams . . . seemed to reach the utmost limits of horror, when they suddenly ceased . . . and he heard . . . her voice, faltering, vibrant, tender, and blissful as she whispered, "It's over!" (748)

Kitty looks "extraordinarily lovely and serene," "trying unsuccessfully to smile," Levin is transported by joy:

> The taut strings snapped, and the sobs and tears of joy which he had never foreseen rose within him with such force that they shook his whole body and for a long time prevented him from speaking. (Ibid.)

The midwife is dealing with the baby:

> In Lizaveta Petrovna's skillful hands flickered the life of a human being, like the small uncertain flame of a nightlight—a human being who had not existed a moment ago but who, with the same rights and importance to itself as the rest of humanity, would love and create others in its own image. . . . In the silence there came in unmistakable answer to the mother's question ["Mama, is it true?"] a voice quite unlike the subdued voices that had been speaking in the room; a bold, insistent, self-assertive cry of the new human being who had so incomprehensibly appeared from some unknown realm. (749)

It is a deeply moving moment. For Levin, it takes a "prodigious effort to realise that she was alive and well and that the little creature yelling so desperately was his son." He is unutterably happy: but he cannot accustom himself to the idea of the baby: "It seemed to him too much, a superabundance, to which he was unable to get used for a long time."

Kitty has recovered, but "there is the same change in her face from earthly to unearthly that is seen on the faces of the dead"— again, Tolstoy equates childbirth with death—"but there it means farewell, with Kitty it was a welcome to new life."

For Levin, it is difficult for him to respond.

> Gazing at this pitiful little bit of humanity, Levin searched his soul in vain for some trace of paternal feeling. He could feel nothing but aversion . . . the beautiful baby only inspired him with a feeling of disgust and pity, which was not in the least what he had anticipated. (750–51)

Kitty, however, laughs, as the baby takes the breast for the first time. Levin continues to be disturbed:

> he was oppressed by a new sense of apprehension—the consciousness of another vulnerable region. And this consciousness was so painful at first, the apprehension lest that helpless being should suffer was so acute, that it drained the strange thrill of unreasoning joy and even pride which he had felt when the infant sneezed. (751–52)

Tolstoy is surely able to give us this sensitive picture of the husband's baffled response, because he is reliving his own suffering as an infant, and also is able to identity with Levin, in his Oedipal response to the rivalry between himself and the new son, at Kitty's breast. The husband is simply not equipped to deal with a baby as primeval as this, because he is a man and not a woman.

A further excellent passage about Mitya follows immediately after the dreadful episode in which Vronsky, devastated by Anna's death, sobs as he recalls her mutilated body. The juxtaposition is highly meaningful, in the light of Tolstoy's experience: to him unmodified sexual love leads to such hideous mutilation: the remedy for death by sexual intercourse is "*family*" in *marriage*. In a sense, also Tolstoy is seeking to overcome his sense of the doom that must follow sexual love (i.e., death of the mother) by making a contribution of tremendous reparation—as in chapter 6, by showing a mother *surviving* with her baby, and successfully leading him toward reality, as his own mother did not. This impulse generates the marvelous nature of the episode. It is a record of "primary maternal preoccupation"—the kind of telepathic state in woman to which D. W. Winnicott drew the world's attention. Kitty *knows* her baby needs her, before she hears him yelling:

> feeling the flow of milk she hurried to the nursery. Indeed, it was not a mere guess—the bond between herself and the baby was still so close—she knew for certain by the flow of her milk that he was in need of food.
>   She knew he was screaming before she reached the nursery. And so he was. She heard him and hurried. But the faster she went the louder he screamed. It was a fine, healthy, cry, hungry and impatient. (816)

The nurse, carrying the baby over to Kitty, who is undoing her bodice, declares that he "knows" her. But Kitty is not listening: her impatience was increasing with the baby's.

> The baby had difficulty in taking the breast and grew angry. At last, after desperate screaming and choking, and vain sucking, matters were settled satisfactorily, and mother and child breathed a sigh of content, and both subsided into calm. (817)

This close relationship is also strongly sexual: to her the baby's eyes seem to "peep roguishly" under his cap and she dwells on the "circular movement of the baby hand with its rosy palm." All this area of the joy of the "nursing couple" has been observed with close attention by Tolstoy. And there follows a penetrating observation of the psychic encounter between mother and child that is unsurpassed in literature:

> She smiled because, though she said he could not know her, in her heart she was sure that he knew not only Agatha Mihalovna, but that he knew everything and understood a whole lot of things that no-one else knew, and which she, his mother, was only just beginning to find out and understand thanks to him. To Agatha Mihalovna, to the nurse, to his grandfather, to his father even, Mitya was just a little human being, requiring only material care: but for his mother he had long been a personage endowed with moral faculties with whom she already had a whole history of spiritual relations. (817)

Levin only enters into this sphere later, when they are bathing the baby and it becomes clear that he knows Kitty:

> Kitty leant over him—his face lit up with a smile . . . Levin was surprised and delighted. . . . (850)

Levin admits to being "disappointed before"

> "I had expected some novel pleasant emotion to awaken in me, like a surprise, and instead there was only a sensation of disgust, pity. . . .
> . . . and there being far more anxiety and pity than satisfaction. I never knew until today, after that during the storm, how much I loved him."
> Kitty's smile was radiant. (850–51)

Levin, of course, spends many of the last pages agitating about the meaning of life, and rediscovering his capacity for a simple faith, at a level he has learned from the peasants. At the end he finds that his life is "no longer meaningless as it was before, but has a positive meaning of goodness with which I have the power to invest it." Again, this is an observation of the universal response of a father to the birth of his firstborn. But we have a feeling that it is the woman who has lived through the experience of meaningful being, without needing to question it or to examine it philosophically. In this she has led the way for her husband, who seems by contrast less involved, as he is

> "seeking to fathom the general manifestation of God to the universe with all its stars and planets. What am I about? Knowledge, sure, unattainable by reason, has been revealed to me, to my heart, and here I am obstinately trying to express that knowledge in words and by means of reason. . . ." (852)

He tells himself that his solution is "a secret for me alone . . . not to be put into words. . . ." Yet, looking into his wife's face, as it is illuminated by a flash of lightning, he tells himself, "She understands . . . she knows. . . ." We recollect Winnicott's phrase "the mother knows": women have another, intuitive, mysterious mode of knowing, and living at the heart of being. Tolstoy shows here that he knows that: amazing that this same writer should also elsewhere write disparagingly of women; should write *The Kreutzer Sonata,* in which he quotes the fanatically hostile Schopenhauer; and make that final flight from woman to Astapovo, where he died.

* * *

Tolstoy, according to Gustafson, "turns his attention (in *Anna Karenina*) to the modern assumption that romantic passion is the first step to marital love and family life, and he explores the age-old confusion between romantic love and the Christian idea of

love" (Gustafson, 110). He sees the novel that Anna reads in the
train as the agent the implants in her mind the romantic impulse
that destroys her: "through self-indulgence and self-protection
Anna brings ruin to her self and to those for whom she cares
and to whom she is responsible." This critic is especially hard on
Anna: "Anna's sin is that she lives for herself and enclosed in
herself" (Ibid., 119)

But even a study of the early scene in the train surely indicates
that the matter is more complex than that, and is more than a
fable enacting the difference between romantic love and Christian love.

Anna's romanticism sometimes leads her to abandon herself to
fantasies, and then be taken over, as by forces outside herself. This
becomes clearer in the chapter (*Anna Karenina,* 29) in which she
settles in the train home after her first encounter with Vronsky.
She hopes soon to be back in her "nice, everyday life." But she is
still in a "worried frame of mind." She tries to read her book,
but finds

> no pleasure in reading, no pleasure in entering into other people's
> lives and adventures. *She was too eager to live herself.* (115; my italics)

She reads of an Englishman, attaining his idea of happiness: a
baronetcy and an estate. She was wishing that she could go to the
estate with him, but

> she suddenly felt that *he* must be feeling ashamed and that she was
> ashamed for the same reason. But what had he to be ashamed of?
> "What have I to be ashamed of?" she wondered indignantly. (Ibid.)

But she recalls Vronsky's face, with the look of slavish adoration
in his eyes, although she repeats that there is nothing to be
ashamed of.

> The feeling of shame was intensified and some inner voice, when she
> was thinking about Vronsky, seemed to say to her, "Warm, very warm,
> hot!" (116)

She laughs contemptuously, and then laughs with joy, "her nerves
being stretched ever more tightly, like strings round pegs." It becomes rather a nightmarelike state, like the state she is in when
she blunders toward her suicide at the end:

> "What am I doing here? Am I myself or someone else?" (Ibid.)

Something seems to draw her to this state and she was free to yield to it or resist. A man comes in, a "thin peasant with a long nankeen coat with a button missing," whom she later realizes is the stoker: but he bears the distinct resemblance to the ghostly peasant with the hammer who haunts her and Vronsky: "after that there was a terrible screech and clatter as though someone were being torn to pieces; then a red light blinded her eyes, and at last a wall rose and blotted everything out" (Ibid.). It is as if she is preexperiencing her own suicide:

> Anna felt as if she were falling from a height. But all this, far from seeming dreadful, was rather pleasant. (Ibid.)

When she gets out of the carriage, she finds Vronsky, who has followed her with "reverential ecstasy": a feeling of joyful pride sweeps over her. Their brief exchange makes her both frightened and happy. She does not sleep the whole night, suffering visions that are "joyful, glowing and exhilarating." When she descends from the carriage, she is startled by the appearance of her husband: "A disagreeable sensation oppressed her heart when she met his fixed and weary gaze, as though she had expected to find him different. She becomes aware of a consciousness of hypocrisy, which she had experienced in her relationships with him: clearly and painfully." It is clear that not only is she trapped in a cold and meaningless marriage, but that she feels falsified by that relationship.

What Tolstoy magnificently conveys through this scene, as in others, is the way in which in individual who has been starved of fulfillment, who feels at the deepest level of being that they have never been awakened, and have a potentiality they have never known, may experience the potential awakening that emerges with ecstasy—with an ecstasy that cannot be repressed. As it emerges, it takes over part of the personality, and thus provokes a duplicity. This must be the experience of many people who escape from unsatisfactory relationships including marriages, and the impulse no doubt generates many divorces. One may also study such forms of awakening in case histories, as patients under therapy revolutionize their lives. But, inevitably, such new directions cause much suffering, distress, and tragedy, as relationships are broken.

It is thus entirely credible that Anna, although in a sense she finds fulfillment, should in the end go mad and destroy herself.

* * *

Why does Anna Karenina kill herself? In one sense, to pay out
Vronsky—she has a "vague fury and craving for vengeance rising
within her" (794). When she imagines that Vronsky is falling in
with his mother's plans to marry him to Princess Sorokin, everything in the house "filled her with loathing and malice" (Ibid.).
When she reaches the railway station, on her last rambling journey, she "thought of how . . . Wretchedly she loved and hated
him." Her bewildered position about her love has become a deep-
ening misanthropy, and she cannot find any positive hold on her
feelings for humanity.

As she decides to throw herself under the train she thinks, "I
shall punish him and escape from them all and myself" (p. 801).

This is psychologically accurate, I am sure—a common motive
for suicide is the impulse to punish others—parents or lovers—
though the flaw in the insane logic is that one will not be there
to enjoy the triumph.

Anna Karenina is clearly insane in that last chapter, about her
wild journey and about her mental confusion: things she sees are
all related to her own situation in a desperate way, and she uses
them to draw morbid conclusions about human nature and aspirations. But to this we must add the hint we get, of Tolstoy's thumb
in the scales—his sense of a malevolent spirit, that haunts Anna
throughout the novel: "A little peasant muttering something was
working at the rails" (802). It is this peasant that she occasionally
dreams about—and even Vronsky dreams of him at one moment.
It is as if by this Tolstoy is saying that this demon is not merely a
figment of the unconscious life of any one character, but an archetypal figure in the universe he has created:

> Immediately after lunch he lay down on the sofa and five minutes
> later memories of the disreputable scenes he had witnessed during
> the last few days became confused and merged with a mental image
> of Anna and of a peasant who had played an important part as a
> beater in the bear-hunt; and Vronsky fell asleep. He awoke in the
> dark, trembling with horror, and hurriedly lighted a candle. "What
> was it? What was the dreadful thing I dreamed? Yes, I know. The
> peasant-beater—a dirty little man with a matted beard—was stooping
> down doing something, and all of a sudden he began muttering
> strange words in French. Yes, there was nothing else in the dream,"
> he said to himself. "But why was it so awful?" he vividly recalled the
> peasant again and the incomprehensible French words the man had
> muttered, and a chill of horror ran down his spine. (380)

The appearances of this ghost, in the minds of both Anna and
Vronsky, echo the original moment of disaster that presages the

tragic end of their love. As Vronsky and his mother are getting out of the carriage several men run past with alarmed faces.

"What? . . . What? . . . Where? . . . Threw himself under! . . . Run over! . . ." people passing by the window were heard saying. (78)

A gentlemen says, "They say he was cut in half": another replies, "I think it was the easiest of deaths—instantaneous."

Anna Karenina hears this and her lips tremble: "She had difficulty in keeping back her tears."

"It is a bad omen," she said.

At the same moment Anna is "tossing her head as if she wished with a physical gesture to shake off something that troubled and oppressed her":—she has only met Vronsky for the first time on the previous day, and yet he has begun to haunt her. It is at her suggestion that he has given the stationmaster two hundred roubles for the widow of the dead railway worker.

So, there is a sense from the beginning of the novel that Vronsky and Anna are linked by death—sudden death, of a suicidal kind: and yet this threat seems to be influenced from outside them, by the peasant with the matted beard of their dreams, who is manipulating something heavy made of metal, while muttering incomprehensible French words. This peasant has an extraneous symbolism in the novel: he seems less a projection of inner dynamics in either Anna or Vronsky, but rather to be an independent dynamic in the world of Tolstoy's novel, a dynamic of the authorial omnipotence we have found in *War and Peace*. In examining this and its origins, we find clues to the origins of Tolstoy's art, and also clues to the way he felt impelled to delineate the love he creates: the malignant peasant represents a force he feels unconsciously there to be, in fate, of the kind that killed his mother and threatens the whole area of sexual love.

Anna forecasts her own death, as a consequence of a parallel dream. Vronsky is somewhat disturbed when Anna tells him this, and he remembers his own dream.

"Yes, a dream," she said. "A dream I had a long time ago. I dreamed that I ran into my bedroom to fetch something or find out something—you know how it is in dreams," she said, her eyes wide with horror. "And in the bedroom, in the corner, stood something."

"Oh, what nonsense! How can you believe. . . ."

But she would not let him interrupt. What she was saying was too important to her.

"And the something turned round, and I saw it was a peasant with a tangled beard, little and dreadful-looking. I wanted to run away, but he stooped down over a sack and was fumbling about in it with his hands. . . ."

She showed how he had fumbled in the sack. There was terror in her face. And Vronsky, remembering his own dream, felt the same terror fill his being.

"And all the time he was rummaging, he kept muttering very quickly, in French, you know, rolling his r's: *Il faut le battre, le fer; le broyer, le petrir.* . . . And I was so terrified I tried to wake up . . . and I did wake up but it was still part of the dream. And I began asking myself what it meant. And Korney said to me: 'In childbirth you'll die: in childbirth, ma'am. . . .' And then I woke up." (386–87)

It is immediately after this that Anna Karenina feels her fetus quicken.

The appearance of this demonic figure does not arise naturally from the depiction of the consciousness of the characters. We may even say that it emerges from the *author's consciousness*, at moments of sexual attraction, sometimes associated with aspects of pregnancy, and with death.

This peasant-demon is even there at the heart of Anna's suicide:

A little peasant muttering something was working at the rails. . . . (802)

He could even be interpreted as the personification of death. (The only title given to a chapter in *Anna Karenina*, by the way is "Death.")

*　*　*

In another sense, Anna Karenina's death is punishment for sexual love—that evil and dangerous indulgence when it is unmitigated by marriage. This is the theory behind Tolstoy's impulse to write the novel, though in effect the art takes on a degree of life that confounds Tolstoy's moral theory.

How does this theory, and how does the upshot of the art, conform with the findings of psychotherapy in our time? Well, first we have to accept that there is nothing inherently dangerous or murderous about sexual intercourse, though it easily becomes the focus of such fears, and the source of much division within the self, and conflict between impulses. So, the conflict within Anna is quite authentically rendered:

> The thought of the wrong she had done her husband aroused in her a feeling akin to revulsion, like the feeling a drowning man might have who has shaken off another man clinging to him in the water. *That other was drowned.* (489, my italics)

Marriage offers certain safeguards, Tolstoy obviously thought at this time: as a recognized commitment, it made it easier for confidence between men and women to be expressed (though it is also possible for an Oblonsky to be deceitful and to hope that duplicity will be connived at). The problem between Vronsky and Anna is that they become duplicitous in a different way: he develops a split between what he says to Anna and his inner feelings, where he comes to hate her, and to resent her demands on him. She on her part ceases to trust him and becomes anxious about "keeping" him. The seductive capacities she exerts with her beauty and charm thus become an anguish to her, and a capacity with which he becomes weary and disillusioned.

They cease to speak to one another over important issues: for instance, it is highly significant that Anna has not discussed with Vronsky her decision not to have anymore children. When she discusses children with Dolly it emerges that she has made this decision alone. Much later she tells Vronsky, who is hoping for more children, "we shan't have any" (780). This is perhaps the greatest indication of the difference between them as a pair who have married and who go on loving one another. One cannot imagine Kitty making such a decision alone.

So, Anna's greatest fear is losing Vronsky:

> "But he ought to tell me so. I must be told! If I know the truth, then I shall know how to act," she said to herself, quite powerless to imagine the position she would be in if she were convinced of his indifference. She thought he had ceased to love her, felt on the verge of despair, and this galvanished her. She rang for her maid and went to the dressing-room. She took more pains over her toilet than she had of late, as though he might, if he had fallen out of love with her, love her again because she dressed and arranged her hair in the style that was most becoming. (568)

Later, when discussing pregnancy with Dolly, she says

> "he loves me as long as he loves me. And how am I to keep his love? Like this?"

She curved her white arms in front of her stomach. (669)

It is because of this predicament that she declares, "what wife, what slave could be more of a slave than I am in my position?" (668).

And in her final soliloquy, she declares to herself,

"My love grows more and more passionate and selfish, while his is dying, and that is why we are drifting apart. . . . Up to the time of our union we were irresistibly drawn together, and now we are irresistibly drawn apart. . . ." (796)

"Nothing can be done about it," she muses. It is this perplexity that makes *Anna Karenina* such a great novel. It is all very well for Gustafson to speak of Anna's "failure to confront or reveal herself" and to condemn her because "in their romance each sought their own needs and thus went their own ways" ("The pursuit of happiness for yourself alone, regardless of others, which in the end is what the fantasy of romance entails, inexorably leads to a world of struggle and strife" [130].) But Anna feels trapped existentially: her life with Karenin, once she is awakened by her love for Vronsky, becomes meaningless, so what could she have done? It is true that "Anna has no faith and never goes to church" (*Anna Karenina*, 143). But even had she been a believer, what should she have done? Her tragedy is that "nothing can be done about it," and that there is no way out, even if she had confronted the reality of her position.

* * *

Now I should like to return to Anna's thoughts as she goes on her crazy last journey, to die at the railway station. Without wanting to detract from the tragic nature of Tolstoy's great novel, I cannot help feeling that something does not quite ring true in this final sequence. It is not only that, as I have tried to show, the little peasant is present here, as at so many crucial moments in the novel, representing an external, almost *deus ex machina*, or *diabolus ex machina* presence. It is rather that Tolstoy seems to show Anna's view of her predicament as clear and true, as right and unsightful, even as he shows her to be so terribly deranged, and it is unclear whether she has found a saving illumination or not.

Light has a complex symbolism in this sequence—the light in which she sees her situation clearly and the light in herself which she extinguishes. (Besides the obvious origins of the event in Tolstoy's own experience, there is a significance in his choice of this particular death for his heroine—subjecting herself to the smashing onslaught of a great machine, as if to the ultimate maleness, and thus in a submission to the violence inherent in the primal scene. The same is true, of course, of some of Dickens's preoccupations, as with the execution of the Mannings, the murderer husband and wife, in relation to the murder of Nancy: underlying such obsessions is an unconscious feeling about sexual love as murderous.)

During her tragic ride, Anna seems to achieve insights into her predicament:

> And now for the first time Anna turned the glaring light in which she was seeing everything upon her relations with him, which she had hitherto avoided thinking about (795)

Here, it would seem, that the author is endorsing the "glaring light":

> "What did he look for in me? Not love so much as the gratification of his vanity."

She goes on, as the author says, not surmising, but seeing things "distinctly in the piercing light which revealed to her now the meaning of life and human relationships." We are obviously meant to compare these insights of Anna's with Levin's contemplation of the meaning of his life, and we get a sense that Anna's capacity to grasp meanings beyond mutual exploitation is limited.

> She remembered his words, the expression of his face, like a faithful settler's, in the early days of their liaison. And everything now confirmed that. "Yes, in him there was triumph over a success for his vanity. Of course there was love too, but the chief element was pride of success. He gloried in me. Now that is past. There is nothing to be proud of—nothing to be proud of, only ashamed. He has taken from me everything he could, and now I am no more use to him. He is tired of me and is trying not to act dishonourably towards me. . . ." (795–96)

"*The zest is gone*" she says to herself in English.

Their illicit effort has been held together only by sensual fire, and Anna goes on to declare that "my desire arouses his disgust, and that excites resentment in me, and it cannot be otherwise."

D. H. Lawrence, as we have noted, believed that Anna and Vronsky should have simply thumbed their noses at "Mrs. Grundy."

Anna and Vronsky's relationship fails because they have only their sensual fire to sustain them, while they are continually undermined by their failure to take into account the complex relationship between themselves as a couple and their inevitable connections with "society": not so much the conventional moeurs, but the inevitable links, of producing children, and of the effect of their relationship on others, from Vronsky's mother, to Karenin, and even Kitty. Anna's self-possession is utterly destroyed by the breakdown of her relationship with her son Seriozha, while the future of Ani her daughter, who is a Karenin legally, is uncertain and a source of unhappiness to her. There is an essential truth in the upshot of this novel over these issues. Sexual love cannot be satisfactorily dissociated from its purpose, which is the production of children, however much contraception has advanced: in denying the connection, women suffer, inevitably, since they have an urge to create children, as a fulfillment of their capacity for sexual love—and so they need the concept of marriage, to guarantee their future. To rely solely on their capacity to attract is to place a great strain on their existential security, and thus to sow the seeds of the collapse of their relationships, through the very anxiety of fearing such collapse, when their partners have undertaken no obligation to remain committed to them. Beneath these problems is the issue of sub specie aeternitatis: the ultimate commitment which marriage celebrates at best.

As Anna goes on, musing on their relationships,

"Up to the time of our union we were irresistably drawn together, and now we are irresistably drawn apart. And nothing can be done to alter it. He says I am insanely jealous and I have kept on telling myself that I am insanely jealous; but it is not true. I am not jealous but unsatisfied." (796)

Anna is surely not sexually unsatisfied: she is unsatisfied in the wider sense, of finding harmony and peace with her man, in a social context, and not being tormented by anxiety about his possible abandonment of her:

"If I could be anything but his mistress, passionately caring for nothing but his caresses—but I can't, and I can't be anything else. . . . Don't I know that he wouldn't deceive me, that he has no thought of wanting to marry the Princess Sorokin, that he is not in love with Kitty, that he won't be unfaithful to me? I know all that, but it does not make it any easier for me. If he does not love me, but treats me kindly and gently out of a sense of duty, and what I want is not there—that would be a thousand times worse than having me hate me. It would be hell! And that is just how it is. He has long ceased to love me. And where love ends, hate begins. . . ." (Ibid.)

Tolstoy portrays Anna as one of those women who make a claim to be loved—like Cleopatra—to whom a normal world is "no better than a sty," and who are prepared to die, in a great final drama, rather than subdue themselves to living on a lesser level. As the same time it is clear that it is Anna's impossible position, vis-a-vis others in life, that makes it impossible for her.

"Well, I get divorced, and become Vronsky's wife. What then? Will Kitty cease looking at me as she looked at me today? No. And will Seriozha leave off asking and wondering about my two husbands? And is there any new feeling I can imagine between Vronsky and me? Could there be if not happiness, just absence of torment? No, and no again! . . . "

She is in a confused and negative-minded state: but she has penetrated to the wilfull and all-or-nothing aspect of her love for Vronsky, which in one sense is narcissistic, immature, and undeveloped, but on the other is a magnificent and defiant assertion of life. At the same time, there is a sense in which, while Vronsky seems unworthy of Anna, there is a limit on their capacity for mutual trust. We may remember how, in talking to Dolly, she proclaims that she will practice birth control, so as to preserve her figure, so that she can hold Vronsky—and yet deny him the children he would have liked, to carry his own name. For we need to remember that as well as destroying her own life, Anna has also destroyed Vronsky's, in the end. Yet who would have wished her, Anna, to have gone on enduring her life with Karenin, unawakened and never knowing what it was like to be loved or to love? Yet in the end, when she compares her love for Seriozha with the "other love" for which she exchanged his, she is filled with disgust "at what she called the 'other love'." (Ibid.)

The clearness with which she saw her own life now, and everybody else's, gave her a sense of pleasure. . . . "So it is with me . . . and all those people. . . ." (Ibid.)

She develops contempt for the people around her, and suddenly becomes aware of the archetypal menacing peasant figure:

A grimy, deformed-looking peasant in a cap from beneath which tufts of his matted hair stuck out, passed by this window, stooping down to the carriage wheels. "There's something familiar about that deformed peasant," thought Anna. And remembering her dream she walked over to the opposite door, trembling with fright. (798)

Later on she reflects that she couldn't conceive of a situation in which life would not be a misery.

But when you see the truth, what are you to do? (799)

Is Anna seeing the truth or not? Or has she lost her capacity to see reality (she has been taking drugs and screws up her eyes as if to avoid certain aspects of reality). When she hears a woman for whom she has only contempt talk of "reason" she applies it to herself and then declares,

"Why not put out the candle when there's nothing more to see, when everything looks obnoxious. . . . " (800)

"Everything is false and evil—all lies and deceit," she declares. At last she selects the exact spot where she will throw herself.

"There, in the very middle, and I shall punish him and escape from them all and myself." (801)

It is interesting, by the way, to note the symbolism of the red bag that Anna carries. Tolstoy had of course seen a red bag accompanying the body of the woman whom he has seen killed by a train, and this had struck him with powerful especial force. No doubt it was an unconscious symbol of the womb, and so of femininity, that womb and that femininity of which his mother was a victim, dying in childbirth. Anna's last moments are haunted by her red bag, and just at the end it actually delays her:

the red bag which she began to pull from her arm delayed her, and it was too late. (Ibid.)

It is as if a last vestige of her feminine capacity to cherish the state of being offers some resistance in her impulse. As she reaches her final determination, strangely:

suddenly the darkness that had enveloped everything for her lifted, and for an instant life glowed before her with all its past joys. (Ibid.)

Now she throws aside her red bag and launches herself to death. She has a moment of horror-struck questioning ("Where am I? What am I doing? Why?") and she tries to get up: but something huge and relentless strikes her on the head.

> And the candle by which she had been reading the book filled with trouble and deceit, sorrow and evil, flared up with a brighter light, illuminating for her everything that before had been enshrouded in darkness, flickered, grew dim and went out for ever. (802)

The whole episode is enigmatic. In one sense, Tolstoy wants to show Anna's progress as a form of atonement for sin—and gives her at the last moment a profound illumination. At the same time he is aware that she has become confused, distracted, and has lost her self-possession: has become locked in a false logic and a malicious cycle, turned against herself. It is as if the little peasant of whom she becomes aware again in the last moment ("A little peasant muttering something was working on the rails")—is he that powerful force of fate that Karenin detects? Is he the sexual instinct that degrades and kills—being impelled ultimately by the death instinct? Is he Satan? Or is he the God of the Old Testament? Or is he one of the Eumenides?

He is perhaps, in unconscious symbolism, that human element which Tolstoy experienced in the primal scene—the brutal father—that he also knew in himself, as a lustful man: that element that threatens to corrupt even the purity of the mother, who died because of his "working." Armstrong reports that with a male child whose mother dies in infancy there may arise many complications of the Oedipus problem, according to psychoanalysts, and this again would have contributed to Tolstoy's association between sex and the threat of death.

The little peasant sticks out like a sore thumb in the pattern of the book, because he represents a certain awful feature of existence that Tolstoy could not solve for himself. In Anna he may be destroying symbolically himself, his own sexuality, while punishing himself for having created such a vivid loving, beautiful, and good-natured, desirable woman. Of course, we may extend our psychoanalytic interpretation further and say that Anna represents in one sense a split-off element in Tolstoy himself, his own femininity: and having brought her into such a claim for "life," he cannot avoid placing her in a situation from which she cannot escape—and destroying her.

This would help explain the strange ambiguity of her last scene,

and the confused symbolism of light and illumination in it. For
Tolstoy was surely near being able to see and find the Anna in
himself, but needed also to extinguish her—because of the terrible dangers symbolized by that red bag she ultimately flings away.

* * *

I have referred to Karl Stern's remark about *The Kreutzer Sonata*,
as being full of "pathological material." This is perhaps especially
so of the moment when Pozdnisheff recounts how he plunged
the dagger into his wife:

> I stuck the dagger with all my strength into her left side beneath the
> ribs . . . I felt and still recall the momentary resistance of the corset
> and something else, and then the passage of the dagger cutting its
> way through the soft parts of the body . . . I immediately drew it out
> again . . . Suddenly the blood spurted out from beneath the corset.
> (Stern, 240–42)

The horrific clarity of this vision suggests that the impulse to do
this to a woman was often present in Tolstoy, in fantasy, because
of his hatred of women. In *Anna Karenina*, of course, he can be
said to do the same to a woman to whom he is much attracted,
in fantasy.

In Anna's last demented moments she has a nightmare, the
force of which seems parallel to the horrible passage in *The
Kreutzer Sonata*:

> At dawn a horrible nightmare, which she had had several times even
> before her connection with Vronsky, repeated itself and woke her. A
> little old man with unkempt beard was leaning over a bar of iron,
> doing something and muttering meaningless words in French, and—
> this was what always made the nightmare so horrible—she felt that
> though this peasant seemed to be paying no attention to her he was
> doing something dreadful to her with the iron. (*Anna Karenina*, 785)

It is interesting to note that Tolstoy says Anna used to have this
nightmare before she met Vronsky: so, he implies, the menacing
peasant cannot be he who exacts vengeance for her crime. We
may take it to mean, I believe, that Tolstoy himself was troubled
by such a dream—and the dream relates, as I have suggested, to
the primal scene.

We are told that not only does a child feel that the intercourse
between parents is sadistic, but that he *wants* it to be sadistic. A
disturbed infant such as Tolstoy seems to have been could perhaps

be obsessed with the idea of sexual intercourse as murder. And that seems to lie behind Anna's nightmare—and behind the mordant description of the murder in *The Kreutzer Sonata*. Both are symbolic of the intense feelings of revenge in Tolstoy's unconscious mind directed against women.

So, in the end, we may return to that perplexing motto of *Anna Karenina*, Vengeance Is Mine: I Will Repay. All of Tolstoy's hatred and disparagement of women relate to the way his mother abandoned him as an infant and are *revenge* for that original suffering: so, the vengeance in *Anna Karenina* is not really God's, but Tolstoy's. It is highly significant that Tolstoy tells us that Anna used to dream about the little peasant before her connection with Vronsky—thus telling us that the motif was there before she became a fallen woman. It was, one might say, in her as Tolstoy created her. And, as we know from the last episode in which Seriozha appears, with Oblonsky, that Seriozha is permanently damaged by her abandonment of him for another creature whom she loves—as Tolstoy himself was damaged by being orphaned. The menacing peasant who occurs so curiously and as if extraneously in *Anna Karenina* is not fate or God's agent of revenge, so much as Tolstoy's impulse to revenge split off into an externalized dynamic, borrowed from the fantasy of the primal scene.

The murder in *The Kreutzer Sonata* is a symbolic act of revenge against women, and that whole novel is a rationalization of Tolstoy's hatred of women, sex, and marriage. But it also parallels the destruction of the charming, intelligent, sensitive, and eminently womanly Anna Karenina by the author whose unconscious motto was Vengeance Is Mine: I Will Repay, although in that novel we have a more fully complex portrayal of a woman, with whom Tolstoy has a deep sympathy, in her existential plight.

He was, of course, moving toward the adherence to the Christian view as expressed in his book *My Confession* (1879), but we need to examine his position in the light of the mythology of his unconscious. Seen in this light the Christian view is seen to have something in it of a rationalization, a defense in part against what was going on in his unconscious mind. When Tolstoy saw the actual mangled body of the mistress of Anna Pirogova in the railway station, he reacted strongly because he saw enacted the brutal fantasies of his own unconscious, that he would have liked to have exacted on women. When he saw the little peasant in reality at the same railway station, he was able to project his own dread and culpability on him, so that he could stand in the place of the father in the primal scene, who he suspected of hurting or of even murdering his mother. Yet, although he idolized his mother, he, too, wanted to murder women in revenge—which he was able to do in fantasy, both in *The Kreutzer Sonata* and in *Anna Karenina*. In the latter novel, however, his perplexed engagement with the truth, without falling into simplistic solutions or propaganda for his false solutions, generates the complex life of a true work of art, a creative exploration of the nature of love and passion, marriage and responsibility, that does not follow the motto offered on the title page, whether one interprets it in the Christian reference or sees it, as I do, as a motif emerging from the unconscious.

*　*　*

Leavis declares that "Kitty and Levin have a clear normative significance," and "provide a foil to Anna and Vronsky." (He also says, to my astonishment, that Oblonsky and Dolly's marriage remains "successful"!) The word normative in such a context implies that Tolstoy was offering or attempting to offer a definition of marriage, and in the Leavis scheme of things, in which the novelist is offering thought about "the nature, the meaning and the essential problems of human life" in a moral way, that is one way of seeing the novel.

But how "normative" is the marriage of Levin and Kitty, and how much can it be said to provide a foil to the "abnormal" or "unsuccessful" relationship between Anna and Vronsky? In answer to this kind of attempt to give the book a "moral" or even "didactic" structure, its own opening sentence provides the appropriate corrective:

> All happy families are alike but an unhappy family is unhappy after its own fashion. (*Anna Karenina*, 13)

—which has an unspoken ironic flavor, representing the query "Are there any families without unhappiness?"

Perhaps we can penetrate beyond the word moral to Leavis's other terms: *sincerity* and the notion that there are modes of action and of character that *offend against life*. Leavis almost gets to the concept of authenticity, though he continues to be confused between the two perspectives. To use phrases such as "Anna was not an amoral German aristocrat,"* "Karenin . . . is a 'social' being,

---

*To say that "Anna was not an amoral German aristocrat" shows a serious confusion in Leavis's critical thinking. I deal with the question in a footnote in

ego-bound, self-important," and to speak of Anna's "perverse and dangerous will" is to refer to a different paradigm from what is implied by "Anna ... in her relations with Vronsky has come to life" and to speak of "fulfilment." Somewhere behind Leavis's remarks in this vein is the perception that there is a way of finding "life" and even that there is the "nature of life and its *implicit laws*" (*Anna Karenina,* pp. 26–27; italics mine)—that there is a natural truth about human beings, with its own injunctions that can be violated. This is a different "model" from that in which a character can *do wrong* ("though Karenin is insufferable, she has done wrong" (p. 20)). This is the model in which an artist engages with "the deep spontaneous lived question."

What Leavis's essay does reveal is D. H. Lawrence's inadequacy, in the face of *Anna Karenina*. Leavis goes so far as to say that Lawrence "refuses to see the nature of the tragedy," declaring that Anna and Vronsky should have spat in Mother Grundy's eye ... and that "cowardice was the real sin." Anna and Vronsky, actually, display enormous courage: courage, however, cannot solve an impossible situation, as Lawrence should have known. Anna and Vronsky cannot solve the problem of bringing their love to fulfillment and secure development in the face of the social conditions and moeurs of the time, including their own psychic makeup in complex with these conditions.

If Anna and Vronsky's love fails, how much, if Levin and Kitty's relationship is offered as a "foil" to their disaster, do that couple achieve, in terms of the conception of "marriage" in the novel? We

---

Where D. H. Lawrence Was Wrong About Woman (1992). It is unacceptable to compare a real woman with a character in a novel. Leavis shows himself obsessed with Lawrence at the time he wrote his very unsatisfactory essay on *Anna Karenina*. Frieda became for him a focus of contention: Leavis did not apparently know that she sustained her admiration for the German sex revolutionary, Otto Gross, who gave her sister a baby and who also had an affair with Frieda, all her life (even though at the end of his life—unknown to her—his nostrils were eaten away with cocaine). Gross's repulsive ideas, that society was to be saved by "polymorphous perversity," influenced Lawrence through Frieda: for instance, his enthusiasm for sodomy, as manifest in *The Rainbow, Women in Love,* and *Lady Chatterley's Lover.* Frieda was worse than amoral. She was a disastrous influence on Lawrence, who obviously loved her, while she was often flagrantly unfaithful to him. In consequence he forsook the tradition of the pursuit of authenticity of the English novel for a "continental" amoralism. Anna as a character has none of the morally inverted impulses of Frieda (see her depicted as Johanna in *Mr. Noon*): she is simply an unawakened woman trapped in a lifeless marriage, who finds herself drawn into a passionate relationship that cannot find fulfillment. But she is a *character* and Frieda was a real person!

have seen that, although Tolstoy attends closely to the subjective consciousness of the tragic lovers as their relationship goes on, there is a sense in which they fail to understand one another, and do not completely put their trust in one another. Vronsky makes increasingly irritable claims for his "freedom," while Anna deceives Vronsky over contraception. In the end they become terrified that the only "hold" they have on one another is their sensual appeal: there is no deep trusting commitment, in their sense of being in harmonious relationship with "society," and its involvement of past and future.

Kitty and Levin experience the marriage ceremony and Tolstoy's delineation of this event is beautifully given:

> Lifting the crowns from their heads, the priest read the last prayer and congratulated the young couple. Levin glanced at Kitty and thought he had never seen her look like that before, so lovely with the new light of happiness shining in her face. Levin longed to say something to her but did not know whether the ceremony was over yet. The priest came to his aid, saying softly, a smile on his kindly mouth, "Kiss your wife, and you, kiss your husband," and took the candles from their hands.
>
> Levin carefully kissed her smiling lips, offered her his arm, and with a strange new sense of closeness led her out of the church. He did not believe, he could not believe that it was all true. Only when their bewildered, timid glances met did he believe in it, because he felt that they were one already. (484)

The ritual, with all its mysterious elements of symbolism and communal sanction, even though they don't understand it, and are bewildered by it, obviously gives them support, through the months that follow—the strangely "morbid" experience of their honeymoon, and the discovery that, in the early period of their married life, they quarrel bitterly:

> directly she opened her mouth, a stream of reproach, of senseless jealousy, of everything that had been torturing her during the half-hour she had spent sitting motionless at the window, burst from her. Then for the first time he clearly understood what he had not understood when he led her out of the church after the wedding: that he was not simply close to her, but that he could not tell where he ended and she began. He realized this from the agonizing sensation of division which he felt at that instant. He was hurt for a moment but immediately knew he could not be offended with her because she was himself. . . . (508)

Naturally, such intense identification, and a dependence as urgent as Levin's, eventually generate resentment. At first he idolizes Kitty, and the portrayal is close to autobiographical experience: as we have seen, Levin attributes spiritual qualities to Kitty as did Tolstoy, when he first related to Sonya, treating her as he was inclined to do, having idolized his lost mother. But by degrees, Levin finds out that Kitty is a real person in her own right, and not simply "himself": he has, naturally, tremendous difficulties over this problem, which is a quite natural one to anyone in a close loving relationship. Indeed, one of the most profound problems in marriage is that of learning to treat one's partner as a person in his own right, rather than as a projection out of oneself, as a man does, for instance, when he treats his wife as if she were merely his own "female element of being."

> Nevertheless, this first period of their married life was a trying one ... quarrels sprang up from causes so trifling as to be incomprehensible, making them wonder afterwards what they had quarrelled about. ... (509)

Levin feels he is too happy: "what have I done to deserve such happiness? It's not natural—too good to be true. ...."

> A feeling akin to remorse fretted him. There was something shameful, effeminate about his present mode of life—Capuan, as he called it to himself. "It's not right to go on like this," he thought. "It'll soon be three months, and I'm doing next to nothing ... I ought to have been firmer and asserted my masculine independence. This way I shall get into bad habits, and encourage her to. ... Of course, it's not her fault. ... " (512)

He begins even to think that, although Kitty is not to be blamed for anything, it is due to her "frivolous, shallow upbringing." He is, however, failing to appreciate that Kitty is preparing herself to "be wife to her husband and mistress of the house, at the same time bearing, nursing and bringing up her children"—a "gigantic task"—and so she does not reproach herself for the "moments of idleness and happy love that she enjoyed now while gaily building her nest for the future."

Both in *War and Peace*, with Natasha, and with Kitty in *Anna Karenina*, Tolstoy shows himself more than satisfied with this concept of women's roles—once the happy days of courtship and idolization are over. In *Anna Karenina* however, Dolly's disillusioned reflections cast a critical light on Tolstoy's satisfactions with the family role of the wife in marriage: this is not to say that the satisfactions of bringing up a family are not great—but that a woman will still yearn for other interests, while if the man's romantic interest in her declines, she is likely (as Dolly does) to indulge in wayward fantasies: and, in any case, the demands of family life gradually become reduced—and what then? Tolstoy's emphasis is undoubtedly unfair and conservative in the extreme—as one might have expected from a man who, in life, mistreated his own wife so abominably, despite her unbelievable devotion (she copied out the manuscripts by hand many times over—doing transcripts of *War and Peace* alone seven times).

Tolstoy is, however, able to show that women are preeminent in dealing with the primary and basic elements of human experience: and that this commands respect. His portrayals of mother-infant relationships are superb, as we have seen. And Kitty strikes a blow for female equality, when Levin is called to deal with his dying brother. The sequence is beautifully done, and shows Levin adjusting painfully to the recognition that his wife is a separate being with her own determination, her own wisdom, and her own capacities and intelligence. "It's out of the question" he says sternly: she mustn't be allowed to associate with his brother's lowly mistress. He supposes that she is volunteering to accompany him because she doesn't want to be left alone: characteristically, he attributes weakness to her:

> "I can't bear to think that you should bring your weakness into it, your dislike of being alone. . . ." (315)

Kitty breaks out into tears of resentment and fury, accusing him of ascribing mean, contemptible motives to her. He bursts out, "to be such a slave!" and she challenges him—"then why did you marry?" He agrees to let her accompany him, but is dissatisfied with himself for not having stood his ground.

In the event, the condition of Nikolai Levin turns out to be more terrible than Levin could have imagined, and he is lying in a dirty room in a disreputable provincial hotel, Levin is overcome with horror. Kitty, however, can cope with such primary manifestations of life and death: she speaks to the brother "in that unoffending, sympathetic, gently animated way natural to women" (p. 519).

Levin cannot look calmly at his brother, and cannot see or distinguish the details of his brother's condition. He feels "powerless to do anything to help."

But Kitty thought and felt and acted quite differently. On seeing the sick man, she was filled with pity for him. And pity in her womanly heart produced not the horror and loathing that it did in her husband but a need for action, a need to find out all the details of his condition and to remedy them . . . and she set to work without delay. (520)

Levin comes back to find the place all in order, with Kitty "pouting her lips and puffing out her rosy cheeks" replacing the stuffy air with the smell of aromatic vinegar, and "the sick man himself, washed and combed, lying between clean sheets and propped up by high raised pillows, had on a clean nightshirt, its white collar fastened round his unnaturally thin neck."

All this induces a new hope in the patient, but there is no hope. The brother is dying. Levin reflects on the text, "Thou hast hid these things from the wise and prudent, and hast revealed them unto babes." Levin knows he has more "intellect" than his wife and Agatha Mikalovna, but when it came to death, he did not know "one hundredth part of what his wife and Agatha Mikalovna knew."

The proof that they knew for a certainty the nature of death lay in the fact that they were never under an instant's uncertainty as to how to deal with the dying, and felt no fear. But Levin and others like him, though they might be able to say a good many things about death, obviously did not know anything about it since they were afraid of death and had no notion what to do in the presence of death. (523)

These are profound insights into the special nature of woman, of "female knowledge" and the woman's capacity to deal with death, and primary life: to deal with those experiences that require a response at the level of being. But the end is revealing. Levin is back in his metaphysical reflections, and he is chewing over accepting the simple Christianity of the peasants. He and his wife see one another's faces in a flash of lightning.

"She understands," he thought. "She knows what I am thinking about. Shall I tell her or not? Yes, I will. . . ." But just as he opened his mouth to speak she turned to him first.
"Oh, Kostya, be nice and go and see if Sergei Ivanich will be comfortable in the corner room. . . ." (852–53)

And Levin decides it is a "secret for me alone, of vital importance for me, and not to be put into words. . . ." Fair enough: but there is just a suggestion that a woman is by nature *terre-à-terre*: her satisfactions are those of household and family arrangements, and in childbirth and childrearing, management, and such skills. The metaphysical torment is for the man who lives (as Tolstoy supposed he lived) on a higher plane—to which the woman must be subservient.

It is as if the man is seeking someone who belongs to the spiritual heights to which, in his imagination, he elevated his mother's image. At the first stages of courtship (as with Pierre's early feelings for Natasha, or with Levin's view of Kitty skating) the woman provides this ideal spiritual goal. After marriage the man finds (as Blake said) that her knees and elbows are only glued together—that she is a real woman, with a woman's needs and a woman's capacities. But for her there is no future "spiritual" role and, like Natasha, she must give up her singing, and even her inclination to keep herself tidy and attractive: in the end she has nothing to say in answer to a philosophical generalization of Pierre's, but a story about how when the nurse took her baby Petya off her, "he laughed and puckered up his face and squeezed up to me—I suppose he thought he was hiding. He's awfully sweet. . . ."

"Is it possible that a man of such value, of such importance to society, is at the same time my husband?" is one of Natasha's last thoughts. Kitty is shown to have the same kind of satisfaction. Yet both their husbands are maddeningly awkward, mercurial, obsessional, and restless creatures. There is, however, it would seem, one law for them, and another for the women, whose whole lives must be devoted to serving these men, so that they can continue to act out their metaphysical and philosophical perplexities, even though under "petticoat government." It is an old-fashioned idea of marriage which we need to rethink—taking account, it must be said, of Tolstoy's best insights.

Perhaps the best of these is the gradual relinquishment, both in Pierre and Levin, of the old authoritarian role of the husband. Both, mollified by suffering, are able to forgive—and thus to escape destructive confrontation. When Levin finds Kitty and Mitya safe after the storm, he is vexed:

> "Well, you ought to be ashamed of yourself! I can't think how you can be so reckless!" said Levin, falling on his wife in vexation.
> "It wasn't my fault, really. We were just going home when there was an accident and we had to change him. We had hardly. . . ." Kitty began defending herself.
> Mitya was unharmed and dry, and still fast asleep.

"Well, thank God! I don't know what I'm saying!"

They gathered up the wet napkins; the nurse picked up the baby in her arms and carried him. Levin walked beside his wife, conscience-stricken at having been angry, and stealthily, when the nurse was not looking, squeezed Kitty's hand. (848)

Tolstoy's portrayal of the suffering of this couple—Kitty's bewildered despair as she is rebuffed by Vronsky and her gradual rediscovery of her love for Levin, and Levin's long period of feeling rejected and overwhelmed by rejection, is superb. So, too, is his portrayal of the *participation mystique*, the mysterious capacity that arises in them, at the crucial moment of courtship, to communicate by chalked letters, because they are so inhibited in utterance (an autobiographical record)—an unforgettable passage. He portrays Kitty, Dolly, Anna (and Natasha) with great tenderness, and exhibits in the delineation of many of his women a marvelous capacity to identify with women. Tolstoy was fully aware of the mystery of women. Karl Stern remarks that Gorki reports that one day a group of men including Chekhov were sitting in the garden and talking about women. Tolstoy listened for a long time in silence, and then suddenly remarked, "I am only going to tell the truth about women when I am standing with one foot in the grave—I shall say it, jump into the coffin, pull the lid and then I'll say, 'Do with me what you want!'"—as if, says Stern, the truth about women were something a man could not possibly say and stay alive! Stern interprets the remark to refer to women's special nature as *mysterium tremendum*—as being mysterious, veiled, and enigmatic.

Yet, despite this capacity, Tolstoy, in his life, treated his own women in such a way that, in any novel, would have made him the worst blackguard. It is indeed strange that we should be considering such a man's "definition of marriage" in his novels.

* * *

One talks of art portraying human beings in pursuit of "authenticity"—that that they feel they have in them to become, in terms that are absolutely right for them. For Tolstoy, however, there is something else—he needs to find a meaning in life that can be put in philosophical terms, or in terms of a philosophy of existence.

This need is expressed for his men—eminently Pierre Bezuhov and Levin, though there is a touch of it in Karenin, and in Prince Andrey. It is significant that for Tolstoy, with his bleak view of women, that he does not portray the same need in his women characters. Furthermore, the question of the meaning of life seems to center in their capacity for relationships and in their children and family life, and they are much more secure in their religious faith and more conformist in this (even Anna cannot escape from her sense of shame, in breaching religious commandments). However, in their dealings with death and birth his women—notably Kitty—display an intuitive capacity for courage, practicality, and sympathy that his men lack. Despite his wide philosophical generalizations, Levin for example is ditheringly useless when Kitty's confinement happens, and even when he is confronted by his dying brother.

But yet in his portrayal of the heart-searchings of his protagonists Tolstoy does give us the experience of philosophical need— of the living presence of that "philosophical space" to which each of us, according to Roger Poole, is entitled.*

Can any of us get further than Levin, in *Anna Karenina*, who is stricken with horror at life—"without the least conception of its origin, its purpose, its reason, its nature?"

> The organism, its decay, the indestructibility of matter, the law of the conservation of energy, evolution, were the terms that had superceded those of his early faith. These terms and the theories associated with them were very useful for intellectual purposes. But they gave no guidance for life. . . . (*Anna Karenina*, 820)

Levin "has never lost this sense of terror at his lack of knowledge." The question he puts to himself is,

> "If I do not accept the answers Christianity gives to the questions of my life, what answers do I accept?" And in the whole arsenal of his convictions he failed to find not only any kind of answer, but anything resembling an answer. . . . (820)

Most men of his acquaintance found nothing distressing in their substitution of science for religion. He finds that, after reading many scientific books, that the men who shared his views got no more out of their convictions that he did.

> Far from explaining the problems without a solution to which he felt he could not live, they set them aside and took up others of no interest to him, such as, for instance, the evolution of organisms, a mechanical explanation of the soul, and so forth. (821)

---

*See *Towards Deep Subjectivity*, Allen Lane, 1972.

Levin tries philosophers who seek a nonmaterialistic explanation of life—Plato, Spinoza, Kant, Schelling, Hegel, and Schopenhauer. He follows the fixed definitions given to vague terms such as *spirit, will, freedom,* and *substance.* But he only has to forget the artificial train of reasoning, and to turn to real life,

> for the whole artificial edifice to tumble down like a house of cards. (822)

He reads a book of theology, but that, too, when he reads a history of the churches, falls to pieces.

Levin feels he cannot live without knowing what he is and why he is here.

> In infinite time, in infinite matter, in infinite space an organic cell stands out, will hold together for a while and then burst, and that cell is Me. (823)

This was an agonizing fallacy, but it was the sole, the supreme result of centuries of human thought in that direction. It was the dominant conviction, the ultimate belief on which all the systems of thought elaborated by the human mind in almost all their ramifications were based. This makes him feel suicidal.

Levin's answer is to go back to the faith in which he had been brought up: "One must live for God and not for one's own needs"—he believes he would have been a brutal creature had he not been brought up by faith to adhere to this principle. The knowledge of what is right and wrong had been *given,* because he could not have got it from anywhere else.

This of course is a fallacy: the sense of right and wrong is a product of one's upbringing: the "stage of concern" which develops in the infant, by the psychological processes explored by Melanie Klein and D. W. Winnicott. There is a natural morality in nearly all of us, arising from love between ourselves and our mothers, as we discover that she is a separate person and we depend upon her. Levin believes that he has been "living (without being aware of it) on these spiritual truths that he had imbibed with his mother's milk": this is true, but it is a moral sense he has imbibed, not a philosophy of existence. And the "truths" he may have taken in with his mother's milk are not to be equated with the truths of Christianity.

The barrier is surely that what is called the scientific viewpoint has been extended beyond its legitimate sphere, to become a general philosophy of existence. Science declares, "let us assume every living thing is to be understood as if it were a machine"—but then has allowed the extension of this to mean "everything *is* a machine." The essence of what a living thing is thus escapes thought: the essential "other"quality that distinguishes live from dead matter is missing. If that quality is grasped, we have to talk of *intelligence,* of an impulse toward ingenuity, development, and invention that needs to be restored to the picture. It is valuable and important to have a statement which places this kind of emphasis on "philosophical space," in the work of a major artist.

* * *

In making a critique of this novel we must defer to its established greatness as a work of art. *Anna Karenina* is a great European novel—if not the greatest. And it is a tragedy of love. As a work of art about love it bears comparison with Shakespeare's *Antony and Cleopatra,* as the portrayal of a passion from which a couple cannot escape, and which yet destroys them, because it cannot be reconciled with the world. Yet we can neither say we would not have had the lovers at all, nor that we take their side against the world: there is a terrible grandeur about their passion. Yet there are also sordid and degrading elements, illumination and delusion, joy and torment. Indeed, the ambiguity of love is encapsulated in such works, and we cannot but be transfixed by the possibilities explored, even if they end in death. Such a work of art certainly makes us feel alive, in the face of being-unto-death, our universal human predicament, because it shows human beings making the choice of what seems to them the overriding meaning in life, to which, if it is necessary, they must sacrifice everything.

Of course, Anna's overpowering love, the focus for which is her mysterious and superlative beauty and her intelligence, and Vronsky's compulsive and progressing love for her, are contrasted with the love between Levin and Kitty, with which it runs parallel throughout the novels and that culminates in marriage, as Anna and Vronsky's cannot. That love is shown to have equal difficulties and pains, of adjustment, not least after marriage. Levin finds his courtship, his renunciation of Kitty extremely difficult, and for a long time, after she has rejected him in favor of Vronsky, he scornfully refuses to forgive her for turning him down. After marriage, his problem is coming to terms with the courage and independence of his wife, with the agonies of her parturition, and the disappointments of parenthood. He strives continually to relate these experiences of love to the wider perspectives of the meaning of life (as Anna and Vronsky do not, their love being intensely manic and narcissistic). At the end Levin finds something of the capacity to believe and to find life meaningful that he has been seeking all his life. He finds a good deal of what he is looking for through his love and his marriage, by contrast with Vronsky and Anna, who simply remain locked in a mutual struggle of egoisms to try to survive their impossible situation, which despite their gains they cannot solve.

Judith Armstrong says that

> As for Anna, her love is also narcissistic, partly because she and Stiva have similarly been deprived of proper family life, having been brought up by an aunt: and partly because, given the social mores of the time, it is a deadend love, a love with nowhere to go. (Armstrong 1988; 89)

But this is not quite right, either. It implies that Tolstoy meant Anna and Stiva to be seen as products of a certain kind of family conditioning—but there is no indication that he means either to be seen as victims of such deprivation with inevitable consequences. Both are benign and admired figures, and several critics have emphasized the way in which Tolstoy himself seems to love Anna. And, again, the second part of her sentence implies that "society" or "social mores" are to blame for the "dead-end" quality of the love between Vronsky and Anna: yet is the fact that (as Armstrong says) Vronsky's aim is to "master" Anna also a product of "social mores"? She says his love is narcissistic because of "upbringing": is this a product of society, or of the character of Vronsky's mother? Of course, Vronsky is in a sense the product of his class and of male-dominated bourgeois society, as are Anna and Stiva. But the unsatisfactoriness of all such attempts to pin down the nature of their weaknesses in simplistic terms reveals only the life and quality of Tolstoy's art, its breadth, tolerance, and wisdom.

It is a mark of our involvement in their passion that we do not feel it is appropriate to ask whether Anna and Vronsky pursue the existential questions about the meaning of life such as Levin pursues. They cannot move out from their preoccupation with their love, to devote themselves to the world, in confidence in their mutual security. And here I would draw a parallel with the lovers in D. H. Lawrence's later novels: nowhere does he portray lovers who, fulfilled in their love, move outward to give their richness to the world—as Levin and Kitty try to do. With Vronsky and Anna, their love tends to burn them up, as a force that fills all their hours of day and night, with problems of how to relate to the world in such a way as to give them the least sense of fulfillment, to enable them to contemplate their "freedom," their satisfaction, and happiness. All their efforts to solve this problem—as by travel, by Vronsky's painting, by his creation of a hospital, seem to make them less secure, of one another, and of their place in the scheme of things. These problems center around "society" and their role in society: but the lack of security there tends to undermine and disturb their sense of their place in the wider scheme of things— their own lives and ambitions, their relationships with those close to them (e.g., Seriohza, Ani, and Vronsky's mother). They do not develop the capacity, so eminent in Levin, to move out from the rich satisfactions in their love relationship, into life tasks, and to contemplate the ultimate meaning of existence. They are not religious, while Christianity becomes their enemy and undoing: but they are also untroubled by the question of whether they "believe" or not: while to Levin it is a central problem, which he seems to solve in the end, even though his wife is *terre-à-terre* enough not to let it torment her, that Levin is not a Christian believer, as she is. Anna, at least, it has to be said, feels a deep sense of shame at having betrayed her marriage vows by infidelity, and this haunts her until the end. But her tragedy is that of a woman who is overwhelmed by "life"—by the very authenticity of her need to love and be loved, and to "live" in that way, not least because she is trapped in a dead marriage, sanctified by the Christian Church. She is trapped in an enigma, an unsolvable puzzle: one, it has to be said, that our modern world has not solved.

At the same time she is haunted by the spectre of *something* that seems to hang about her like fate—as symbolized by the peasant of whom she (and Vronsky) are made to dream. I have discussed the question of the motto of the book: Vengeance Is Mine: I Will Repay, and the way Anna is overtaken by some extraneous power, that has a demonic quality. The sense that a "brutal force" often intervenes in our lives seems to be an unconscious element in Tolstoy's view of existence. From the beginning, when the railway worker is killed at the station, Anna seems to be dimly aware of the menace of fate to her: at the very first moment in the railway station, her brother noticed with surprise that her lips were

> trembling and that she had difficulty in keeping back her tears. . . . tossing her head as if she wished with a physical gesture to shake off something that troubled and oppressed her. . . . " (*Anna Karenina*, 79)

This theme of demonic possession develops, as Anna begins to give way to Vronsky's lure, and to the lure of relishing his love for her. As she is overwhelmed, she finds that she has the capacity to lie, with great skill, to her husband, to deceive him—but then, brutally, to tell him that she has a lover, and hates him. It is as though she is "taken over" by some force and by "another woman" in herself, as we have seen. This is a paranoid element in the novel.

Exploring this novel has taken us into very deep waters—involving Tolstoy's view of women, which was fed by his fascination with the abominable philosophy of Schopenhauer: and we have examined the possible psychological origins both of Schopenhauer's hatred of women, and Tolstoy's. With Tolstoy, I have suggested, many of his major artistic preoccupations involve a rationalization of his problem of suffering from the loss of his mother at eighteen months. I am by no means the first critic to make this association, but I believe the insights of object-relations and existentialist psychoanalysis bring further light to this problem. However, we also have to consider the ambivalence, between Tolstoy the man with strange and eccentric opinions (who told his sons "A sound healthy woman is a wild beast," and "the most intelligent woman is less intelligent than the most stupid man"— Edwards 1981, 294) and the man who was sustained by women, his wife in particular, and who was the great sympathetic artist who could give us Anna Karenina, Dolly, Kitty, and Natasha in his novels, and portray especially the delight and charm girls and young women bring to the world.

* * *

Interestingly enough, both novels, *Anna Karenina* and *War and Peace,* move toward their conclusions with the male protagonist becoming involved with their baby offspring, at close quarters. The mother's attention to the baby, after her acts of primary maternal preoccupation, are set against the man's tendency to go away to attend to affairs of the world, and to his philosophical ruminations. In *War and Peace*

> when Nikolay and his wife came to look for Pierre, they found him in the nursery, with his baby son awake on his broad right hand, dandling him. There was a gleeful smile on the baby's broad face and open, toothless mouth . . . sunny radiance of joy flowed all over Natasha's face, as she gazed tenderly at her husband and son. (*War and Peace,* 1464)

The baby, with the wobbling head in the little cap, is absorbing Pierre's whole attention.

Nickolay declares his wife Marya cannot feel the charm of these little creatures:

> "Oh, Pierre is a capital nurse," said Natasha; "he says his hand is just made for a baby's back. Just look."
> "Oh yes, but not for this," Pierre cried laughing, and hurriedly snatching up the baby, he handed him back to the nurse. (Ibid., 1469)

In *Anna Karenina* the baby also has "an accident" as they are coming back from a trip into the garden in a storm.

> "It wasn't my fault, really. We were just going home when there was an accident and we had to change him. We had hardly. . . ." Kitty began defending herself. (*Anna Karenina*, 848)

Levin, who has been angry with is wife out of fear that something terrible has happened to the baby in the storm, is conscience-stricken, and stealthily, when the nurse is not looking, squeezes Kitty's hand.

Levin is later summoned to the nursery. He is filled with feelings of joy and tranquillity, and all the mental preoccupation with "an emancipated world of forty million men of Slavonic race" seems trivial, compared with what is going on in his own soul. Before entering the nursery he sees two stars in the already darkening sky and remembers a philosophical thought that has occurred to him:

> that if the chief proof of the existence of a Deity lies in His revelation of what is right, why is that revelation confined in the Christian Church alone? How about the Buddhist, the Mohammedan faiths, which also preach and do good. (858)

He hasn't time to formulate this thought before entering the nursery.

> Kitty, with her sleeves tucked up, was bending over the bath in which the baby was splashing about. . . .

Misha has that day begun to show unmistakable, incontestable signs of recognizing his nearest and dearest: Kitty demonstrates this, and Levin, for the first time, feels love for him, not least because he has felt such fear during the storm. Kitty's smile is radiant.

It is, surely, highly significant that an author whose impulse developed out of the anguish of spirit produced by the loss of his mother in infancy should make these incidents with a new infant so significant at the end of each of his great novels. The existential security of the mothers in each case is deeply appreciated by the male protagonists and their dealings with their sons are seen to stand in complement to their philosophical musings, and to their elevated responses to the beauty and mystery of life. The awakening perceptions and responses of the very young infants are seen as the awakening of the human perception of reality, and of the immense perspectives the human mind is capable of: and the links between love and the appreciation of reality are made clear. At the same time, the rather pitiful nursery reality, with which the women have to cope—the "accidents" of babyhood—is brought home to us, as a sine qua non of civilized existence, and the grounds of all human life. The attention Tolstoy pays to the man's participation in response to his very young infant, in complex with his penetrating depiction of the mother's special role in nurturing, both physical and psychic, is surely very original and very modern. It is surely a major contribution to the mutual understanding between the sexes, and a gesture toward the increasing participation of male partners in the upbringing of children (the portrayal of Nikolas Rostov in relation to Marya, their children, and Nikolinka is equally sensitive). This is an extraordinary contribution to civilization from a man who so despised women!

5

Conclusions

In drawing on insights from psychoanalysis and more particularly from objects-relations dynamic psychology and from existentialist psychotherapy I have not, I hope, tried to explain Tolstoy's dichotomies in the sense of explaining them away. I hope I have shown how they arose—out of the same origins from which sprang his impulses to seek the truth, to explore human experience, and to ask Why? and What for?—meaning, What is life for? They arose out of the same formative experiences in his infant life which left him with problems not only over women, but with the whole Earth, the whole of reality, and with the meaning of existence.

The great novels came at a particular moment when he was guided by his capacity as an artist, between the anarchic revolutionism of his early life and his conversion to Christianity, leading to his later asceticism and fanaticism. He is dominated in writing them by the need to explore to find out human truth, and he is not dominated by his guilt, his misogyny, his fears, or his impulses to control, exploit, or destroy women. Later, as happened with D. H. Lawrence, he uses his skill as a writer to subject his literary power to propaganda, and to indulge in fantasies of hate against women—as he does, I believe, in *The Kreutzer Sonata*, which I see as a work that is dominated by the psychotic. I have doubts about *The Death of Ivan Illich*, which, though I am told it is a great existentialist work, I can only find to be willfully and morbidly preoccupied with death, and, so, tedious. Even *The Cossacks* seems to be an awkward and miserable tale, although it has some immediacy, about the savage life of the Cossacks. *Resurrection* also seemed to be tedious, and too much of a moral tale—essentially lifeless.

In *War and Peace* and *Anna Karenina* we find a tender, rapturous portrayal of the young women whose beauty and vitality becomes an inspiration for men, Natasha, Kitty, and Anna, and a sympathetic portrayal of those women, like Dolly and Sonya, who fall

258

short of fulfillment, in the social circumstances of the time, but who are heroic and stoic and who bear their suffering with dignity. With Tolstoy in these novels we explore the suffering of men and women who are afflicted by the pains of discovering their humanness. In this respect the portrayals of Pierre Bezuhov, Prince Andrey, Levin, Anna Karenina, Vronsky, and Dolly are unsurpassed in literature. And there are sympathetic delineations of other minor characters, of Karenin himself, of Denisov, of Nikolay Rostov, of Petya, and of many others, as well as of innumerable soldiers, poor people, and servants. The portrayal of the various spheres of Russian society is exceptionally penetrating, and leaves one with a special feeling for the character and quality of this very different society—very different, that is, from the society of the West. Of course, Tolstoy was racked by guilt, and he examines and exposes his guiltiness in Pierre, Anna, Denisov, and Levin. But his central theme is an existentialist one—an urge, as acted out in Pierre, Andrey, and Levin, to try to find whether life can have any meaning, and, if so, how one can seek this meaning and organize one's life to find it. He is the novelist of devotion to solving the problem of existence—a stance that makes nearly all the literature of the present time appear trivial and worthless.

Yet he himself had been a delinquent, drunk, and womanizer, or, perhaps rather, a visitor to the normal vice dens of bourgeois society. Respectable bourgeois society of the time had another face, even as it assumed moral righteousness. In a discussion of Monet's Paris Vivian Perutz reports that the usual figure taken for the number of unregistered prostitutes outside the brothels in that city is 30,000 (the population was around 2,000,000). There were 2,648 registered prostitutes. This author says that the fundamental cause of this abundant supply of loose women was poverty. So, we can perhaps suppose that a parallel situation existed in Moscow and Leningrad, in the late nineteenth century, and that it was common for men of the "civilized" upper classes, of Tolstoy's aristocratic class, and of Vronsky's kind as well as bourgeois men, to go off after their drunken frolics to the brothel: and Tolstoy, like Levin, felt he must show the diary of his escapades in this area to his wife, when they got married.

Moreover, Tolstoy was also guilty of an affair with a peasant-woman in his household. He had severe practical daily difficulties with his women, as we have seen, finding himself unable to restrain his lust, and yet fearing the sexual act to be debilitating and destructive: ultimately murderous. As we have seen, he caused his wife untold distress and suffering, at times seriously threatening her health and even her life, by his antics. And while he often expressed repentance he was still unable to control himself when impelled to commit the grossest offenses.

At a deeper level, as we have seen, he is preoccupied with the Winnicottian theme, of men taking risks, to compete as it were with the essential risks women take in giving birth to everyone of us. It seems to be a fruitful insight, which indicates how envy of women drives men to war, and to commit the horrors of war, so graphically conveyed in *War and Peace*.

It is difficult to draw attention to this strange perplexity in Tolstoy's life, in today's world and to draw satisfactory conclusions. Despite his intense propaganda against women and sex there is nothing in the great novelist Tolstoy that is dehumanizing: his campaigns, even at their most repulsive, are offered in the name of serving higher spiritual goals. Even in his most ascetic propaganda people are to be saved from sexual indulgence for the good of humanity and of their souls. It is true that in *The Kreutzer Sonata* he offers intense rationalizations and then indulges in a fantasy of perverted satisfaction in his hero's wife-murder. But even this story is far from the kind of indulgences that pervade our culture today, in which women are subjected symbolically to rejection and subjugation—to hate—in a thousand films, novels, and plays. Indeed, one might almost say that misogyny, expressed in the coarsest and most loutish terms, is the criterion for success in today's London literary culture. Perhaps one might boldly declare that one cannot have a truly civilized culture when every writer seems impelled to "do dirt on life" and especially on the female element being by gross sexual explicitness, taken to be the criterion for commercial and artistic success. Yet the indulged impulse to reduce women, as a symbol of being, of sensitivity and creativity, to abuse in our society goes largely unnoticed in its significance. The consequences of this abuse is not examined, even though it might have the direst implications, and expresses some vengeful impulse that threatens civilization, as if humanity has become hostile to its best and more feminine qualities, and was renouncing being. Meanwhile even our consideration of the significance of this trend is confused by the observations of some feminists that belief in the special ways of knowing that women are blessed with, or that they have a higher moral capacity because they can become mothers is, as just registered, regarded as "protofascistic."

The capacity to portray women in such a respectful and admiring way, making them at times the focus of an almost divine inspiration, by a writer who in his life and psychological dynamics feared and hated women, is the great enigma of Tolstoy's art. To Tolstoy, clearly, as he shows through Levin, Pierre, and Prince Andrey, women, and love for them, was the focus in his quest for a sense of meaning in life. Yet he devised all manner of philosophical reasons, drawing on Schopenhauer and others, for despising her and for placing her under strict control, out of fear. Even in his greatest novels, in *Anna Karenina*, in the end, he kills his heroine, or gets her to kill herself; in *War and Peace* with Natasha he strips her of her fire and of her charming capacity to inspire, and makes her a dully hausfrau: thus symbolically putting her under control. But while she has lived, she has filled us with a sense of women's beauty, charm, vitality, courage, and truth. Anna Karenina is duplicitous and evades reality, but in her yearning and in her passion conveys the spirit of being intensely alive and in pursuit of an authenticity whose claims are undeniable, even if they lead to death. We shall never solve these perplexing ambiguities, for they are the essence of being alive, and it is this that Tolstoy captures.

* * *

The anguish that lurked in Tolstoy's mind, from his early experiences as a child, generate some of the key passages in both of the great novels. One is struck, time after time, by juxtapositions of birth and death or of love and death which seem to spring from a spirit in which these are inextricably linked. In *War and Peace* the very scope of the novel is expressed with "The unsettled question of life and death hanging, not only over Prince Andrey, but over all Russia, shut off all other considerations," (*War and Peace*, 1163). This is at the moment when Natasha, who embodies for Andrey both the inspirational and ideal aspect of women, and her most treacherous fallibility, breaks through to him at last, because he is mortally wounded, to reveal in him his love for her, to invoke his forgiveness ("I love thee more, better than before. . . ." [1162]) and to nurse him: "the doctor was forced to admit that he had not expected from a young girl so much fortitude, nor skill in nursing a wounded man" (p 1163). While women are treacherous, if exposed to sexual love, once the possibilities of sexual love are removed, they can play a superb role, from their natural abilities and inclinations, to deal with sickness and death. In *Anna Karenina* Kitty is recognized to have the special woman's capacity, to face the real needs and the ghastly reality of the dying: "she immediately clasped in her fresh, youthful hand his huge skeleton of a hand, pressed it, and began speaking to him in that unoffending, sympathetic, gently animated way natural to woman" (*Anna Karenina*, p 519). She has to fight for the right to take on this role, against all the conventional codes that stated that it would be too shocking for a respectable married woman to associate with the sometime prostitute Masha who is Nikolai's mistress. Kitty takes practical steps to make the dying consumptive comfortable, and Levin thinks "Thou has hid these things from the wise and prudent, and has revealed them unto babes." He regards himself as "wise and prudent" but realizes that despite his intellectual ponderings he "yet did not know one hundredth part of what his wife and Agatha Mikalovna know": they "knew . . . what sort of a thing was life and what death was" (p 523). The comparison of Kitty to "babes" is by no means disparaging, but a critical disparagement of his own sophistication and wisdom, of the adult man's world, which are useless in the face of death.

This kind of special capacity of women, to be sympathetic and caring, and yet to be able to be practical and not to flinch from disconcerting truths has, of course, been the basis of their developing claim for equality and freedom—as by becoming nurses in the great battles of the Crimea and World War I: today, alas, they seek to go beyond this and become combat troops, turning the aspiration for equality into seeking to ape male destructiveness.

Recognition of these female capacities by Tolstoy would seem to spring from his special preoccupation with the dangers of sex, childbirth, and the very vulnerable emotional susceptibility that goes with these functions. Anna Karenina's tragedy develops from her need to fulfill herself in love: her love for her children is examined in relation to her predicament as a wife and lover:

> the sight of this child (Anna) made it plainer than ever that the feeling she had for her could not even be called love in comparison with what she felt for Seriozha . . . on her firstborn, although he was the child of a man she did not love, had been concentrated *all the love that had never found satisfaction*. . . . (p 567; my italics)

As an artist, Tolstoy recognized that women need to find such satisfaction, even if it leads to such an impossible situation as that of Anna Karenina, and eventually destroys her.

In childbirth, women find the ultimate challenge of being. When Kitty is lying on her confinement bed, he implicitly compares her with someone on their deathbed.

she drew him to her side with a look. Her look, already bright, grew brighter still as he approached. *There was the same change from earthly to unearthly as is seen on the faces of the dead;* but there it means farewell, with Kitty it was a welcome to new life. . . . (p. 750; my italics)

With *Anna Karenina* one could almost draw a diagram of the conflicting swings of development between birth and death, what makes for life and what for death. Toward the end the fulfillment of Levin's love for Kitty and their marriage rises as triumphantly as the love between Vronsky and Anna becomes baffled by their inability to solve the complex problems of their relationship to others and society, of Anna's relationship to her children and their future, and her inability to get, or to face, a divorce: and their increasing exasperation with maintaining their love relationship in the face of the frustration and suspicion that turns it into hate. Tolstoy seems to be at this stage still hopeful that marriage was a means of controlling the dangers of sexual passion. Anna and Vronsky suffer the alienation that must torment people who cannot find satisfaction and fulfillment in their contribution to the world and to the lives of others. So, they come to be left only with physical attraction and with the anxieties of sustaining desire and commitment that tend to exert a burning out and somewhat narcissistic energy, cut off from the relief of feeling that the emotional life fits into the world and is approved by the world, so that there is relief from the exigencies of mere physical bonds; and, of course, in the contribution to the future, by "giving out" to children. Cut off from all these outgoings toward the future and creative interaction with other human beings and society, they come to be enclosed in a *huis clos* of intolerable dependence one on another that exhausts and burns out their love. It is this complex reality of the position of lovers, in the complex dynamics of living in the world, that D. H. Lawrence failed to appreciate, in his attitude to Tolstoy's novel and to its upshot.

So, Levin and Kitty move into the new world of the "helpless being" born to them, and into their need to adjust to this challenge of life, while Anna and Vronsky fall into mutual distrust and alienation, ending in the suicide of Anna and Vronsky's sacrifice to the Turks: toward mutual vengeance and self-destruction. It is the *risks* inherent in sexual love with which Tolstoy is concerned—not only the risk of pregnancy, but the risk of damaging other lives, especially those of children, a long-term consideration we have failed to take note of in modern society and civilization.

Levin suffers guilt, because he has made his wife pregnant "'If not I, then who is to blame?' he thought, involuntarily seeking a scapegoat to punish. . . ." [p. 740]. He finds the answer to his philosophical yearnings in the commitment to the exigencies of family life:

> "be it faith or not—I don't know what it is—through suffering this feeling has crept just as imperceptibly into my heart and has lodged itself firmly there. . . ." (p. 853)

He feels the same satisfaction in commitment to the demanding routines of life as he experienced in mowing with the peasants, and such as Pierre Bezuhov finds in his relationship with Platon Karataev.

Tolstoy, in making this emphasis, is saying the same thing as the contemporary existential psychotherapist Irvin Yalom, who sees the answer to the problem of life in "engagement."

> Engagement is the therapeutic answer to meaninglessness. . . . whole-hearted engagement in any of the infinite array of life's activities not only disarms the galactic view [i.e., the view that the universe is a mere machine operating by the impersonal laws of entropy and evolution] but enhances the possibility of one's completing the patterning of events of one's life in some coherent fashion. To find a home, to care about other individuals, about ideas or projects, to search, to create, to build—these, and all other forms of engagement, are twice as rewarding: they are intrinsically enriching, and they alleviate the dysphoria that stems from being bombarded with the unassembled brute data of existence. (Yalom 1980, 482)

Levin is appalled by the imminent death of his consumptive brother, and declares that he will soon be dead himself:

> He saw death or the advance towards death in everything. . . . Darkness had fallen upon everything for him: but just because of this darkness he felt that the one thread to guide him through the darkness was his work, and he clutched at it and clung to it with all his might. (*Anna Karenina*, 377)

This is one way of avoiding a sense of meaninglessness. The other is love. Levin has already been rescued from hopelessness and despair by seeing Kitty one morning being driven past on her way to Yergushovo.

> He could not be mistaken. There were no other eyes like those in the world. . . . (299)

He looked up at the sky . . . spread half across the sky was a smooth tapestry of fleecy cloudlets growing tinier and tinier. The sky had turned blue and clear: and met with the same tenderness but with the same remoteness his questioning gaze.

"No," he said to himself, "however good that simple life of toil may be, I cannot go back to it, I love *her*." (300)

This love culminates in Kitty's giving birth to Levin's child, and his deep satisfaction in gloating on their safety, after the storm, at the end of the book. Kitty's confinement, and the early life of little Mitya, are haunted by danger, but it is in participation in these events that Levin finds a peace that allays his essential terror.

The birth of little Anna, Ani as she comes to be called, however, has a quite different effect, of promoting a degree of suffering which brings all the relationships round her into question. The particular nature of this birth, at the level of being, is given a symbolic color by Vronsky's terrible failure as the rider of the mare Frou-Frou in the race, when he fails to keep his posture as a rider in rhythmic harmony with his sensitive animal and breaks her back. What is symbolized by this Vronsky's ingrained self-satisfaction as a passionate lover with its consequent element of indifference, and his unconscious resentment at the way Anna has inflicted submissiveness on him, as a woman, when he cannot marry her. As we have seen, he kicks the horse in the belly, symbolic of his hostility to the woman's inevitable pregnancy—for it is at that moment, just before the race, that Anna has told him she is with child.

Anna's pregnancy is haunted by jealousy of Vronsky (as when he escorts a visiting prince round the night shows), resentment over her husband's coldness ("He understands nothing, feels nothing"), and by the fear of death ("I shall die, and I am very glad I shall die, and set you free and myself as well" [386])—in this there is a degree of self-pity, which in turn goes with her increasing unwillingness to face reality, and her taking resort to morphine. She reports her dream of the little peasant at the very moment her fetus begins to quicken (386–87): and, of course, this fatal little peasant is heard muttering at the moment of her death.

So, this parturition is fraught, and, since Anna gets puerperal fever and nearly dies, it is a death-haunted delivery, such as Tolstoy was preoccupied with all his life, because of the disaster of his own origins. This is a dreadfully harrowing scene. Karenin is summoned to her bedside where he finds Vronsky, and the two men are reduced to utter misery. Vronsky is weeping: Karenin is faced with the sight of suffering which fills him with nervous emotion. Anna, in her delirium, becomes dissociated and split, speaks of dying in such a way as to fill Karenin with suffering, yet she confesses "There is another woman in me, I'm afraid of her . . . I'm not that woman. . . ." while Karenin feels "a new happiness he had never known." Anna is perplexed by the fact that both her lovers are called "Alexei," and makes them take one another's hands: Karenin draws Vronsky's hands away from his face and it is "terrible with its look of agony and shame." The scene is painful and confusing: it is terrible for Karenin and for Vronsky not least because of Anna's confused duplicity. The doctor expects Anna to die. Karenin forgives Anna and confesses his desire for revenge: he promises to "turn the other cheek," but while Vronsky is persuaded there is something lofty and inaccessible in Karenin's outlook on life. It becomes clear later that his is not a real coming-to-terms, with forgiveness, while the effect of Anna's feverish duplicity is so to confuse the two men so much that Vronsky goes home and tries to shoot himself, in desperate perplexity. Karenin finds that Anna is still afraid of him and really loathes him: yet he is deeply concerned for his wife's baby by her lover, but then cannot bring himself to divorce her or to let her have Seriohza: Anna on her part resolutely refuses a divorce and at the end of this part of the novel the situation is still grim, the alienation deeper, and the situation is still haunted by death: "Oh, why did I not die? It would have been better?" cries Anna (461). (In the end, of course, by her vengeful death, Anna makes Vronsky's life meaningless: "life which is not simply useless but loathsome to me. Anybody's welcome to it," he declares.)

This agonizing scene is, significantly, followed by the marriage of Levin and Kitty. It is clear that the upshot of the novel is that since sexual love is such a force for division and conflict, for threatening chaos, marriage is the only possible answer. Later, of course, Tolstoy even abandoned this hope, but only after he had tried, in this novel, to confront the realities of the relational agonies such as human beings are capable of experiencing, in their struggle to satisfy their need to love. Even for Levin and Kitty, the road is hard, but they in their mysterious harmony, represent the best human beings can achieve. What makes these scenes so marvelous is Tolstoy's capacity as an artist to allow his characters to behave in the kind of way he knows people behave in real life, being mixed, confused, and fallible. While he has a firm moral foundation, rooted in the recognition of the human urge for authenticity, he is by no means writing moral fables in these two great novels. They are great art.

* * *

I have tried to write out my response to Tolstoy's great novels in the hope of paying tribute to his art, and in answer to the question, "How can a man with such negative and fanatic attitudes to women write such marvelous novels as these two, in which women characters play such a convincing and illuminating part?" I don't know whether I have offered any answers to that, but I believe that my invocation of certain ideas from the field of psychotherapy may have helped me to give my readers some insights into Tolstoy's problem with women. It may be that in the course of my excursion into these novels I have said something insightful about them as art.

The time is hardly propitious for those of us who wish to try to confront such problems. Today is a time when people suppose that by watching a television play of *War and Peace* they have possessed Tolstoy's masterpiece. Yet nearly everything I have concerned myself with in this study attends to the record of the "inwardness" delineated in the prose that has to be cut out for a film production. The mere plot and some of the dialogue, however well dressed, acted, and "shot," would seem comparatively ridiculous, and would not embody the genius of the artist, which is in his dealings with the inwardness of consciousness, as captured in words.

The justification for writing literary criticism must be that one hopes, by the example of one's close attention to the meaning of the words on the page, to convey one's respect and enthusiasm and to enrich and illuminate the response of others. So, one hopes by writing a volume like the present one, to contribute to the satisfaction of reading books, as a collaboration with the artist.

These two novels are for me the most satisfying books I have ever encountered, and this is a response I would hope to encourage in others, who come across these two formidable works of art. They enrich one's understanding of human nature, and of one's own nature, more than any other novels in the world, and for that one must be eternally thankful. Civilization itself is the richer for Tolstoy's literary efforts in these works, and we must hold on to this whatever dangerous nonsense he uttered in other directions.

Bibliography

GENERAL

Bowlby, John. *Attachment and Loss.* London: Hogarth, 1969.

Empson, William. *Seven Types of Ambiguity.* London: Chatto and Windus. 1946.

Fairbairn, W. R. D. *Psychoanalytical Studies of the Personality.* London: Tavistock, 1952.

Farber, Leslie H. *The Ways of the Will.* London: Constable, 1964.

Forrester, John, and Lisa Appingnesi. *Freud's Women.* London: Weidenfeld and Nicolson, 1992.

Gallie, W. B. *Philosophers of Peace and War.* Cambridge: Cambridge University Press, 1978.

Guntrip, Harry. *Personality Structure and Human Interaction.* London: Hogarth, 1961.

———. *Schizoid Phenomenon, Object-relations and the Self.* London: Hogarth, 1968.

Holbrook, David. *Human Hope and the Death Instinct.* Oxford: Pergamon, 1971.

———. *Where D. H. Lawrence Was Wrong About Women.* Lewisburg, Pa.: Bucknell University Press, 1984.

Kohut, Heinz. *The Search for the Self,* Edited by Paul Ornstein. New York: International Universities Press, 1978.

Lawrence, D. H. "Reflections on the Death of a Porcupine." In *Phoenix.* London: Neumann, 1936.

Marcus, Stephen. *Dickens from Pickwick to Dombey.* London: Chatto and Windus, 1965.

May, Rollo. *Love and Will.* New York: W. W. Norton. 1969.

Perutz, Vivian. *Édouard Manet.* Lewisburg, Pa.: Bucknell University Press, 1993.

Poole, Roger. *Towards Deep Subjectivity.* London: Allen Lane, 1972.

Stern, Karl. *The Flight from Woman.* London: Allen and Unwin, 1966.

Straus, Erwin. *Phenomenological Psychology.* London: Tavistock, 1966.

Strickland, Geoffrey. *Structuralism or Criticism?* Cambridge: Cambridge University Press, 1981.

Ulanov, Ann, and Barry Ulanov. *The Witch and the Clown.* Wilmette, Ill.: Chiron, 1987.

Winnicott, D. W. *Collected Papers: Through Paediatrics to Psychoanalysis,* London: Tavistock, 1958.

———. *Playing and Reality.* London: Tavistock, 1971.

———. *Home Is Where One Starts From.* London: Penguin, 1986.

Wolfenstein, Martha. "The Image of the Lost Parent," in *The Psychoanalytic Study of the Child.* Vol. 28, pp. 433–66.

Yalom, Irvin D. *Existential Psychotherapy.* New York: Basic Books, 1980.

ABOUT TOLSTOY

Adelman, Gary. *"Anna Karenina:" The Bitterness of Ecstasy.* Twayne's Masterwork Series. Boston: J. K. Hall, 1990.

Armstrong, Judith. *The Unsaid Anna Karenina.* New York: St. Martin's Press, 1988.

Bayley, John. *Tolstoy and the Novel.* London: Chatto and Windus, 1986.

Benson, Ruth Crego. *Women in Tolstoy: The Ideal and the Erotic.* Urbana: University of Illinois Press, 1973.

Bloom, Harold, ed. and introduction. *Leo Tolstoy's "Anna Karenina"* New York: Chelsea House, 1987.

Christian, R. F. *Tolstoy: A Critical Introduction.* Cambridge: Cambridge University Press, 1969.

Edwards, Anne. *Sonya: The Life of Countess Tolstoy.* London: Hodder and Stoughton, 1981.

Eikhenbaum, Boris. *The Young Tolstoy.* Translated by Gary Hern. Ann Arbor: Ardis Press, 1972.

———. *Tolstoy in the Seventies.* Translated by Albert Kaspin, Ann Arbor: Ardis Press, 1982.

Evans, Mary. *Reflecting on Anna Karenina.* London: Routledge, 1989.

Gibian, George. *Tolstoy and Shakespeare.* The Hague: Mouton, 1975.

Gifford, Henry. *Tolstoy.* Oxford: Oxford University Press, 1982.

Greenwood, E. B. *Leo Tolstoy: The Comprehensive Vision.* New York: St. Martin's Press, 1975.

Gustafson, Richard F. *Leo Tolstoy: Resident and Stranger.* Princeton: Princeton University Press, 1986.

Hardy, Barbara. *The Appropriate Form: An Essay on the Novel.* London: Athlone, 1964.

Jones, Peter. *Philosophy and the Novel: Philosophical Aspects of "Middlemarch," "Anna Karenina," "The Brothers Karamasov," "A la Recherche du temps perdu" and of the Method of Criticism.* Oxford: Clarendon Press, 1975.

Knowles, A. V., ed. *Tolstoy: The Critical Heritage.* London: Routledge and Kegan Paul, 1978.

Larrin, Janko. *Tolstoy, An Approach.* London: Methuen, 1944.

Leavis, F. R. *Anna Karenina and Other Essays.* London: Chatto and Windus, 1967.

Lucas, Victor. *Tolstoy in London.* London: Evans Bros. 1979.

McLean, Hugh, ed. *In the Shade of the Giant: Essays on Tolstoy.* Berkeley: University of California Press, 1989.

Mandelker, Amy. *Framing* Anna Karenina; *Tolstoy, the Woman Question and the Victorian Novel.* Columbus, Ohio States Press, 1993.

Matlaw, Ralph, ed. *Tolstoy: A Collection of Critical Essays.* Englewood Cliffs, N. J.: Prentice-Hall, 1967.

Polner, Tikhon. *Tolstoy and His Wife.* London: Jonathan Cape, 1946.

Redpath, Theodore. *Tolstoy.* London: Bowes and Bowes, 1960.

Rowe, William W. *Leo Tolstoy.* Boston: Twayne, 1986.

Silbajovis, Rimvydas. *Tolstoy's Aesthetics and His Art.* Columbus, Ohio: Slavica, 1991.

Steiner, George. *Tolstoy or Dostoevsky.* London: Faber, 1959.

Stenbock-Fermov, Elizabeth. *The Architecture of "Anna Karenina": A History of Its Structure, Writing and Message.* Lisse, Belgium: Peter de Ridder Press, 1975.

Troyat, Henri. *Tolstoy.* London. W. H. Allen, 1968.

Wasiolek, Edward. *Tolstoy's Major Fiction.* Chicago: University of Chicago Press, 1978.

Wilson, A. N. *Tolstoy.* London: Hamish Hamilton, 1988.

Index